Writings

Commentary from Jack Engelhard the Voice of America's Conscience

---

"Jack Engelhard is the last Hemingway; a writer without peer, and the conscience of us all."
- John W. Cassell

by

JACK ENGELHARD

DayRay Literary Press
British Columbia, Canada

Writings:
Commentary from Jack Engelhard the Voice of America's Conscience

ISBN-13 978-1-77143-553-6
First Edition

Library and Archives Canada Cataloguing in Publication
Title: Writings : commentary from Jack Engelhard the voice of America's conscience / by Jack Engelhard..
Names: Engelhard, Jack, 1940-, author
Identifiers: Canadiana (print) 20230137539 | Canadiana (ebook) 20230137563 | ISBN 9781771435536 (softcover) | ISBN 9781771435543 (PDF)
Classification: LCC PS3555.N395 W75 2023 | DDC 814/.6—dc23

Jack Engelhard may be contacted through the publisher at either:
www.dayraypress.com or **www.ccbpublishing.com**

Front cover artwork: Diplomatic handshake between countries: United States and Israel.
Picture © MattiaATH | CanStockPhoto.com

Jack Engelhard's columns reproduced herein were previously published by *Arutz Sheva English site (israelnationalnews.com)* and in the Communities section of *The Washington Times*, respectively, except for the columns entitled *Notes from the Days of Our Youth*, *The Holocaust in the Age of Forgetfulness* and *The Obit Uris Never Got.*

DayRay Literary Press is a literary imprint
of CCB Publishing: www.ccbpublishing.com

DayRay Literary Press
British Columbia, Canada
www.dayraypress.com

International Bestselling Novelist Jack Engelhard
Author of *Indecent Proposal*

Translated into more than 22 languages and turned into a Paramount motion picture of the same name starring Robert Redford and Demi Moore.

Writings

Commentary from Jack Engelhard the Voice of America's Conscience

Legendary American novelist Jack Engelhard is equally regarded for his high standard of journalism, which for many years appeared as Op-ed columns in the *Philadelphia Inquirer*, and also in such publications as *The New York Times*. Today he enjoys a large worldwide following for his columns that appear on the popular Israeli news/opinion website *Arutz Sheva/Israelnationalnews*, English edition. There he is recognized for his discerning eye on politics and culture in both the United States and Israel, where he has served as an American volunteer in the Israeli Defense Force (IDF).

In *Writings* Engelhard pulls no punches in this collection of columns about the political climate here and abroad that affects people worldwide. He is our conscience of today, pointing out distortions and corruption of our government and leaders. He is never afraid to tell us the truth no matter how difficult it is to face.

Also featuring

Engelhard's Guide to Writing

and more bonus essays

Praise received for Jack Engelhard's books

"Precise, almost clinical language…Is this book fun to read? You betcha."
- *The New York Times,* for *Indecent Proposal*

"The prose is vivid, cool and muscular, the story is great. In all, the fine tension between desire and high moral principal make *Indecent Proposal* a well-crafted book... well-wrought characters, exhilarating pace...it's beautifully written."
- *Philadelphia Inquirer*

"*Compulsive* is enormously enjoyable, and so easy to get into."
- Kenneth Slawenski, (Random House) bestselling author of
J.D. Salinger: A Life - www.deadcaulfields.com

"A towering literary achievement."
- Letha Hadady, author, for *The Bathsheba Deadline*

"Engelhard zeroes in on a news anchor who resembles Megyn Kelly. It's fiction, but WOW!"
- Bonnie Kaye, author, for *News Anchor Sweetheart*

"The refugee stories Engelhard preserves are boyhood memories of an almost Tom Sawyer character… adventurous, humorous, sometimes wonderfully strange."
- Chris Leppek, *Jewish News (Denver),*
for *Escape from Mount Moriah*

"What a great story. If you missed the 60s – if you missed the excitement, the passion, the radicalism, the thrills, the hopes and dreams – this book brings it all alive. I could not put it down."
- Kmgroup review, for *The Days of the Bitter End*

"Savor it…it may be the best, sharpest, most vivid portrait of life around the racetrack ever written."
- Ray Kerrison, *New York Post* columnist
writing for the *National Star*, for *The Horsemen*

Also by Jack Engelhard

Indecent Proposal: Fiction.
Translated into more than 22 languages and turned into a Paramount motion picture of the same name starring Robert Redford and Demi Moore.

News Anchor Sweetheart: Fiction

Compulsive: A Novel: Fiction.

Escape From Mount Moriah: Memoir.
Award-winner for writing and film.

The Days of the Bitter End: Fiction.

Slot Attendant: A Novel About A Novelist: Fiction.

The Prince of Dice: Fiction.

The Bathsheba Deadline: Fiction.

The Girls of Cincinnati: Fiction

The Horsemen: Non-Fiction

* * * * *

A new Spanish language edition of *Indecent Proposal* was released in 2013 in both print and e-book editions and made available for purchase worldwide.

The author wishes to express his gratitude and thanks to translators Frederick Martin-Del-Campo and Laura Mitre for their fine work in this and other projects.

Acknowledgements

For Jack Engelhard's Op-ed columns contained herein that were previously published by *Arutz Sheva* (israelnationalnews.com), acknowledgements are respectfully given to the following:

Uzi Baruch,
Editor in Chief and CEO,
Arutz Sheva (israelnationalnews.com)

Rabbanit Shulamit Melamed,
Director General,
Arutz Sheva (israelnationalnews.com)

Ido Ben Porat,
Deputy Editor,
Arutz Sheva (israelnationalnews.com)

Yoni Kempinski,
Managing Editor,
Arutz Sheva (israelnationalnews.com)

Rochel Sylvetsky,
Senior Consultant and Op-ed Editor,
Arutz Sheva English site (israelnationalnews.com)

The author thanks Jeffrey Farkas for his support,
he wishes to also thank Lindy Snider,
and expresses his gratitude to compiler Bonnie Kaye.

Dedicated to Leslie, my wife

Introduction

We are living in modern times that are unlike others. The simplicity of the past is no longer part of our present. Due to "technology and social media," news is no longer the news but rather political commentaries espoused by people both on the left and the right.

Society is constantly bombarded by opinions that are not worthy of being called "the truth." That's why it is a rarity to find a true professional like Jack Engelhard who is willing to put his reputation on the line to share those truths and frailties that our society faces daily.

Jack is a phenomenal award winning author of novels that have sold millions of copies including the book, *Indecent Proposal* which was turned into a Hollywood motion picture. There are few Jewish writers in our century that can combine the enjoyment of fiction alongside the harsh reality of journalism that we live in. Perhaps this is why he was awarded with the Ben Hecht award several years ago for excellence in journalism. Ben Hecht was a champion of the Jewish people during the Holocaust in the 1940's when the American Jewish community feared that roaring too loudly in the face of anti-Semitism would only create more attention against the Jews living here. Hecht constantly alerted the world to the extermination of the Jews and served as a gadfly in the midst of other Jewish journalists who labeled his actions as "idiocy and recklessness." He didn't care. Hecht put all of his efforts into informing the world of the incomprehensible disaster going on in Europe through various media and plays when the world turned a blind eye.

Like Hecht, Jack Engelhard serves as a conscience to the Jewish community both in the United States and in Israel. He spent time in Israel serving as a volunteer in the Israeli Defense Forces. In these columns from his articles in the Israeli newspaper *Arutz Sheva*, you will see Jack's talent to see through our realities in a society that is producing Jewish hatred from both the left and the right. He pulls no punches in his columns about the political climate here and abroad that affects Jews worldwide. He is our conscience of today, pointing out distortions and corruption of our government and leaders. He is never afraid to tell us the truth no matter how difficult it is to face.

It is hard to find true literary heroes in our life. That is why as a former Jewish activist leader, I am proud to know this man who has made such a difference in the world through his words and actions. He certainly has influenced my thinking over the years knowing that we have someone who can champion the truth. Enjoy the pages ahead.

Bonnie Kaye, M.Ed.

Notes from the Days of Our Youth

-by Jack Engelhard

Dateline, somewhere outside Philadelphia; a midsized newspaper conglomerate serving the neighborhoods weekly.

Mid 1950s, and I've got a job. The pay doesn't cover expenses to get there and back, but if people ask if I'm working, I can say, yes, I am.

Mack is the foreman over there on the dock and on a Friday, just as I'm clocking out, he hands me a package and says, "Take it to the editor."

"Where?"

"The newsroom."

I'd never been there, but keep walking until I reach a place that actually says Newsroom. I step in and already it's a different world. There's a cathedral-like reverence about it all. People are seated at their desks typing away. The room is quiet and noisy all at once. Once in a while someone shouts out "Boy," meaning Copy Boy, and that's what he does, picks up copy from one desk to another, from reporter to editor.

I spot the man who must be the editor. I start heading in his direction to deliver the package, but am rudely stopped.

"Where are you going?" someone asks.

I tell him.

"You'll have to wait. Mr. Franklin is writing."

What a man, Mr. Franklin. He can't be disturbed because he is writing. A revelation. Writing turns a man into a king.

The newsroom, then, is a sanctuary, a kingdom.

Writing is holy.

This is the life for me.

* * *

Dateline, Cincinnati, late 1950s

I've written something that feels right. It's about my parents, Holocaust Survivors, who, now in America, get to vote for the first time.

Some of it I made up. But the patriotism was correct for the place and the times.

The short stories I had written and sent off to New York all kept coming back. Fiction wasn't working, not yet, so let's give something factual a try.

I showed the piece to Kuana, the big Hawaiian, black belt in judo but also in literature, and my best friend.

"I like it," he said.

This was historic.

"Good enough to get published?"

He suggests I take it to the *Cincinnati Enquirer*.

"It's that good?"

"I think so. Show it to the columnist you're always talking about, Ollie James.

Ollie James' column was a daily feature on the Op-ed section of the paper, and these were written in a casual style I so admired and wished to emulate, and, over the years, perhaps I did. The photo of him showed him to be a jolly fat man, a man always ready with a wisecrack, but with Midwestern brevity, lightness, neighborliness and charm.

"Mail it?" I ask Kuana.

"Why wait? Take it to him in person."

"Is this done?"

"Find out."

I drive to the building, then tell the guard in the lobby that I am here to see Ollie James, and just when I expect him to laugh in my face, or escort me out the door, he says, "What's it about?"

"I'd like to show him an article I wrote."

He turns away to make a private call, and returns to say, "Take the elevator to the eighth floor."

On the eighth floor, I introduce myself to the receptionist, expecting her to tell me that Ollie James is not available but to leave the article with her.

Instead… "Mr. James will see you shortly."

Mr. James will see ME?

I sit and wait, and reconsider the article. Maybe I should just leave. Because, on second thought, it's just awful. Dreadful. Pathetic. Go home.

Spare yourself the embarrassment.

I am actually ready to bolt when a man appears, tall, severe, his face etched Lincolnesque.

"You're here to see me?" he asks gently.

Wrong man. The man I had expected is short, fat and jolly, and I keep looking for him down the hallway, tapping a trick cigar.

Not this guy.

"I was hoping to see Ollie James."

"I am Ollie James."

I am about to say, no you're not, when he says, "I understand you have something to show me."

So this is the real deal. Turns out his job as columnist is only part-time. He is the editor.

"When would be a good time to show you a piece I've written?"

Would he be taking it back to his desk and get back to me in five weeks with the customary rejection?

"Now is fine."

There is still time to run and tell him I'd rather forget the whole thing.

The article is worthless.

"Let's have it," he says, politely, and so, I hand it over, and here he is, reading it on the spot.

The following morning, it was in the paper, even read over the radio, and at our usual hangout, Sugar 'n Spice, Kuana is celebrating me as a new literary hero.

I find myself signing autographs.

Days like that come around once in a lifetime.

* * *

Dateline, South Jersey, early 1960s

The Suburban Newspaper Group covers the region, township by township, in and around Moorestown, with a staff of about 10 editor/reporters.

I got the job saying that I'd been published in Cincinnati, which was true, and that I had a novel under consideration in New York, also true, in that anybody can say as much.

That does not mean that an offer is forthcoming, but I gave it some flair and put it over, and there I was, my first job, a real job, for a real newspaper.

My career has begun. Maybe. This is to be my first assignment, ever.

Jay Dunn, associate editor, explains what I should expect at this Board Meeting out in Delacore Township, where it's open warfare between Democrats and Republicans.

At issue, and it is crucial, the building of a new road that would cut through farms and farmland. Democrats say yes. Republicans say no.

A dozen times Jay goes over all the particulars. I jot it all down. All of this is new to me, and I am dizzy from so many names and so many facts.

The first job is to find Delacore Township. I don't know the region. Somehow, I get there, and the place is mobbed. Who is who, I don't know.

A woman, smiling, asks me who I am. I explain.

"Oh, you're a reporter."

I am? By golly, yes, I am.

She directs me to the reporters' desk, where about a half dozen of them look me over, approvingly. I take my seat, and the meeting begins.

I open my notebook and start taking notes. What notes? I'm scribbling away hoping somehow, some way, something will make sense.

The others jot down a word or two. More than half my notebook is already full.

When I get back to the newsroom, I am in a panic. The other staffers are back from their assignments and typing away.

Some are done and hand over their work to Costello, the editor.

Jay Dunn approaches me at my desk, where I have not yet written a word, and hadn't even slipped in paper into the typewriter.

I am frozen.

"How did it go?" he asks, worried.

"I don't know."

He leaves, even more worried.

Costello, at the other end, starts eyeing me. Deadline is fast approaching. I am still in a state of shock.

He walks over and says, "Go home."

Was I fired? If so, my career as a journalist was over the same day it had begun. Or did he mean take a break and start fresh tomorrow. There was still an evening edition.

But getting to my car, I took "go home" as the end.

They say that we must never count on miracles. Then how else to explain what happened.

As I'm driving home, it came to me as the writing on the wall. The story wrote itself in my mind, word for word, sentence by sentence, paragraph by paragraph.

As soon as I got home, I dashed for the typewriter to get it all down, as given.

Costello said nothing when I handed him the copy. He read it and placed it in the file for the evening edition.

Prelude

The Holocaust in the Age of Forgetfulness

-by Jack Engelhard

Dateline, Current Day – As many times as I have read the Book of Ecclesiastes (Koheles), not until now, upon reading an article by David I. Klein that the Holocaust is a vague remembrance in The Netherlands, Anne Frank territory, did it reach me, the awesome power of King Solomon's seven words, such as… "A generation goes and a generation comes."

Goes on… "but the earth abides forever," and "there is no recollection of former times."

The statistics show that in The Netherlands, and also in the United States, and surely elsewhere around the world, Holocaust awareness has plunged to the level of forgetfulness.

Forgetfulness is the word.

We are not talking about Holocaust Denial. That is another category, for another time, about which we have touched on plenty.

Our focus is on people with open hearts and open minds.

"No recollection," applies mostly to the upcoming generations, that, year-by-year, replace the old. The old forget. The young don't know.

"But the earth endures forever." Take that to mean, life goes on. People, namely the young, have other business, other interests, other pursuits.

Drive by any schoolyard, the boys playing ball, the girls playing hopscotch, and ask yourself, can these children be reached?

No malice intended. They mean no disrespect. They come on the scene eyes to the future, not the past, and the memorials we erect can only do so much to instill awareness.

There's a fine line between educating the young, and going on with it until we say too much, and we turn them off. We become a nuisance, a windbag.

For those of us who know, especially those of us who survived, this hurts, the knowledge that so many know nothing, or don't care, and that too much information backfires.

Beware the lament, "Oh that again."

We have no choice but to persist against the worst crime in history, and to make sure, yes, through education, that it never happens again, and won't, thanks to Israel.

King Solomon's message hits in other ways, and speaks directly to those of us who find our days slipping past.

Forgetfulness, indeed.

Who will be there to pick up where we left off? Will there be anyone to remember that we were here and did something?

Or are we doomed to be forgotten without a trace?

When the accusers come, who will rise in our defense? We won't be around to speak for ourselves… if there is anything to say.

Have we made more enemies than friends? Sometimes it seems that way. It's unwise to review the past, and yet we do so to our peril and despair.

More often than not, we have failed.

We yield to our most horrible nightmares… while still awake.

The worst of it is when, in our weakest moment, before our first cup of coffee, we run out of excuses only to admit that, now and then, we were to blame.

That hurts most of all.

The father judges but often the most severe judgement comes from ourselves. Kafka was right.

We are haunted by the mistakes we made and we are troubled three o'clock in the morning of the friends, loved ones and even acquaintances who misunderstood us.

If only there were some way to make amends, but most of them are gone.

What's there to cheer when the past is so much longer than the future? For the young, there are no assurances, either.

From the bricklayer to the barber to the writer, did we do anything of worth? In the end, the writer's words splash and wash away like raindrops.

That is forgetfulness.

In your prose, you against the world? That's a laugh. The world always wins.

Is anybody listening?

If so, do they take it the wrong way?

We were gifted with life. How much of it did we squander? The days slipped by too fast. We were given one chance, and Fitzgerald was right.

There are no second chances.

We begin with dreams, with hopes to achieve, and with promises to succeed, only to realize that nobody cares.

That too is forgetfulness.

Wisdom comes with age? So does regret.

But to our Creator, who assigned for us the Works to be done, to our credit, we say, "Here I am."

Our prime… our best years… are they ahead or behind? God only knows.

Says King Solomon, "So remember your Creator in the days of your youth, before the evil days come."

But he ended his Book of Koheles on a high note: "The end of the matter, when all is considered, fear God and keep His commandments, for that is man's whole duty."

Contents

Writings

Commentary from Jack Engelhard
the Voice of America's Conscience

Even at *The New Yorker*, You Can't Be Woke Enough

***Jul. 27, 2022 – Once good writing was the criterion, and we never knew, or cared, who was left, right, Democrat, or Republican.**

Well, she isn't claiming sexual harassment. That's refreshing.

But that could come next in Woke USA. Though as the always excellent Giulio Meotti documents in the *Arutz Sheva* pages, Woke-ism is rearing up in Europe as well.

Is Israel being spared this fast-moving poisonous culture?

Moving on, since we only know what we read, says here that a staffer at *The New Yorker*, Erin Overbey, just got fired for complaining that the magazine lacked "diversity."

Huge story in the book and literary world.

She's seeking redress from the union.

She also griped about "gender inequality" in the workplace, according to the report.

Editor David Remnick views it differently. He says she's a constant headache. A real kvetch.

No, take that back. I was only interpreting. He says she was let go "for a pattern of misconduct disruptive for the Company," and for "self-plagiarism."

"Self-plagiarism" is a wrinkle. It's when you present old material of yours as something new.

Whatever the reason, Editor-in-Chief Remnick must not have seen this coming, certainly not from inside his own confederacy of leftists.

Since he took over the magazine in 1998 from the flashy Tina Brown, he's been the perfect Liberal, which means that everything he does is in keeping with political correctness.

Obviously, though, in a world where every person is watching every move you make, harshly, as Kafka would say, you can never be perfect enough.

---

* Originally published in *Arutz Sheva* English site (israelnationalnews.com).

You are always guilty.

You are always the accused.

Never mind what you did.

You always did something.

For Remnick, this thwack from his staffer, must sting as an Et Tu stab in the back. Seems that she sent out wholesale tweets and emails to register her complaints.

Management noticed.

It's doubtful that Remnick toured the newsroom taking a census… how many are White, how many are Black, who's a man, and as for women, suddenly, what is a woman?

Are there enough transgenders to fill the quota?

Apparently, never enough, and never enough Minorities. If he'd watch more television, Remnick would learn from the rest of corporate America how it's done.

Virtually all commercials, these days, feature Minority performers. That's the way to go… to avoid being called out.

Remnick must be wondering what more he could have done to be a more perfect Woke specimen.

Until he came on the scene, *The New Yorker* had been apolitical and a haven for literary introspection.

It's where we first read Hannah Arendt's "Eichmann in Jerusalem," and Salinger's "A Perfect Day for Banana Fish," and Shirley Jackson's terrifying "The Lottery."

Good writing was worshipped, and we never knew, or cared, who was left, right, Democrat, or Republican.

Until David Remnick came along and imposed his leftist dogma, trampling high literature with low politics.

The hint came in 2004, when, as it says in Wikipedia, for the first time in 80 years, *The New Yorker* endorsed a presidential candidate… John Kerry.

Yes, John Kerry, and under Remnick's heavy-handed leadership, it's been that way ever since… politics, and leftist orthodoxy week after week.

Finally, to his chagrin, he found someone even more perfectly liberal than he could ever be, and she's coming for him.

Hell hath no fury as a leftist scorned.

Oy Vey! Thomas Friedman is Upset with Israel

Jan. 20, 2023 – He is the Korach of our times, and so is the rest of his paper, plus even the media in Israel, Hebrew and English ...except *Arutz Sheva.

Marcus, an old friend, and a friend of Israel, was terribly upset. He phoned to say, "Did you read Tom Friedman today?"

"I try not to read him any day."

Friedman, of *The New York Times*, has written the same column about Israel over and over again, though usually with some new twist.

What is it this time?

Today what's his oy vey complaint? With him, on Israel, it is always oy vey. The sky is falling.

"He says Israel's democracy is doomed."

That one again?

I'd heard that before, about a hundred times. Israel is finished. Kaput. The party's over. It's time to call it a day.

Time to hand Israel over to the Palestinian Arabs, an ancient civilization, since around 1964. Even the Beatles preceded them.

Meantime, an artifact has emerged that dates back to King David, 3,000 years ago. In Israel, when they dig for electric wiring, something like this usually comes up.

From column to column to column, on Israel, Friedman finds nothing but imperfections.

His petulance today, says Marcus is, "All because Netanyahu won the election and his right-wing ministers are about to make drastic changes. Read it and find out. Hurry."

Over the past week or so, I'd read dozens of articles on the subject, how Israel is alarmingly on the verge of losing its right to consider itself a democracy for any number of reasons.

---

* Originally published in *Arutz Sheva* English site (israelnationalnews.com).

The main reason is that Netanyahu and his ministers are working on a plan to simmer down the high court, which has amassed far too much power for itself.

A good number of conservatives, in and out, agree that it's high time the members of the high court act as judges and not as legislators, too often the case.

Meantime, before I had a chance to catch up with Friedman, the phone rang again, and this time it was no friend.

"Told you," he says, "the Israelis have finally done it. This time they're cooked. The whole world has come out against Netanyahu and what he's up to."

Oy vey, oy vey.

The entire world, huh? So what else is new?

In fact, only the Left has gone nuts… not only about this, but about anything Netanyahu does. They resent his election and want him removed, pronto.

Yair Lapid, the man Netanyahu replaced, keeps calling for unrest, and demonstrations, and boycotts, and is proving himself a really sore loser.

In Tel Aviv, leftists have been loudly demonstrating, also to topple the government because, as here in America, if things don't go their way, they turn nasty.

Their way or the highway.

What is it about the Left that they can't take no for an answer, even after the people have spoken?

Same deal with Tom Friedman.

In his column, Friedman calls on Biden to get tough with Netanyahu. No more fooling around, and if Netanyahu keeps it up, namely, the effort to revise the high court, plus even an inkling to annex Judea and Samaria, the so-called 'West Bank,' he should realize that the United States will cut off relations with Israel, and will no longer support or be a friend of the Jewish State.

Israel's democracy, says he, is severely at risk. Biden must act to save Israel… as he is saving America?

That's Friedman today… and that was Friedman yesterday, last week, last month, last year, 10 years ago.

But this time, calling on Biden to intervene, he really means it, as do his fellow Leftists in America, Israel, everywhere.

You can practically hear their Gevalt.

So I asked one of my relatives in Jerusalem how he feels about the situation.

"What situation?" he asked.

"You know… Bibi… the high court…"

"Oh, well, here we call it just another day in Israel."

"So what's all that commotion I hear in the background… a riot no doubt against Bibi and his ministers."

"Not quite. Yossi won his wings for the Air Force. So we're having a party. Our family, as you know, does get loud."

So they do. God bless them.

Biden is Losing the Media, and Thus the Country

***Jan. 15, 2023 – The switch, to aggressive reporting, happened in a blink, and it came crashing about a week ago.**

Calamity Joe faces a resentful media.

No more are they asking which flavor ice cream he prefers, as they did there at the beginning.

"Mr. President… Mr. President… what do you like best, chocolate or vanilla?"

That's as far as it got for investigative reporting from America's docile media. Joe had them at hello.

Now is it goodbye?

Before our eyes we are watching Joe and his presidency unraveling domino by domino as more questions are being asked about his neglect toward classified files… a serious breach.

So serious that it could bring down his presidency… especially so with the Republican House on the hunt.

There is blood in the water… all the way from China.

The switch, to aggressive reporting, happened in a blink, and it came crashing about a week ago when *CBS Evening News* broke the story about mishandled classified documents.

What were the documents doing in Joe's former office… when they should have been turned over to the National Archives?

Joe's alleged malfeasance is one part of the story. The other part is the media and how they turned to activists after so many years on snooze control.

They turned on him, the thinking goes, because they find him unfit to run again, and are thus preparing America for a fresher face, someone like Pete Buttigieg.

---

* Originally published in *Arutz Sheva* English site (israelnationalnews.com).

Pete, today's Transportation Secretary, is equally incompetent, and he is gay, therefore perfectly suited for the highest office, thanks to the Democrats.

Identity politics uber alles.

Better, they reason, a young fool than an old fool… and whatever Joe did to ruin the country, Pete, or perhaps Kamala, can finish the job.

Either way, the media woke up and for the first time found imperfections in good old Joe… actually, the first time they found faults in any Democrat.

The answers coming from Joe's press secretary, Karine Jean-Pierre, were found wanting and misleading, in what used to be called a "credibility gap."

After *CBS* came *NBC* and even *ABC*, and together they found and exposed Joe as the hoarder of classified documents, stashes of them here, there, and everywhere.

Not so fast, though.

Originally, they tried to play it down. No big deal, they said. Why… only a few pages were found, compared to Trump's larger haul of forbidden material at Mar-a-Lago.

Biden good. Trump bad.

Oops. Now they have found 20 such secret materials on Joe's properties.

To divert attention, *The New York Times* began running stories meant to prove that the Biden family is not crooked.

Joe, the paper alleged, knew nothing about Hunter's shady business deals, and for sure Joe never shared, nor got rich, from the proceedings. Never. Never. Never.

Not a chance that China has got its paws all over father and son.

The rest of them, however, continued to assail Joe… an amazing turn of events and a lesson to what happens when you poke the sleeping giant, the media.

You don't want the media turning on you.

Lyndon Johnson's presidency came to an end after Walter Cronkite, note, *CBS*, visited Vietnam and came back to say the war was "wasteful."

Johnson declined to run for a second term.

Richard Nixon was undone by Watergate. He resigned after being exposed by Woodward and Bernstein and *The Washington Post*.

Both presidents were caught being dishonest.

Joe can't give a straight answer… not even on ice cream.

Tough Guys Don't Dance in Israel

***Jan. 10, 2023 – Poor Abbas… what happened to the good old days when he could make promises he'd never keep and still get the Israelis to pay up?**

Finally, an Israeli government that is not afraid to say, this land is our land.

Romancing the Muslim Brotherhood, as per Bennett/Lapid/Gantz, came to an end when Benjamin Netanyahu emerged triumphant and filled his Cabinet with tough guys who don't dance with terrorists, nor share leadership with members of the Muslim Brotherhood, nor are apt to play Ring around the Rosie with the PA, Fatah, Hamas, and Islamic Jihad.

Jews on trembling knees. No thanks. It's been tried. Never works. Oslo, for example.

That's when, 1993, Israel caved to Leftist pressure from home and abroad and elevated a group of bums and cutthroats, the PLO, to the level of respectable diplomats.

File that too under the category of Never Again.

Do not, then, expect Israel's newly installed security minister, Itamar Ben-Gvir, to shake the blood-soaked hand of Mahmoud Abbas, duplicating Rabin's mistake with Arafat.

Instead, Ben-Gvir took a step toward correcting Dayan's mistake by paying a visit to the Temple Mount, but which *Al-Jazeera* termed "storming Al-Aqsa."

They do know how to hyperventilate the language, don't they? Nothing subtle.

Neither is Ben-Gvir.

From Ben-Gvir's point of view, so sorry to hurt your feelings, but we are entitled to go wherever we want in our own country.

Next, he's ordering the police to take down Palestinian Arab flags hoisted anywhere in public places. This after they celebrated the release of one of their own brother terrorists with cheers and flag-waving,

---

* Originally published in *Arutz Sheva* English site (israelnationalnews.com).

a sight that has to be most disturbing to Israelis who have suffered so long from these same people… at home, in their own country.

Nothing says eyesore as a PLO flag waving somewhere in Israel.

Message… Israelis have feelings too and were thus hurt and terribly displeased when the Palestinian Authority, through the UN, summoned Israel to the World Court to be chastised for the "occupation." No more Mr. Nice Guy, under this administration, the government retaliated with sanctions.

In other words, Abbas is stuck with no money, from Israel, to pay the electric bill… and for whatever it costs to incite adults and teach kids to hate Jews.

Obviously, he did not know that these new guys can't be fiddled.

These guys play for keeps… and fat chance for a Palestinian Arab embassy in Jerusalem.

They were such an easy mark, such a soft touch, that Abbas could foster his draconian pay to slay program without much consequence for Israelis being murdered at home and on the roads. The Israelis, the leadership that is, turned aside to avoid rocking the boat internationally… and shrugged it off as the price of doing business with an eventual "peace partner."

Those delusions have expired.

This time, this Israeli government is diverting tax dollars for the PA to the victims of Palestinian Arab terrorism.

What took so long?

Abbas is moaning about the unfairness of it all, and says that drying up the funding for his terrorists and their families could put the Palestinian Authority out of business.

What's his next move? The UN again? The World Court once more?

Let him try and see what happens now with new sheriffs in town.

How Netanyahu Turned the Flood Against Him into A Puddle

***Jan. 5, 2023 – The story is as much a triumph of the Right, as it is a defeat of the Left.**

After all the Bibi bashing, look who's on top

For the Left in the United States, they will always have Trump. In Israel, they will always have Netanyahu… to kick around.

In fact, whatever you say about Trump, the same goes for Netanyahu, except that Bibi got to the finish line first.

"What tipped the scales for Netanyahu?" Answer: "Israelis voted to win back their country and the sanctity of their Jewish heritage."

For many, the result was news to cheer.

However, if you're ever having a good day, to ruin it all, watch the evening news on either *NBC*, *CBS*, or *ABC*, to catch up on What Did Trump Do Today To Upset Them So Much.

Ditto for Netanyahu in Israel… who remains the main target of the Left especially after he's given them a thrashing, and wound up on top.

This they will not forget or forgive.

With them, it is always something, though lately, around here, it has been the same thing, Jan. 6.

Nothing new there, but they will always find a twist to smack Trump around one more time.

But how many times can you hook the same fish?

People who've been in the news business for some time develop a nose for which headlines stay fresh, and a knack for which news gets stale.

As it is, the animosities have boomeranged, and the media are stuck with overkill. Will they learn from this? Surely not.

Thus the question… have the Leftists used up all their marbles… lost their mojo… lost their wallop… to the point where nothing they say means anything anymore?

---

* Originally published in *Arutz Sheva* English site (israelnationalnews.com).

It would seem so in Israel where the Leftists control the media and the legal system, and ganged up on Netanyahu using all their tools, and so huffing and puffing they tried to bring him down, but failed, and failed, why? One reason: "The Israelis saw with alarm their Land, their Good Earth, being corrupted.

"Leaders that they never voted for were making plans to undo Israel's Jewish sanctity."

So the Israelis turned Right, their actual default position, and true enough that, but they also told the Leftists, enough with your sanctimony, your sourpuss kvetching.

The Left, it would surely seem, had played its "Never Bibi" hand once too often, so that the people grew weary and said…

"Bibi's desire for better coverage. That's it? That's your scandal? What else you got? Oh cigars."

The population tuned out. Call it a numbing effect.

The Left's one-trick-pony message had grown dull… and this is where we are in the United States as well.

Whatever they say, does it mean anything anymore?

Case in point… like the "scandal" over Netanyahu's cigars over there, so too over here, Trump's taxes, a scandal which also never materialized.

The House, then under Democrat control, released the data, only days ago, which showed that, over the past few years, Trump paid hardly any taxes at all. However you feel about this, or about Trump… Trump deniers will always think the worst… even if Trump may have a legitimate case… fact is, this should have been a big story.

Yes, stop the presses.

They'd been begging for ways to finally get Trump… hang Trump… bury Trump… and here it was, on a platter.

Taxes… that is how they get you, and how they got Al Capone.

Hence, Trump was ripe for a shellacking across the dials, from one news cycle onto another, as it was, day and night, during the Russia frame-up.

Strangely, not this time.

On *ABC*, the network, through David Muir, that never misses a chance to praise Biden but malign Trump, the story wasn't even the top item.

The piece ran somewhere in the middle as ho-hum, as if Muir and the editors figured they'd used it all up on the guy, nothing more to give, and so it was across the dials.

The New York Times gave it about a day and a half… no more than that over embarrassment that over the years they'd laid it on too thick.

To their chagrin, he'd begun earning sympathy points.

Netanyahu wearied them down the same way, until their storms of discontent against him turned into no flood, but a puddle.

UN vs Israel – New Year, Same Old Story

***Jan. 2, 2023 – The UN has an Israel fixation caused by Israel's only crime – being Jewish.**

Look at it this way – the score could have been 193 to nothing.

That's the figure Israel's part-time "peace partner" and full-time terrorist Mahmoud Abbas keeps going after as chairman of the Palestinian Authority.

Instead, the tally at the UN General Assembly came to 87 against Israel, 26 in favor, and 53 abstentions.

That is still lopsided, and if you are a bettor, and the UN versus Israel is your game, you probably collected.

What was it all about? New Year, same old story – Israel is an "occupier" in Judea, Samaria, and Jerusalem, the land of its Hebrew fathers, by the way.

All that territory, they say, is in the wrong hands, and belongs to the Palestinian Arabs, who have no Bible and no history of nationhood in or around the Holy Land.

It became the Holy Land thanks to Abraham, Isaac, Jacob, Joseph, Moses, David, and many other men of towering distinction, and women of valor, up to today's IDF.

Details like that are no bother at the UN, which referred its latest anti-Israel proposal to the World Court in The Hague.

The World Court, which, as Napoleon would say, has no army, so who's afraid? Well, it can make trouble simply through bad-mouthing somebody, anybody.

Any bets on which side those judges will take?

The World Court happens to be a satellite of the United Nations. So much for a fair trial.

But didn't they do all that before?

Seems like only yesterday, in fact it was 2016 when this time the UN Security Council passed Resolution 2334, same deal as today. Israel in the wrong.

---

* Originally published in *Arutz Sheva* English site (israelnationalnews.com).

We read that outgoing PM Lapid and incoming PM Netanyahu each, separately, took to the phones pleading with world leaders to vote nay for the latest UN travesty.

Why make so much effort over something that amounts to nothing? On Israel, the UN has zero credibility, and since Resolution 2334, the year 2016, Israel has grown even mightier.

True, it is understood, that nobody wants to be disliked. We'd all rather have friends than enemies. That goes for individuals, and nations, too.

No wonder, then, that Israel reached out for some love, and got 26, as meanwhile 87 nations turned their backs, among them Arab nations that signed peace treaties with Israel.

Go figure… and what's the deal with Ukraine's Volodymyr Zelenskyy? Seems that he told Netanyahu that he'd vote favorably for Israel conditionally… only if Israel supplied him with more defensive equipment, which is some chutzpah, seeing how Israel is itself constantly under the gun on all its borders.

Israel already gave and Israel must always weigh its balance between Russia and anybody else. Some consideration for Israel's tight spot would have been appreciated.

In the end, Zelenskyy voted to abstain. This did Israel no favor, and proved how fickle some people, some nations, can be. Zelenskyy is an ingrate.

That was a gratuitous slap, as it was during the Dark Ages when the Chief Rabbi of Toulouse had to present himself, once a year, to the cathedral for a ceremonial slap across the face.

For the crime of being Jewish… and for a grudge that persists to this day. As we have just seen at the UN.

Israel must continue to make friends, as it did through the Abraham Accords, but if there's a lesson here, it's that Israel must never count on being adored.

From strength to strength is the only way.

The Migrants and the Holocaust

***Dec. 28, 2022 – Why I don't bleed for the migrants.**

The breaking news is that Title 42 has been extended, by the Supreme Court, thus averting a surge of migrants that would have become torrential.

Still they come here in droves, illegally, mostly men, and say, "Feed me."

From Honduras, Guatemala, Haiti and elsewhere around the world they come and expect, and are often granted, instant gratification.

Not for them the waiting 10 years for the proper papers. Biden says come, and they come, by the millions.

I remember those 10 years when Father would come home exhausted after visiting another lawyer, another ambassador, another diplomat, all to no avail for a visa.

The doors were mostly closed.

Roosevelt knew the situation, but he did not care. Canada's government declared, humorously, "None is too many."

For most Americans, like those who got their news from *The New York Times*, the Holocaust was a distant thing. Somebody else's business.

The Times usually mentioned it, if at all, on page 36… a paper owned by Jews, but Jews afraid of rocking the boat.

They did not want to be identified with Those Jews.

So the murder of Six Million by the Germans, by all of Europe, became noticed only gradually among Americans. It took years to grasp the full horror.

It was in those days when Mother found out that she had relatives on Long Island. These were well established, prosperous Americans, and certainly they would be happy to meet a European cousin who had just arrived from France, through Spain, through Portugal, aboard the Serpa Pinto, carrying a suitcase that had been packed in a hurry.

---

* Originally published in *Arutz Sheva* English site (israelnationalnews.com).

Suitcases, to this day, are a dreaded sight among the remaining Holocaust Survivors. The suitcase is a symbol of all that was left behind.

So a meeting on Long Island was arranged, and there is no telling how Mother got there; she spoke no English. The relative, Mina, retained some Yiddish.

The home on Long Island was grand, as it had been for Mother and her family back in Toulouse, France, before the arrival of the French police and the German Gestapo.

Mina had invited Mother for a chat.

In the kitchen, over coffee and cake, Mother explained this, calmly… how all was lost.

Mina listened patiently, even sympathetically, but without fully understanding how this could be so, so terrible. She knew, of course, about Hitler, about Jews being deprived of homes and businesses… she'd read about it in the paper… but about concentration camps and Jews being hunted and whisked off the streets, of that she knew but faintly.

Was it really that bad?

For Mother, this was a revelation. America was not a different country. It was a different world.

She realized that it would take time to tell the story, but Mina had not the time. A European story was not her story.

She was an American, and soon she would have to pick up the kids from school, prepare dinner, and get ready for an important gala to which she and her husband had been invited.

This was not the chat she had in mind.

Mother understood this, but she could not help crying when she told about her family… also Mina's family… that had, one by one, been wiped out by the Nazis.

Mina listened, with growing impatience, and some irritation, about events that were far from her own life, but so close to Mother's, and it became unbearable for Mina, to learn how Tanta Erna was exposed to the Gestapo when she dared to visit her three sons, all in hiding, separately, and all doomed together.

Mina too began crying, truly for the tragic loss, but also, mainly, in fact, for the serene life of hers that was being uprooted by this tale from Europe.

This was an intrusion she had not expected and did not need.

"I've heard enough," she screamed.

Mother said, "I did not mean to upset you. But you asked to be told how it was."

"But not such details."

Never would they meet again.

Biden's Chutzpah
Over the Jenin Accident

***Dec. 14, 2022 – Lapid rushed to offer his condolences to the family, and to the world, in case you are wondering why he was voted out of office.**

In David Rosenberg's recent article "Itamar Ben-Gvir Pushes Back on US Demand for 'Accountability'" he states, quite clearly, that Israel admits that through an accident, its forces killed a teenage girl in Jenin.

End of story? No. The Biden Administration, through its State Department, demands further investigations and "accountability."

Like what? Presumably, Biden demands hand-wringing sorrow for a Palestinian Arab girl who was on a roof, not the roof of her own home, next to a terrorist and crouching in the line of fire between the IDF and her brother terrorists.

She may have been an "innocent" bystander. If we forget that they so frequently use children, girls, and women as fodder; human shields.

In our world, 16-year-old girls are being readied for the Prom. Their world we will never understand.

We say to life. They rally for death… and Israel is given permission to defend itself, so long as no harm comes to the enemy.

For collateral damage in the fog of war, the Israelis are always to be faulted. The other side gets the benefit of the doubt.

In any case, outgoing prime minister Yair Lapid rushed to offer his condolences to the family, and to the world, in case you are wondering why he was voted out of office.

Israelis prefer strong leadership, rather than being portrayed as "Jews on trembling knees."

Meantime, Palestinian Arab terrorists continue their murderous campaign against Israeli civilians and off-duty soldiers.

The highways and byways are unsafe. For Jews. In their own country.

---

* Originally published in *Arutz Sheva* English site (israelnationalnews.com).

So where is Biden on this? We've yet to hear his State Department demand accountability from the Palestinian Authority.

Nor does Biden insist that the PA must stop its pay-to-slay pogrom… or else the financing will be cut off. To the contrary.

The PA has hit the jackpot through Biden's generosity from American tax dollars. Trump had turned the spigot off.

This teenage girl in Jenin. We already know her name. But we do not know the names of the IDF guys who day after day must go in against terrorists armed to the teeth, but in they go fully aware that harm's way is the only way. They put their lives at risk for G-d, family and country, and many of them are teenagers as well.

Outside of Israel, where are the tears for them… the thousands maimed and killed to protect Israel against Palestinian Arabs who are taught to hate and kill Jews from the cradle onwards? Jenin, population around 40,000, in Samaria, in what used to be Biblical En-Gannim, a stronghold for the Levite tribe of Issachar, is now occupied by Arabs.

They are administered by the PA, but ruled by Hamas and Islamic Jihad.

Any wonder that it is a flashpoint of terror!

Jenin was handed over to the Arabs in 1995 as part of the Taba Agreement, a period when Israel was willing to trade land for peace, but got no peace.

Today, there is no such thing as cleaning house, because, among diehard segments, they continue to breed.

The IDF has no choice but to keep them from running wild throughout the Land.

So Biden demands accountability.

The one word that comes to mind is chutzpah.

Biden has yet to answer for Afghanistan, his reckless pullout that left thousands behind and which caused the murder of 13 US service members.

In the military, leaving your people behind is cause for court-martial. From a president, it is cause for impeachment.

How can such a man demand accountability from anyone… anyone but himself?

Naturally, he's been in the clear, with the media covering for him. That will change when the Republicans take over the House, Jan. 3, 2023, and start digging.

Yes, it is time for accountability. Not the sort he had in mind.

Jews Need Not Apply

***Dec. 10, 2022 – Once again, Jews seeking employment face a Gentlemen's Agreement that they thought had faded away long ago.**

Just when I thought I was done writing about anti-Semitism, at least for a month, Bonnie Kaye pulls me back in.

Bonnie, dear friend and tireless fighter for Israel and Jews everywhere, alerts me to a news item which shows that Jews seeking employment face a Gentleman's Agreement.

Gentleman's Agreement, from the book by Laura Z. Hobson, is code among employers. Done through nods and understandings, Jewish applicants face hiring quotas and restrictions.

Think of it as knowing winks and secret handshakes among human resource managers.

Nothing overt, unless you are Jewish and can tell you've been typified… as are 25 percent of Jewish job-seekers who won't get hired in America today. So says this news item.

Hobson made a strong case for how it was around the 1940s, and her book aroused a sensation.

Some believed, and some doubted that anti-Semitism to such degrees existed in America… and so soon after the Holocaust, which should have been a lesson as to what bigotry can do.

The movie came out in 1947, and it caused an uproar. It starred Gregory Peck as a reporter pretending to be Jewish in order to find out if it's true; that Jews face prejudice.

He finds out all right. Friendships go cold. Family members turn off. Hotel clerks can't find him a room, and he can't get a job.

Was it really that bad? I'm thinking Hyman Rickover, admiral, and Father of the Nuclear Navy. He faced prejudice throughout his years of service, and yet he succeeded.

So Jews did find work and Jews did succeed… our success rate higher, far higher than among any other minority group… so that finally Jews, despite small in number, failed to qualify as a minority, and

---

* Originally published in *Arutz Sheva* English site (israelnationalnews.com).

were thus denied minority benefits, even for those who lived at or below the poverty line. There were, and there are, plenty of those, too, among our people.

The Jewish answer… think medicine (Salk), think science (Einstein), entertainment (Hollywood, Broadway), think any other field, and find Jews who create something out of nothing.

They create worlds of their own.

That is the upside.

The downside is that prejudice against Jews is a fact, to the point where Jews cannot feel entirely comfortable.

Back to Hollywood. Even though Jews created Hollywood, out of nothing but tumbleweed, and thus ran Hollywood, they never felt completely at home.

During the Red Scare of the 1940s and 1950s… the blacklist era of HUAC and McCarthyism… the tycoons tried to keep "The Hollywood 10" employed.

These were mainly screenwriters and directors who were, or were thought to be, communists, at a time when communism was anathema.

Finally, the moguls caved, for fear of being taken as un-American, which they weren't, and for fear of being tainted as Jewish monopolizers.

Never mind that they had built the business from scratch and had made America the entertainment capital of the world.

As columnist Hedda Hopper told Samuel Goldwyn, "Your real name is Goldfish, isn't that so?"

She was prepared to "expose" the other studio heads as well, to her 30 million readers, and to Congress. All were patriotic Americans. But Jewish.

Funny how nothing much changes.

Today, these hiring managers, at least 25 percent of them, track Jewish applicants with the same tricks.

They can tell you are Jewish by your name and "superior attitude." An old story. In Hemingway's *The Sun Also Rises*, Robert Cohn is frequently described as feeling superior. His "Jewish superiority" is all over the novel. Which is strange, but a sign of the times. Because whenever Cohn appears on the scene, he is viewed as a tag-along, inferior.

Peter Viertel, Jewish and himself a fine writer who ran with Hemingway, a great writer, and that group, laughed when asked if his pal was anti-Semitic.

"In those days," he said, "weren't they all?"

These days?

I remember my first interview, as a 15-year-old, and the man said, "You think you are the chosen people, don't you?"

They still use that today as a form of blacklisting.

Let's be fair. At around the same time, back in Montreal, which led to my memoir, I was turned down by a Jewish manager because my father, who worked 18 hours a day in the leather trade, was a Torah scholar, an "accusation" I could not deny, but it cost me a job, because, according to that man, Torah scholars tend to be preoccupied by Torah and Talmud.

That sounds like a plan, our plan, right Jeffrey? Let's forget that we have gotten too old and too sick. Stick to the plan, with G-d's help.

Torah and Talmud round the clock. Next Year in Jerusalem.

How the Red Wave Fizzled

***Nov. 11, 2022 – This means the same inflation, the same fuel and food prices, climate hysteria, crisis at the border. The migrants will keep coming.**

Turns out that abortion was a bigger deal than we thought. Bad luck for Republicans when the Supreme Court abolished Roe v. Wade. Big mistake.

Not the act, but the timing, June, just as the midterms were gearing up, only to give Democrats a hot potato, like Jan. 6, to run on.

A few weeks later came an act of stupidity. As the conversation was quieting down, GOP Sen. Lindsey Graham introduced legislation for a national 15-week abortion ban.

The bill went nowhere in the Senate, but fellow GOP senators wished he'd shut up.

Some, or many, wish Trump would do the same.

Over at the *New York Post*, columnist John Podhoretz blames Donald Trump… says he's a "vote repellant." That's why Republicans under-performed in Tuesday's midterm elections.

Ditto, *The Wall Street Journal*, which says, "Trump is the Republican Party's biggest loser."

Maybe so, but it's the media that from day one never let-up their withering campaign against him.

So that finally, through repeated slurs and nitpicking, he became box-office poison… to a segment that bought and voted the slanders the Networks were selling.

It's the media, stupid.

Meantime, Joe Biden can't get the smirk off his face.

The all-teeth gloating is a pathetic sight, and now, seemingly victorious, he's preparing to make no changes.

Therefore, Americans are to expect the same of everything.

---

* Originally published in *Arutz Sheva* English site (israelnationalnews.com).

This means the same inflation, the same fuel and food prices, the same climate hysteria, and the same crisis at the border. The migrants will keep coming.

He thinks he won.

No, he didn't.

I agree with Robert Spencer that the blue votes were the result of a generation that came of age, 18 to 35, after being trained for adulthood from Leftist indoctrination camps… the universities. These are the thumb-sucking Pajama Boys and Girls who needed Safe Spaces, and counseling, if someone with a different opinion entered the room.

If a pro-Israel or pro-USA speaker showed up in town, or at the dorm, they'd run for their pacifiers and hide under their beds. Later, they'd riot.

The Palestinian Arabs are their favorite people. They know nothing, zero, about Israel. But are always ready to expound.

As adolescents, and throughout the school system, they learned to jeer at Hatikvah, and to turn their backs, or take a knee, at the playing of the Star-Spangled Banner.

Today they vote. Yesterday they were groomed, processed, manufactured, indoctrinated, and packaged to serve as machines for the Party.

Fetterman lived with his parents until he was 49 years old. That's why they voted him into the Senate… a fellow Pajama Boy.

In New York they voted for Hochul to remain governor because her opponent Zeldin favored law and order.

Pajama Boys favor the criminals, and BLM, and the anti-white racism of Critical Race Theory. They defund police, deface statues, and can't figure out what a woman is.

A woman is a woman and a man is a man is a concept too deep for them.

They graduated with degrees in gender studies and Black History, which teaches that genders come like Heinz, in 57 Varieties, and that all white people were slave owners.

As these people get older, do they get wiser?

If not, Republicans have no chance far into the future.

Trump: The Lost Tycoon

***Nov. 8, 2022 – Why no praise for keeping the nation safe and prosperous as president, and why scant praise for his pushing the Abraham Accords?**

Imagine if Joe Biden got the same treatment for just one day that Donald Trump endured every day for six years.

For starters, there'd be televised congressional hearings over Biden's misbegotten, even traitorous withdrawal from Afghanistan.

Such things are not done by commanders in chief.

But through his recklessness, thousands were left behind, straight into the arms of the merciless Taliban. Many are still trapped.

Thirteen US service members were murdered in Kabul during the chaotic retreat that was the handiwork of sloppy Joe.

Imagine the tearful testimonies from survivors and loved ones… all of them, including the lawmakers, pointing fingers at Biden.

There'd be talk for his impeachment.

In such an imaginary world, or rather, an imaginary America, *The New York Times* and the rest of the media would play up Biden's disgrace round the clock, gleefully.

In fact, he would be impeached.

How about Hunter Biden? Joe would have to explain, to Congress, and to the American people, to what extent he enriched himself from his son's shady business dealings.

It's impossible to believe that he knew nothing when in fact the two traveled together around the world… on Joe's vice-presidential airplane.

Top level emissaries from Russia, Ukraine and China would be brought in to testify against Hunter and Joe… and Joe Biden would be impeached a second time.

On that and on the migrant fiasco, Joe Biden would be on the hot seat, the media gloating at his discomfort.

---

* Originally published in *Arutz Sheva* English site (israelnationalnews.com).

Alas, such an America does not exist… we were just dreaming. (Though now, with the House in the hands of the GOP, some dreams may come true, eventually.)

Like the rest of us, Trump lives in the real world… and the real world is an unforgiving place.

Where is his reward for keeping the nation safe and prosperous during his time in office, and why was there scant praise for his pushing through the Abraham Accords?

No Nobel Peace Prize? Obama got one for doing nothing.

No other American president other than Trump did as much for Israel and Middle East peace.

As for me, I can understand Trump's bitterness. I can forgive the flaws of a man so frequently battered.

I don't know if he's the right man for the job the next time around. Maybe, as they say, he's too much Donald Trump… the battler… the tweeter… his personality overbearing.

I do know that I will not join the braying mob… those Deep State hypocrites.

I may not vote for him, as I did before, but I stand with him as someone who knows slander, baseless accusation.

Being Jewish helps.

From the outset, Trump was a condemned man. So to this day.

In boxing they would call it punch drunk, when a fighter can't see straight anymore from relentless hits below the belt.

Such a moment was Jan. 6. That's when, dazed from six years of being pummeled by false charges, he lost control and gave in to his worst instincts.

That was not the Donald Trump I knew in and around New York City when he was known as a tycoon… friendly, warmhearted… and just another one of the boys at Katz's Deli.

He was the most charitable man I met.

Something happens to a man after years of constant hectoring. Something snaps when he takes blow after blow, and finds himself staggering down for the count.

They threw everything at him. Twice they impeached him for no reason and sent out the man Robert Mueller with 50 million dollars to come back with dirt on him.

He came back with nothing, and it was the same with undesirables like Adam Schiff and Michael Avenatti.

They grew famous and rich and became daily TV personalities by way of promises that the next day they would have the goods on him. They tried, but that day never came.

Trump was clean.

But the battering took its toll, and for Donald Trump the country he loved became a blur of enemies… a confederacy of people out to get him.

Now, with his hat in the ring for 2024, they're revved up all over again. How much cruelty against one man is the country willing to accept again and again?

What Tipped the Scales for Netanyahu?

***Nov. 6, 2022 – Israelis voted to win back the country and the sanctity of their Jewish heritage.**

The sum of it is that one morning the Israelis woke up to realize, in a flash of awareness, that the country was stealthily being taken from them.

The moment of clarity turned them handily to the Right, topped by Netanyahu. Better yet, call it a moment of sanity.

This was like coming to your senses after a hangover… or awakening in a rush from the malaise of the past few years, the years of Bennett, Gantz, and Lapid.

In America we call them Joe Biden… and it was Gantz who characterized the pull-out from Gaza/Gush Katif as a good thing… never to be forgotten. Nor to be forgiven at the polls.

The Left had figured it to be a two-way romance, until the Israelis went voting to say no, the flirting has been done, and we are sober again.

Ditto here, where Americans are learning from Israelis how a crooked thing can be set straight… when election time comes around.

What did it do for the Israelis? They saw with alarm their Land, their Good Earth, being corrupted.

Leaders that they never voted for were making plans to undo Jewish sanctity.

We can start with the day when Naftali Bennett served as prime minister, but only after striking a deal with members of the Muslim Brotherhood, who were meant to serve with him, but instead served over him, a case of the tail wagging the dog. Israel is 80 percent Jewish, 20 percent Arab, but it was the Arabs who called the shots.

How could this happen? But it happened, and the Israelis marked it as something to remember under the category of betrayal of trust.

---

* Originally published in *Arutz Sheva* English site (israelnationalnews.com).

Yair Lapid was part of the ticket, and when he took over as unelected prime minister, with no mandate, he doubled down on mendacity.

At the United Nations, Lapid told the world that he is eager to go forward with a two-state solution.

Music to the ears for Israel's enemies who dream of chopping Israel in half… but certainly a harrowing thought to most Israelis… who took note of this, too.

They would remember a sell-out so blatant, spoken so boastfully, egregiously so when he added that the Israeli people support a two-state solution.

No they don't… as became obvious when they booted him out of office.

While running for the job, Lapid addressed Arab citizens with an extraordinary appeal; vote for him and Jews will have no chance to utter prayers on the Temple Mount.

This was not news. It was a signal that, for him, they come first.

Israelis took note of this, too.

Then came strike three.

Lapid, still serving as a caretaker prime minister, announced that he was prepared to abrogate Israel's Nation-State Law, a measure which prioritizes and treasures Israel's Jewishness.

Israel then, in his hands, would become nothing special, but just another country. No more shining city on the hill.

For Americans, this was Joe Biden saying that the migrants washing up through Mexico are a benefit to America, when in fact they are a detriment.

Their presence, by the millions, illegally, diminishes American Exceptionalism.

For Israelis, Jewish Exceptionalism was direly at risk under Lapid or any other Leftist in power.

As voters, they knew exactly how to make things Right.

How Elections Bring Out the Worst in People

***Oct. 31, 2022 – Through appeals and tactics like comparing Bibi to Hitler, the Left is showing itself to be desperate. But no standards at all?**

So Mehmet Oz is a snake, and Benjamin Netanyahu is Hitler.

That's how they're campaigning around here in Pennsylvania, and there in Israel. Here and there, so far as the Left is concerned, anything goes and decency is off the table.

If you like Dirty Politics, enjoy. This is the time of your life, days apart, from the United States to Israel.

Somehow, during this period, normal people lose all self-restraint and turn to savaging their opponents.

In Israel, the Leftists fear Benjamin Netanyahu all over again, and since they've tried everything else, but he's still standing, unbowed… it was time to go medieval on him.

No, worse. It was time to associate him with the most horrible name in the history of the world, Hitler.

Columnist Ruthie Blum spelled it out wonderfully, and so did Dov Fischer.

Thus, two gentlemen MKs who belong to the Religious Zionist Party, Itamar Ben-Gvir and Bezalel Smotrich, who might join his government, would therefore, by such reckoning, be Himmler and Eichmann. Would you want your country run by Hitler, Himmler and Eichmann? Through appeals and tactics like that, the Left is showing itself to be awfully desperate.

The Religious Zionist Party is scorned by the Left for being religious and Zionist. Religious and Zionist, some might say, "What's wrong with that?"

Nothing. Sounds perfect, in fact, for a Jewish country.

---

* Originally published in *Arutz Sheva* English site (israelnationalnews.com).

Except that being in favor of a strong Israel is considered radical, by the Left.

Netanyahu, for instance, led Israel for 15 years, and, go ahead, argue, but for much of that time, Israel became the Shining City on the Hill.

For all that time he faced dubious charges from a dubious judicial system. Somehow, lighting up a cigar, he survives to run again.

No, he wasn't and isn't perfect, like his detractors, but even during the Obama years he never caved for a two-state solution. He never brought that up at the UN, as did Lapid.

So now he's Hitler, and from where did that originate? G-d Bless America, and we sure need all the prayers we can get during our decline and fall under Biden.

Yes, Bibi is Hitler originated from Trump is Hitler, and so ran the political culture throughout Trump's term in office… and onward, as he too may seek a comeback.

He's dangerous, they say. He's reckless. So how many wars did he start, how many quagmires did he lead us into?

Zero.

The Networks won't let up, warning about the dangers to our democracy if "right-wing extremists" gain power come Nov. 8 midterm elections.

(The Left are NEVER extremists.)

They say it through the News You Cannot Trust, and through the political commercials that befoul our radios, televisions, newspapers, and social media.

They tell voters we need more Democrats in the House and Senate to keep the nation safe for abortion, for migrants, for transgenders, and certainly for Critical Race Theory.

That is their version of democracy.

Their version of a free press is the freedom to tell only one side of the story, their side, and to obstruct the other side. (Maybe Elon Musk can make a dent on Twitter.)

That way, Democrats are always the heroes; Republicans the villains. So runs the cycle of news, views, and campaigning.

The ads keep coming, and they keep getting dirtier, and we assume rock bottom has been reached when the Fetterman campaign referred to Mehmet Oz as a “snake.”

That’s in Pennsylvania, where Democrat John Fetterman is up against Republican Dr. Mehmet Oz for Senate, the result viewed as a winner-take-all for the entire Senate of the United States.

Accordingly, the political focus is on Pennsylvania, and the bull-seye is on Philadelphia, which is all Democrat except for two or three people.

Whither Philly goes, so goes the nation… all else being equal.

But even those burghers have had enough of the negative advertising. They’ve got their Phillies in the World Series, which is plenty to root for and cheer.

The team is up against the Houston Astros.

If you’re from around Philly, now there’s a group you can really hate.

In Israel, will voters finally make a choice that sticks?

From America to Israel, the future begins when you cast your ballot.

Is Israel An Arab Country?

***Oct. 23, 2022 – How else could any Israeli PM, even an unelected caretaker one, promise Arabs he would not allow Jews to pray on the Temple Mount?**

The Americans I talk to are baffled over what's going on there in Israel… specifically, on Lapid saying that if re-elected, Jews would be forbidden to pray on the Temple Mount.

First, Lapid was never elected. As it is in Israeli politics, he cut some deals and Bingo.

So Lapid gets to stay prime minister until the elections November 1, when anything can happen.

A candidate needs to score 61 Knesset seats to secure a clear-cut victory, which is one homerun less than Aaron Judge's 62 for the Yankees.

But the Knesset can be terribly inhospitable for a contender with a dream, and it's been forever since anyone has reached the magic number without jumping through hoops.

Hence, the backroom arm bending to form coalitions, even if it means sharing unholy leadership alliances with members of the Muslim Brotherhood… as with Bennett.

Next, Jews have been forbidden to pray on the Temple Mount for some time, so why is this news?

Shocking… but it was meant as a red-flag, a wake-up call.

Generally, these are pro-Israel Christians who get dizzy when trying to keep up with Israeli politics.

Israel was, is, and always will be a Jewish Country. It's all there from the Hebrew Bible, to the Balfour Declaration and elsewhere, onto the thousands who died on the battlefields, 1948/49, 1956, 1967, 1973… all for the purpose, to this day, through the IDF, of establishing and maintaining Israel as the homeland for the Jewish people.

Never did these Jews fight and die for Israel to become part Jewish, part Arab. That's ridiculous.

---

* Originally published in *Arutz Sheva* English site (israelnationalnews.com).

But strange and ridiculous things happen when the leftists run the show, as in America, as in Israel. Over here, Biden has his own two-state solution in the works, which is to bring in millions of illegal migrants in order to diminish American exceptionalism, but to promote America as a third world country.

Over there, Lapid, if "re-elected," intends to turn Israel into just another country through amending Israel's Nation-State Law, which, to keep it simple, prioritizes Israel's Jewishness.

No more of that, for Lapid.

Under the Law, passed 2018, other citizens are assured equal rights, but must understand that Israel is Jewish.

Too Jewish, according to Lapid.

Thus, he supports a two-state solution "to separate ourselves from the Palestinians."

Has he never heard of Gaza and what happens when you give them territory? Give them even more and they become thorns and thistles to Israel overhead and underfoot.

So far as his promise to keep the Temple Mount safe for Arabs at prayer, but not Jews… where throughout the Holy Land are Arabs forbidden to pray?

There is no such place. Arabs can pray everywhere they want, which indeed does beg the question, whose country is this anyway?

Meanwhile, as in the United States, November is coming up fast. Here, Republicans are expected to win the House, perhaps the Senate.

But Democrats have one big edge… the full support of the media, which daily brings up Jan. 6, but never Hunter Biden.

Over here, they're all about stopping Trump from coming back. Over there, they want to make sure, even by law, that Netanyahu has no chance.

Do we?

Martha's Vineyard to Migrants: Get Off My Lawn!

***Sep. 18, 2022 – We warned you about Ken Burns misusing the Holocaust. Martha's Vineyard is Auschwitz.**

So illegal migrants crossing over from Mexico are Holocaust Survivors and Martha's Vineyard is Auschwitz?

We said it days ago in the column "Beware hidden messages in Ken Burns' US and the Holocaust."

In it, we expressed concern that his three-part series, running on PBS as of Sunday, Sept. 18, is at once a thorough examination of America's misbehavior against the Jews during the Holocaust, but also, for Burns, a chance to turn the migrants into Jews, Trump into Hitler, and Republicans into Nazis… foremost, Texas governor Greg Abbott, and, by way of Texas, Florida governor Ron DeSantis.

Their states are in the throes of a migrant invasion, thanks to Biden, and what they've done is ship busloads and planeloads northward so that the rest of America can share the burden and the pain.

For Burns, in reasoning that is weird, such moves echo Kristallnacht.

Burns' hidden motives became apparent when, earlier, he toured various news programs to promote his documentary.

We wrote: "Ken Burns ought to be congratulated for taking up the cause. Generations who don't know what happened [the Holocaust] should be taught.

"Generations who know but forgot, should be reminded.

"But the left-wing politics within the film is an asterisk on an otherwise noble enterprise."

At the time, Burns only provided a hint on just how far left he'd gone, and to what extent he'd be willing to misuse the Holocaust.

Trifling the Holocaust is a sin, in some places a punishable crime, and here, a scandal.

---

* Originally published in *Arutz Sheva* English site (israelnationalnews.com).

How so?

For more than a year, ever since Biden opened the border, by the thousands and into the millions the illegals have trampled the four border states, California, New Mexico, Arizona, Texas.

Many are relocated to Florida. You know this if you've read the *New York Post* and watched *Fox News*.

Barely a word of it from the other newsrooms.

Gradually, over the past few weeks, mainly Texas and roundabout Florida have been shipping them, trickle by trickle, to blue cities like New York, Washington, DC, and Chicago, to alert the rest of the country and the media that attention must be paid over a crisis that is far, wide, and nationwide.

The Democrat mayors of those sanctuary strongholds are outraged, not at Biden for his open border policy, but at those Republican governors and the chutzpah to have America face the truth.

Can Democrats handle the truth? Not when the migrants come home to roost. Then, aha, it's different. (Get off my lawn!)

Still, though, liberals and their media slept through the migrant storm… until Gov. DeSantis dumped 50 of them onto a town famed for its wealth, its tranquility, its pastoral beauty, and recognized for such liberal residents as the Obamas… in a word, Martha's Vineyard, in Massachusetts, outside Boston. In other words, you want migrants, we'll give you migrants.

Only 50? But enough for the local grandees to complain of being violated and demanding that something be done about a "humanitarian crisis." Where's liberal empathy now?

Suddenly, this became news. Big news. THE news. Migrant crisis? What migrant crisis? Oh, THIS migrant crisis… and now it even topped the evening news.

More so when Gov. Abbott of Texas dumped 100 of them outside Kamala Harris' residence a day after she, the immigration czar, insisted the border is secure.

Enter Ken Burns.

By some tortured logic, he made a direct correlation between the Holocaust and the "themes of today," with this on *CNN*: "When you look at the story we're telling on US and the Holocaust, the time to save democracy is before it's lost."

Remarked one wag alongside an image of serene Martha's Village: "This? This is Auschwitz?"

More from Burns: "This is what's so disturbing about DeSantis – to use human beings, to weaponize human beings."

What's really disturbing, Mr. Burns, is how you are using and abusing and exploiting the Holocaust.

Oscars, Grammys – Something Rotten in the State of America

***May 4, 2022 – Who watches the works of garbage and filth that won the awards? Your kids do.**

Sinatra, this isn't.

Go ahead, call me a prude, but I must say, Sunday night's big event, the Grammys, was just too much.

The Oscars and the slap heard around the world, that was one thing, but the Grammy awards for America's best musical performers were grotesquely obscene.

Tasteless, is that the word? Or, where does a culture go after it has reached rock bottom… is that the message?

What do I know? I won't watch. I only know what I read in the papers. Nothing that I can share in a decent publication.

Who watches this garbage? Your kids do.

One performer in particular, had he done the act in Central Park, would have been arrested for indecency. He did it on TV, as an ARTIST, so it gets an ovation.

This was pornography, courtesy of *CBS-TV*, for the glorification of bacchanalia. Mom, Dad, and the kids, come, they say, gather around for the finest vulgarity in dress and lyrics.

Who knows what they're singing? Usually it's filth, and often there's a zinger or two against Jews and Israel.

Half the time there is no telling the men from the women. This too, courtesy from the Woke swamp, is what's happening, and spreading, even to the schools.

You expected Jan Pierce singing *A Din Toire Mit Gott*? Richard Tucker – *Rozhinkis Mit Mandlen*? Leo Fuld… *Where Can I Go*?

Carnegie Hall was filled to catch such towering performers. Class all the way.

Those days are gone. Down the tubes in a rabbit hole of smut.

---

* Originally published in *Arutz Sheva* English site (israelnationalnews.com).

Where ARE we going? You tell me.

Sinatra did not need a full orchestra and a thousand dancers gyrating ridiculously behind him. Nor did he need vulgarity to make a nation swoon.

All he needed for props, to captivate an audience and a generation, was a stool and a cigarette.

Cigarette? Isn't that hazardous to America's health?

So is this… this that's going on.

This much is for sure… anything goes, and there is no shame. The thing is, what happens in America does not stay in America.

American culture is catchy and travels around the globe.

This used to be a source of pride… Fred Astaire et al. Now, in the face of all this ribaldry, it's an embarrassment.

I feel the need to apologize to my friends and relatives in Israel. This isn't Truman's America, nor is it even Nixon's America.

When in the 1973 War Israel was in a dire spot, and desperately needed equipment to be airlifted, Nixon overrode Kissinger, saying, "Send them anything that flies."

Something's gone haywire since then… and yes to the holier-than-thou critics, Israel needs America, as America needs Israel. It's the way of the world.

Back to the music…

Once upon a time there was Elvis. America wasn't quite ready for his suggestive movements up on stage. Ed Sullivan booked him, but made sure to show him only from the waist up.

Finally, due to the fact that he had real talent, America came around and applauded, with the understanding that there were limits.

Surprise! There are no limits.

Any fool can dress up like a donkey with tassels, do his or her Rap, and make millions for being so adored.

Prime civilizations last about 500 years. Are we somewhere around mid-point, or actually, the tipping point?

Please, Not Another "Scholarly Study" on Anti-Semitism

***Apr. 29, 2022 – Oh no, according to the news release, this is going to be the mother of all "studies." That means millions of meaningless words.**

I don't need an ADL "study" to explain the rise in anti-Semitism.

Alarming? Yes, the spike in anti-Semitism in the US and around the world is alarming. The reason for it is simple; the erosion of Judeo/Christian values.

There, that's the story. Period. So you don't need Jonathan Greenblatt and his ADL …Anti-Defamation League… to pursue the question with a "study," and not just any study.

Oh no, according to the news release, this is going to be the mother of all "studies." Big Thinkers from all over have been invited to produce their thoughts, in a million words or more, as to the causes and mystery of anti-Semitism. Let me try, please, to end the suspense. No, the butler didn't do it… if you know anything about Jonathan Greenblatt.

This is the Greenblatt who was at home in Silicon Valley, who served under Obama, who wanted Tucker Carlson to be fired, who accused Trump of being an anti-Semite… all for being too "right-wing"… and still the same Greenblatt who favors chopping up Israel into a two-state solution… so?

So, what can you expect after all the Big Thinking has been done?

Greenblatt et al will blame it on White Supremacists. There, I ended the suspense on this, too. Easy, because under Greenblatt, the ADL is entirely Liberal, Progressive, Woke.

Blaming the Right, never the Left, is how academics make their livelihoods. Yes, it's a living, though we don't know how much these Deep Thinkers are being paid for this massive new project, which is

---

* Originally published in *Arutz Sheva* English site (israelnationalnews.com).

expected to resolve anti-Semitism once and for all… after several years of Intensive Study. No, wait.

Let's hear from Greenblatt in his own words on the significance and magnificence of the work ahead…

He calls it "a scholarly approach to examining the root causes and solutions for combating modern anti-Semitism." (Did Sasha Baron Cohen write this as Borat?)

"Scholarly" means that preferably you graduated from, say, Yale, where, by the way, a group of law students protested AGAINST free speech.

Earlier, such students rioted to stop any Jewish or Israeli from speaking freely. Now, they're muzzling free speech of any kind.

So the good news is that anti-Semitism is nothing special to this generation. They tolerate nobody they consider to be White.

They hate Christians, too. Not as much as Jews, to be sure, but we are not so exclusive, after all.

They deny the Bible. Holiness to them is CRT; Critical Race Theory. This preaches that White People altogether, not only Jews, are inherently racist and evil.

That's coming to the classrooms, which forbid even a whisper of religion.

Then, entering the Supreme Court is a judge who can't or won't define the word Woman. Indeed, a godless generation, a godless education, and this is what you get.

These are people who were raised to suck their thumbs and to go hiding in safe spaces when they come up against anyone who disagrees with them.

Case in point… the Twitter operatives who lost their comfy/lefty world to Elon Musk, and it's driving them crazy.

Likewise, Walt Disney in Florida, where the Progressives who run the billion-dollar operation aimed at kids, insist that sex re-education is proper for five-year-olds.

So far as "root causes," has anything changed since Pharaoh?

Moving along, Greenblatt says the study "will build on the ADL's over a century of research into core anti-Semitic beliefs and attitudes."

So, this is nothing new? You've been doing this research for over a century… and learned what? Nothing.

Go ahead. Do it again. Maybe in another hundred years you'll come up with something.

Seriously, Does Biden Know He's the President?

***Mar. 31, 2022 – Is Biden aware that when he talks every word counts? No, he is not aware, but we will suffer the results anyway.**

In a minute or so we'll get to President Joe Biden and whether his casual off-the-cuff remarks can trigger the end of the world.

I mean the ultimate showdown between the United States and Russia.

You know, nuclear-tipped rockets flying and landing back and forth… you and me right in the middle.

All because our president suffers from loose lips.

A foggy president is a danger to ourselves and to our truest, most valuable ally, Israel.

But first we must get to what's really bothering America, still, even back to last Sunday when Will Smith slapped Chris Rock.

Slapped him across the face after Chris Rock said something about Will Smith's wife during the Oscars.

Solid right hook from the actor who played Muhammad Ali in a movie.

The *New York Post* devotes an entire section, article after article, for "The Slap Heard Around The World."

Fortunately, both men are African American. If, say, Will Smith were White, there'd be riots. As it is, what we've got is a misunderstanding between two very rich and very successful entertainers, Will Smith the actor, Chris Rock the comedian, a contretemps that has made it to the top of every news cycle… and is still going strong.

Ukraine, sure. That's being covered, and so are the nuke talks between Team Biden and the mullahs of Iran, in which the concessions exclusively come from us, not them, diplomacy, if that's the word, that can spark here too a war of the worlds, only this time between us and Iran… with Israel caught in the middle.

---

* Originally published in *Arutz Sheva* English site (israelnationalnews.com).

Must I provide the details, after everybody else has already provided an opinion? Americans already know the story. Israelis are just as savvy.

The envelope, please? Well, the consensus has it that Will Smith went too far. He has finally apologized, but faces disciplinary action from the Academy.

He could be sentenced to 30 years hard labor in Siberia, or a week watching *The View*. If it were me, I'd choose Siberia.

What strikes me about all this, as always, is that in America we have the luxury to focus on so much that is mundane, frivolous and silly.

Most other nations are not so lucky; Israel facing a new round of deadly terrorist attacks, for example. This charmed life of ours too often we take for granted.

Nothing of this Will Smith/Chris Rock business is life-changing for you or for me.

But this is…

Enter Joe Biden.

After overindulging on too much cultural popcorn, I got caught up on the latest political firestorm from *Fox News*.

To learn that Joe Biden has been making one gaffe after another.

I say *Fox News* because the Big Three Networks find no imperfections, ever, in Joe Biden.

Most seriously, while in Poland, was Biden's off-script comment: "For G-d's sake, this man [Putin] cannot remain in power."

This would be okay if he was talking to his wife around the dinner table after a tough day at the office.

Out loud, was this a call for regime change, from the leader of one nuclear superpower to another? Is Biden aware that such loose talk starts wars?

Is Biden aware that when he talks every word counts? No, he is not aware, when he says that he is only expressing moral outrage and a "personal" observation.

But there are no "personal observations" when a man becomes President of the United States. Everything he says in public is taken as policy and doctrine.

A president never speaks only for himself. He speaks for the nation… and you can bet Putin took it “personal."

Putin must be counting down toward lift-off ever since Biden called him a “killer” with George Stephanopoulos on *ABC-NEWS*.

Obviously, this man Biden has no inkling of the power of his office, and still wakes up every morning surprised that he is president.

As are the rest of us.

Can You Define Woman? Supreme Court Nominee Can't

***Mar. 27, 2022 – Judge Jackson, do you really need a biologist for this… the most basic question and answer since Adam and Eve?**

I'm not a biologist, but I can tell a woman when I see one.

Gender confusion is where we are today, courtesy of Woke Madness.

As for me, over the years, many people have complimented me for my uncanny sense of detection. For example, I can spot a woman a mile away.

This is a skill well beyond Postmodern Progressives like Ketanji Brown Jackson… and guess what? She's a judge.

What's more, she is slated for the Supreme Court, and of course, she went to Harvard.

At the hearing before the Senate Judiciary Committee where her qualifications for the job were being tested, most of her responses were longwinded and agonizingly muddled.

It got even more convoluted when Sen. Marsha Blackburn of Tennessee asked Judge Jackson, "Can you specify a definition of the word woman?"

In other words, is she willing to admit that men and women are different? Otherwise, she's a far-gone leftist

The room held its breath. Suspense was in the air. Judge Jackson seemed puzzled, perturbed, blindsided, baffled. A Google search would help, but she was on the spot.

Define a woman?

Seemed easy to me, as it would be, say, for any Quiz Show contestant, most of whom are educated, hardworking Americans… but never went to Harvard.

They'd have the answer in a snap, and though the top prize would not be a seat on the Supreme Court, most likely it would be a NEW

* Originally published in *Arutz Sheva* English site (israelnationalnews.com).

CAR… and if you think the concept of a “strong woman” began last year, then you don’t know Sarah, Rebecca, Rachel and Leah from the Hebrew Bible.

We’d be nowhere without Moses’ sister Miriam. More, some other time about how “The mirrors of the women” in the wilderness were not vanity, but G-d’s “legions.”

It used to be so simple, remember? Daddy was a man. Mommy was a woman. That’s how we grew up. How did we know the difference?

When there was a mouse in the house, Mommy would scream; Daddy would chase it down. That was one way we knew.

Mommy ran the kitchen; Daddy ran the garage and kept polishing the car… and there was nothing complicated about any of this.

Daddy fixed a flat tire. Mommy fixed the cut and dried our tears.

I imagine that Judge Jackson grew up the same way.

But then she went to Harvard and at Harvard, Yale and the other Ivy Leagues, they teach you everything all over again.

Some might say they teach you to be stupid.

Everything you thought you knew, forget it, say the intellectuals, the sophisticates, the professors, who also attended Harvard.

They taught the Judge… and millions of others now ruling our world… to trust them, and not your own eyes or your own intellect and impulses.

This could be hazardous when at your early years you knew never to cross against a red light, but after attending college, now you freeze and get confused between red and green.

Because red and green are suddenly interchangeable… even meaningless.

Like the difference between man and woman.

Or rather, as they say, there are no differences.

So, when she was asked to define the word woman, Judge Jackson finally collected herself to assert, “I cannot.” Why not? “I am not a biologist.”

You need a biologist for this… the most basic question and answer since Adam and Eve?

Does someone like this fit the criteria for the Supreme Court?

You be the judge.

Living With the Crime of the Century

***Mar. 21, 2022 – The *Times* cover-up and denial of Hunter Biden's laptop, aided by *Facebook* and *Twitter*, has destroyed any trust we had left.**

This is a tale between two newspapers, *The New York Times* versus the *New York Post*. The *Post* won… but too late.

The biggest losers are the American people.

Had the American people known the unsavory facts about Hunter Biden and his father, Joe, Trump would be enjoying his second term… and it does not matter if you love or hate Trump.

What matters is that the 2020 Election was cooked by the media to deny voters the right to the truth.

So they voted eyes wide shut, and that's as close as it gets to the crime of the century.

You should care if you care about the sanctity of the vote… which was dashed by a code of silence among the *Times*, the colossus of social media and the networks.

If you care about America, and if you want the best for Israel, you know the wrong man occupies the White House.

He started with the fiasco in Afghanistan to now, the looming fiasco in Iran… leaving Israel holding the bag.

Joe in the White House, we're living every day with the disastrous result of that heist… when the entire media conspired to suppress the *Post* when, back in October, 2020, the paper, led by reporter Miranda Devine, ran headlined investigative reports which found Hunter getting rich by accompanying his father, then vice president, to capitals overseas, and then reportedly sharing the booty with Joe.

Proof of all that, writes the *Post*, is contained in Hunter's laptop that he had abandoned in a Delaware repair shop. In it, emails reveal and substantiate the dirty dealings.

"The Laptop from Hell," as Miranda Devine has it in her book.

---

* Originally published in *Arutz Sheva* English site (israelnationalnews.com).

The findings were so sensational and so irrefutable, so that the *Post* was confident that it was doing a public service by alerting the people to what they'd be getting in Joe Biden.

Voters were still making up their minds between Biden and Trump.

Today, some 10 percent of Biden voters say they'd have chosen otherwise had they been informed… enough to change everything.

The *Post* was also confident that a story like this was sure to awaken the rest of the media.

Nope.

When it wasn't being picked up, *Post* editors went to *Twitter*. *Twitter* not only refused to carry the story; it banned the *Post* and *Post* editors from its forum. Likewise, *Facebook*.

They dismissed the Hunter/Laptop story as fake news… Russian disinformation… obviously to protect their man Biden.

Beginning with the *Times*, the blackout was widespread… and effective enough to rig the election for the highest office in the land.

Finally, this past week, grudgingly, Biden securely in office, the *Times* came around to admit that the *Post* was correct all along so far as Hunter and his revealing laptop.

Only the *Times* neither mentioned nor thanked the *Post* for its first-rate reportage.

Nor, as it had failed during the Holocaust and Stalin's famine in Ukraine, did the *Times* apologize for its journalistic neglect and malfeasance.

But the harm had been done. Read it and weep.

Soon in America, Russia-Ukraine to Be Just Another Show on US TV

***Mar. 13, 2022 – America, the land of "silken worries," as my mother used to say. Who wants to worry about war when there is basketball?**

As the world teeters on the verge of nuclear war, meanwhile, back in the USA, people are upset because at *Wheel of Fortune*, host Pat Sajak was rude to a contestant.

Gevalt!

America, the land of "silken worries," as my mother used to say.

Or, "America is a picnic, only the Americans don't know it," as I used to say… and if you think March madness is about Ukraine, and what's going on there, yes, but the official March Madness happens in America every year, from March into April, when day after day the best college basketball teams vie for the national championship.

So it's tip-off time again.

Millions will be watching. Millions will be wagering… and the real world will just have to wait. We have other business to attend.

Gone fishing.

Then there's college spring break, and then baseball, and then Ukraine… which will be available on the evening news for 15 minutes.

For the networks, and for jaded viewers, this is "good television." How much longer will Ukraine still be Top Story, Breaking News, or even News?

Paradoxically, we care. We give generously. But life goes on.

Maybe this is for the best. Our love of sport and frivolity is what keeps us from wallowing in despair even during the worst of times. The Israelis have the talent for this, too.

Despair is forbidden, said the Rebbe. Gloom is not our way.

We can't go on; we will go on, to borrow from the Irish writer.

We're not like the rest of world. They do Wagner. We do Elvis.

---

* Originally published in *Arutz Sheva* English site (israelnationalnews.com).

During World War Two, the jitterbug was all the craze.

At the height of the Cold War, America rocked and rolled and twirled the hula hoop, as readers learned from the 60s classic *The Days of the Bitter End.*

That is power. That is the might of saying nothing can bring us down, nothing can stop us. We are special.

Take your best shot. Try us. Go ahead, make our day.

On the other hand, too much silliness, and we are doomed.

As the world burns, we fiddle.

We trifle along obsessed on race and gender; the Left stays up nights worrying about transgender people, who are 0.06 percent of the population.

Gender… you'd think that was figured out between Adam and Eve. Not good enough, and on race, it will never be good enough.

Given what's going on, you'd think we'd be worried about our military preparedness, now especially when there's talk of a nuclear showdown.

Are we up to speed? Leaderless, even the Taliban had us on the run.

Most of them who make the news are worried about Whiteness and white supremacy. As if that's got anything to do with the price of potatoes, bread, milk and gas.

Elsewhere, they don't have time for such trivia. There, the game is life or death.

Only in America do we have the luxury to pursue lightness of being.

Are we grateful?

Or are we really spoiled rotten from over-abundance? Tyrants and criminals re-arm; we defund the police.

Too big, too rich, too much time on our hands to consider the consequences, we elect morons to lead us… up a creek without a paddle.

You wanted Biden. You got Biden… with Kamala into the bargain, and as more evidence that we are a nation in decline, decay and disarray.

John Kerry… you think we're rid of him? He's back like a recurring nightmare; this time serving Biden as Climate Czar. What's his worry?

The climate, of course, and he has a message for Putin, to please stop dropping bombs… it's hurting the climate.

In the real world, like China, they rank number one on math. We rank 37th.

Batter up. Play ball.

Finally, I Disagree With Everybody

***Mar. 7, 2022 – They tell me Putin is not a villain. They tell me Zelensky is a good guy. And then the Russians and the Ukrainians both killed Jews.**

I did not think there'd be two sides to this story… Russia versus Ukraine.

I think that's because of my American upbringing… y'know… good guys, bad guys… cowboys versus Indians.

The cowboys were the good guys… until it turned out just the opposite.

A thousand history books had to be re-written. Movie scripts had to be revised.

Nobody knows the future, and the past keeps changing.

Depends who you talk to, but the people talking to me, tell me I am wrong for cheering the Ukrainians in their conflict with Russia.

Those who share my view… I can't hear you!

Don't I know? Yes, I know the Ukrainians are historically anti-Semitic. I know what they did before, during and after World War Two.

So what am I supposed to do about those images showing children clutching their dolls and toys as their tiny legs try to keep up with their mothers fleeing into Poland?

That reminds me of me.

Am I supposed to feel nothing… and Poland, you want to talk about Poland? I know about Poland, and Latvia, and Hungary, and Lithuania, never mind Germany, and all the rest of them that had a hand in the Holocaust, and who collaborated willingly and enthusiastically when it came to the Jews.

Often enough my relatives, and yours, too.

I know what it's like being a refugee. I don't need the history books. I wrote one or two of those history books.

---

* Originally published in *Arutz Sheva* English site (israelnationalnews.com).

But I am always ready to live and learn, especially from people who are so much wiser than me, and are therefore so quick to correct me.

These tell me that President Zelensky is no hero. If so, I'll need to know more. He should have capitulated, they say, and thus spared his nation the agony.

He should have cut and run, like that president of Afghanistan who knew when his time was up.

Where I come from, that is called chicken.

Good enough, I guess, if you take King Solomon at his word… better a live dog than a dead lion.

That is still yellow.

Putin is no villain, they tell me.

I'm listening.

So happens I do know that Putin is a friend to the Jews. He has outlawed anti-Semitism throughout Russia. I have written about this with gratitude.

He wept bitterly at the funeral of his Jewish judo master.

He may even have learned Krav Maga from the system's originator, Imi Lichtenfeld, whom I met in Netanya for my black belt and for my book which includes Imi and Krav Maga.

So yes, he's got his good side, and so much of our literary culture is Russian… think Boris Pasternak, Isaac Babel, Tolstoy!

If you read Tolstoy, you know the Russian upper-class think westward, and pretend themselves to be French. The Russians, under the Soviets, liberated Auschwitz, and also granted forms of equality to its Jews, and also murdered its Jews. See, "Night of the Murdered Poets"… and doctors… and others.

Back at the Philly newspaper, the Russian man next door used to spit every time he walked past me, uttering, "Yid."

So Russian anti-Semitism is no secret, either.

We are talking Europe, remember? One day Beethoven; next day, Hitler.

Frankly, I do not think much has changed. Given the chance, they'd do it again. There would be only Israel to stop them.

The United States would be no help. Look how helpless we are even now; a lion that can only roar.

Because we cannot get entangled into something that can lead to bombs away and as predicted, we are already at a nuclear stare-down.

Anyway, I am still open to both sides of the argument. Meanwhile, still I hurt for those children. This did not need to happen.

Make Way, Kamala Harris to the Rescue!

***Feb. 21, 2022 – Here comes Kamala to save Ukraine.**

In desperation to illustrate that he's not the same weak-kneed Joe who fled Afghanistan, Biden sends in the clown to stare down Putin.

The message? Kamala Harris is coming, to demand that Putin stop his takeover against Ukraine.

The warning label says that as vice-president she's the most powerful woman in America. So there!

She's an "empowered woman" and empowered women... super women... politically... is what we produce here in America.

Well, okay. She's not demanding. She's asking. It's the most Team Biden can do. Getting Europe to stand together as deterrents is all we've got... and even that's no use.

Because Russia is EU's company store.

So exactly how does the Biden Administration intend Europe to put up a united front against Putin when it's Putin who supplies the EU with most of its fuel?

This is the fact. Look it up. "Russia is the largest supplier of fuel to the countries of the EU, with about 35% of total imports."

More from sourcing: "All of it arriving via multiple pipelines, many of which cross through Ukraine on their way to countries in central Europe."

Ukraine – get that?

Ukraine, by the way, still has to answer for its behavior during World War Two. Some other time for the particulars.

But on that score, Putin has outlawed anti-Semitism throughout Russia. He meets regularly with Lubavitch Chasidim. His martial arts training partners have generally been Jews.

Putin wept at the funeral of his Jewish Black Belt master.

So let's be careful before pointing fingers on what constitutes civility. In our society, at present, it's unsafe to walk, drive, operate a business, or wait at a subway platform.

---

* Originally published in *Arutz Sheva* English site (israelnationalnews.com).

Back to the topic at hand…

Trump warned Germany against cutting a deal with Russia known as Nord Stream 2 Pipeline… which places Germany at Russia's mercy for Germany's gas.

Trump saw this day coming, a day when there'd be no mercy.

Just like that, and Germany and the rest can be out in the cold… quite literally.

So here we are, America, the world's number one superpower, with no power except to wag a finger and warn Putin that if he persists, he'll suffer "unprecedented economic costs."

That came from a canned speech Kamala delivered in Munich before fellow worry-warts, and where she met up with Ukraine President Zelensky.

She was there to give him a hug, a pep talk, and assurances that she, personally, cares.

What could he be thinking, without saying, when a dingbat VP shows up to save his hide?

A former comedian, Zelensky is sure to see the comedy in all that bedevils himself, his country, and the world. His stand-up might go like this…

One: I asked for Kissinger, and Biden sends me Kamala. That's like getting a pie in the face.

Two: She is the epitome of American confusion, decay, and decline… all in one Progressive package.

Three: A Kamala is what you get for leadership when gender and race take precedence over skill and smarts. Only, or mostly, in America… land of the cancelled First Amendment.

Four: No thank you, America. Keep your Woke craziness to yourselves.

Five: Woke may work for you, but around the real world it's shameful.

Six: While you've been busy defunding your police, tearing down your monuments and your history, have you noticed how diminished you are to the rest of the world?

No wonder Putin feels free to do as he likes.

Seven: Picture Kamala as the face of all that… and with the cackle for a laugh.

Eight: Is this the same Kamala who was the border czar for the US-Mexico border?

Nine: If she's as effective for that as she is for this, we're all headed for hell in a handbasket.

Ten: Is there no leadership of substance left in America?

From China to Israel, With Love

***Feb. 16, 2022 – What amazes me is that China's leaders should give Israel a second thought. Their population is one and a half billion. But they do.**

I'm still not sure I read this straight…

About the leaders of Communist China reaching out for good PR, for China, from Chinese citizens who are in Israel as students.

During these Olympics especially, they want China presented to the Israelis as warm and cuddly.

Then forget the rest, like the Wuhan Virus, detention camps and the heavy hand it exerts on its people and its neighbors.

Seems to be the fact that they want to impress the Israelis, urgently. They need Israel's approval.

Since when? Since David was king, or even going back to Moses… even Abraham.

China admires Israel's advancements in technology… and everything else.

What amazes me, is that China's leaders should give Israel a second thought. Their population is one and a half billion.

Does President Xi Jinping know?

Population-wise, it's no contest.

Maybe we shouldn't tell them that Israel's population is nine and a half million.

Let them think Israel is a colossus.

As it is in China… with the ambition of replacing the United States as the world's number one super-power.

Not good. But it is the way of the world that you take what you can get, so meanwhile, China is Israel's third largest trading partner.

That is good.

For some, like me, it is an astonishment to reflect that this country, Israel, that has never known a moment's rest, is today counted a mensch unto the nations.

---

* Originally published in *Arutz Sheva* English site (israelnationalnews.com).

This happened so fast—within 73 years… (without counting its Biblical heritage.)

Other nations need that amount of time to get their socks on.

The respect may be grudging… but respect it is, and it was earned through the blood of her Jewish sons and daughters, the sweat of her fathers, and the tears of her mothers.

This hurts, as only some of us can understand.

As I have it in this novel… *Indecent Proposal*… she says, "The whole world isn't Auschwitz, Josh." He says, "Neither is it Bryn Mawr, Joan."

China, we're reminded, appreciates a kinship with Israel as two nations that go back centuries.

Then there's affinity for the fact that both countries share the same continent.

What?

I remember the Las Vegas TV reporter sitting next to me on the plane, near stupefied when, on landing in Tel Aviv, it turned out we were in Asia.

"Can't be," she insisted.

But it is, and the disbelief is common among Americans, especially Jews, visiting Israel for the first time, and imagining it to be like a trip to Katz's Deli.

They expect heimish, and heimish it is… but you are still in a foreign country!

No… you're not in Kansas anymore.

You're not in Brooklyn, either, or Miami.

Israel is the real deal.

Israel IS the Broadway of the Middle East… the lights never dim, and the show is a hit and never stops.

You're in the western part of Asia… China is in the east. Two different worlds, really, but nonetheless.

Speaking of misconceptions… back when I was editor at KYW-news radio in Philly, good thing I checked Harry J's script before he went on air.

"Harry," I said, "I caught your typo."

"What typo?"

"You have it here that the world's 140 million Jews are preparing to celebrate Passover."

"It's not Passover?"

"It is Passover. But it isn't 140 million Jews."

"Of course, it is."

"Harry, I don't know where you looked it up, but there are no more than maybe 14 million of us around the world."

Finally convinced, he scratched his head, and said, "For such a small people, you sure are big."

Harry was a good guy, and I still take it as a compliment.

Apparently, so does China.

Please Stop Trampling the Holocaust

***Feb. 2, 2022 – The Holocaust is not for amateurs. May I make a suggestion? Just shut up!**

Using the Holocaust to make a point… about something else… is a sickening cheap shot.

You would think an astute journalist like Lara Logan would know better than to compare Dr. Fauci with "angel of death" Dr. Josef Mengele… but that's what she did.

For that, she was dropped by her talent agency UTA.

You would think lesson learned, but only days later, along comes Robert F. Kennedy, Jr., son of Camelot's Bobby Kennedy to invoke Anne Frank to promote his anti-vax agenda.

He too got smacked, even from his wife, Cheryl Hines, and rushed to apologize.

You would think, by now, people would know that playing with the Holocaust is playing with fire.

Instead, making the biggest headlines, now comes Whoopi Goldberg to make some outrageous remarks; saying the Holocaust wasn't about race… then "apologizing."

Insiders, we learn, want Whoopi fired. I say no. First because the cancel culture is too much of a drag on our entire culture.

Next because it will incite a slew of Whoopi defenders who always need one more thing to hang on the Jews. We'll be hearing about "outsized Jewish power and influence."

Late breaking… she has been suspended. Okay, we'll see what comes of this.

Anyway, what wisdom do you expect from the scolds and yentas on *The View*?

Meanwhile, the impulse to play fast and loose with the Holocaust dates back decades, but had its heyday during the Trump Administration.

---

* Originally published in *Arutz Sheva* English site (israelnationalnews.com).

How many different times and how many different ways was Trump aligned with the Austrian house painter?

To be Jewish is to take it from all sides, from Holocaust deniers to Holocaust opportunists.

May I make a suggestion?

Just shut up!

Just because you're on television, or because you're a public figure or a celeb, that doesn't make you an expert on everything, or anything.

The Holocaust, for example, is not for amateurs. The people who endured it are the professionals.

Only they know what they're talking about, and I'll tell you this; even they have trouble describing an event so immense.

As told by one survivor… "You are asking me to describe a day in Auschwitz? I can't even describe a minute."

Was it about race? Who cares? The Holocaust was about murdering every Jew on the planet, period. The simplicity of it is staggering.

Too staggering.

The Holocaust is about the triumph of evil. The rest of the world took part in it in one form or another. Goodness did not prevail.

The St. Louis… the voyage of the damned… went from place to place, with no takers. The Jews were sent back. The mad Austrian evil genius, yes, Hitler, knew this would happen.

He knew the world better than did the philosophers and the theologians. His experiment worked.

Goodness is a theory. Wickedness is a fact.

Therefore, he could continue and even accelerate the killing, secure in the knowledge that he had the world's approval.

At the Wannsee Conference, the ministers had the conquered world all mapped out… Jews marked for death country by country.

There was talk around the table that in some countries, the local Christian population might rise up to defend their Jewish neighbors.

Not to worry, chuckled mastermind Reinhard Heydrich. We can always count on the burghers, on local anti-Semitism.

He too knew the world.

He also knew… they all knew… that the Jews were foremost in science, that their contributions in medicine were a benefit to all humanity.

That made no difference.

The Jews were loyal citizens in whatever the host country, and served bravely and honorably in the military, certainly for Germany.

That made no difference.

So, in Christian Europe, nearly overnight they dropped the cross and marched with the swastika. In too many cases, Hitler, not Jesus, was their preferred savior.

That fast people can turn on a dime. That too is a lesson from the Holocaust.

Has the world returned to its senses?

Let's just say, that this time, the ship St. Louis would know exactly the one place to go to receive a warm welcome. Am Yisroel chai.

Pardon My French

***Jan. 26, 2022 – The Germans were the bad guys, but the French were, too. The round-ups, the expulsions - and today they lead the EU in Jew-hatred.**

You must remember this, the scene in *Casablanca* when, defying the Germans, Madeleine LeBeau rises up to belt out the French National Anthem, "La Marseillaise."

Goosebumps all around. Gotta love the French, you're thinking. Vive la France.

Not so fast for my beautiful and multi-talented sister, Sarah. She was there, and to this day, can tell a different story.

She was there, in Toulouse, for the Vichy Laws that dehumanized the Jews and turned us into preys to be hunted.

She was there when aunts, uncles, cousins, were whisked off the boulevards never to be seen again.

She was there when her best friend Incarnacion called her, Salle Juif, Dirty Jew.

The family made the great escape into the Pyrenees when Sarah was nine years old.

I phoned her this morning soon after I read the news that France, today, leads the EU in Jew-hatred… well, tied with Poland.

"I'm not surprised," she says.

But France, mon amour… the art, Matisse, the literature, Proust, the music, Piaf, the romance of Paris…

"The Paris we know was created in Hollywood."

No pride, Sarah? After all, for a time you were French.

"No pride at all."

Sarah is proud of just two countries… "the United States and Israel."

Amen to that!

So, what comes up when you think of France?

"Danger."

---

* Originally published in *Arutz Sheva* English site (israelnationalnews.com).

But the Germans were the bad guys. The French…

"The French were just as bad. The round-ups, the expulsions until more than 70,000 were sent to the camps."

But don't you remember your crush on Yves Montand?

"But we enjoyed him from the convenience of America. From America, France can be wonderful. It was different when you were there."

No fond memories at all?

"When we went to pick up mother from the hospital and my new baby brother, you, the roads were roped off for Jews and people were saying the Jews started it all."

Sarah tells her story in the book, *Sarah and Abraham*, a book about being there; mine, *Escape from Mount Moriah*, is about arriving and adjusting to the new world.

Even Sarah concedes that it's not that simple.

"There was Godliness from many people. The French priest, Father LaRoche, risked his own life to facilitate our escape. In the Pyrenees, nuns and priests risked the danger to shield us."

From the movies, we also get the paradox that is France.

You couldn't help but cheer the French when, as told in the movie, *The Train*, starring Burt Lancaster and Jeanne Moreau, the Germans came to confiscate France's art treasures.

Every effort was made to save the paintings for France, the art described as "precious" throughout the film.

Wonderful suspense, and absolutely you rooted for the French to win. Until you realized, all that for the paintings… where was it for the Jews?

In the movie, *Mr. Klein*, Alain Delon is Mr. Klein, a non-Jewish rapacious Parisian art collector who gathers up the treasures left behind by Jews being rounded up and deported.

Things go wrong when the authorities mistake him for a Jewish Mr. Klein.

Throughout the red tape entanglement, our hero begins to understand the loneliness of being Jewish of this time and at this place.

Big finish, as he is herded off to suffocate at the Velodrome d'Hiver en route to Drancy and then Auschwitz.

But as he is boarding, word comes that the mis-identity has been corrected. He is free to go home.

Instead, he voluntarily follows the crowd into the deadly transport.

Good ending. But not a happy ending. No such luck to this day.

Look Who's Coming to America

***Jan. 20, 2022 – He was known to be trouble before he terrorized four Jews in a Texas Temple, but everyone can get into America today.**

Now, people are asking how that terrorist from the UK got into this country in the first place.

He was known to be trouble, even before he terrorized a rabbi and other members of a Texas synagogue.

Apparently, though, his "papers were in order."

That could be so because, you see, he was not "really" a terrorist as defined by the Progressive rule book, which prefers the term, activist.

Only an activist? Welcome to America.

That's how language can turn harmful and deadly when downsized and garbled to meet politically correct specifications.

When everybody speaks a different language, and when people have forgotten the difference between good and bad, and between kosher and treyf, you get the confounding of tongues… if you remember your Genesis, and the Tower of Babel chapter, when the world collapsed for the lack of clarity.

Some will say that the hostage-taker being discussed was indeed on a terrorist watch list, at least back in the UK.

But no way would we in Woke America call him an Islamist terrorist, if we can help it.

Over here, according to the Progressive theologists… the people who run our culture… only "white extremists…" namely parents who attend school board meetings… are terrorists and can be called such. We hear it every day. Turn on the News, network to network, and watch the media dance to the rhythm of Jan. 6, just so they can keep whistling "white supremacist" against all Republicans.

Language policing, post Orwell, swept across the United States and the world during and in between the Intifadas when Israeli civilians were being murdered in their homes, schools, synagogues, walk-

---

* Originally published in *Arutz Sheva* English site (israelnationalnews.com).

ing, driving and dining… but by whom? Everybody knew it was the Palestinian Arabs who were doing the stabbing, the shooting, the ramming, the kidnapping and the hostage-taking.

This put the media on the spot. These were a new generation of journalists. In a word – far-out Liberals.

They were not the brawling, boozing Ben Hecht "Front Page" types, warriors for the truth and the facts… and then go out and party.

Instead, the new breed arrived somberly and judgmentally as watchdogs for "equality," and as activists to make "the world a better place."

For the sake of all that, good and evil were placed on the same level, or nearly so.

Virtue was ambiguous.

So, in newsroom after newsroom, all was confusion, as when, for example, to call a spade a spade.

The matter was in heated dispute from one newsroom to the next.

Until finally, outfits like *CNN* and *The New York Times* went all in for the "Palestinian Cause" and war-mongers like the PLO's Hanan Ashrawi were termed "moderates."

To understand is to justify, and the media understood… understood, in their twisted minds and hearts, why it wasn't terrorism or an act of depravity when Arabs murdered Israelis.

At worst, they'd call it "militancy."

Or, as Rabin and Peres saw the bloods in Jerusalem crying to the heavens, "sacrifices for peace."

Tell that to the victims and their families who will never "understand" how murder can ever be "justified."

Language, then and now, made all the difference between right and wrong, and now we are still dealing with Islamic terror but on whose vernacular?

Under the Progressive philosophy… i.e. the Biden Administration… the benefit of the doubt belongs to anyone who wants to come to America.

Accordingly, everybody is welcome… undocumented, whatever. So now… now the sophisticates worry how that one hostage-taker got in, a legitimate concern.

But what about the thousands still getting in through our southern border?

(Not a single question about that from the quislings during the two-hour press conference with Biden.)

Who are these people? Will we find out when it's too late?

Let's hope the Texas synagogue hostage taking is one-and-done. Won't happen again.

We can dream, can't we?

At least that's what the Left is counting on.

Whose Land is This Anyway?

***Jan. 12, 2022 – Who fought, bled and died for Zion and whose country is this anyway? And who is running it?**

From the beginning the Israelis were admired as rugged pioneers who "made the desert bloom."

To this day, planting a tree in Israel is a symbol of rebirth and permanence.

That's what we do when we go to Israel to visit or to stay. We plant trees.

But not everybody is happy about this, three Arab communities in the Negev in particular, who say… not in my backyard.

To many of them, of course, the entire Land of Israel is their backyard, and so they riot when they don't get their way.

They demand a halt to Israel's forestation project, and as discussions continue between the government and the Bedouin, the planting has indeed been suspended.

The question is… which government? Which government is in power… the so-called Jewish one run by Bennett/Lapid… or, do elements of the Muslim Brotherhood really call the shots?

It's come to this? Yes, it has.

Because in order to form a government by hook or by crook, Bennett/Lapid needed up to four more Knesset votes, and got them from Mansour Abbas and his Arab Ra'am Party.

Within a tug-of-war coalition like this, Israelis wake up every morning wondering who's got the upper hand, and who gained an advantage overnight.

While they slept, which Israeli religious site along with Homesh Yeshiva has been marked for the bulldozers?

Who fought, bled and died for Zion and whose country is this anyway?

Parenthetically, some years back, as American volunteers for the IDF, a group of us arrived late back at our hotel where we were invited

---

* Originally published in *Arutz Sheva* English site (israelnationalnews.com).

to stay rather than on base in Haifa. Our Madrich (group leader) began accompanying us to our rooms. The desk clerk shouted, "Stop." Why? It was past visiting hours.

The heated exchange continued when our Madrich announced firmly that "I can go wherever I want, whenever I want. This is my country."

"For the time being," responded the Arab clerk. (More about all that in this thriller.)

So, there it was then, and here it is now.

I've got friends in and around NYC who, in bewilderment, keep asking me who is really in charge of the country. I tell them to stay tuned. It varies day to day.

On this day, it's the Arabs, seeing how the coalition capitulated in the Negev, which proves that Bennett/Lapid are only half the show… and often the lesser half.

When the Muslim Brotherhood speaks, they listen, and obey. They have no choice. Should any member of the Ra'am Party bolt, poof goes the entire government.

On that exact threat, the Israelis caved, and stopped planting in the Negev, upon further notice. Or upon deciding once and for all if Israel is to remain the Jewish/Zionist dream and reality.

If the Jews are so smart, say my friends, how could they be so stupid? The Negev, which is about half of Israel geographically, is sovereign Israeli territory.

Jews are 80 percent of the country… the rest 20 percent… so how did the Jews put themselves in such a spot where others can dictate to them where they can or cannot plant trees?

Or houses… or neighborhoods… or communities… or yeshivas…

In a word, my friends… politics.

Don't ask me to explain. It's too complicated. Or maybe it's too simple. The best of us, I'd suggest, become Einsteins in science and other fields.

That leaves politics for the rest… usually not the best and the brightest, but energetic and power-hungry just the same.

That doesn't go for all. Once in a while, so far as leadership, we get lucky… in both Israel and the United States.

But in the United States, we still voted 80 percent for Biden, and would do so again, so yes, how can people so smart be so stupid.

In Israel, my friends and relatives are worried that at this rate, and through various political shenanigans, the Jewish nation of Israel is beginning to unravel and slip away from them.

G-d forbid, they say. But they do worry… and it does not have to be all at once… only through one uprooted yeshiva and one tree un-planted at a time.

Jan. 6 is Purim for Dems. Trump is Their Haman

***Jan. 10, 2022 – Did you hear graggers go off throughout Democrat strongholds each time Biden mentioned Trump's name?**

January 6 is turning out to be a joyful day for Democrats; soon to become a national holiday judging from what we saw and heard last Thursday.

Biden, Kamala and all the media you can't trust tried to commemorate Trump's folly of Jan. 6, 2021 as a sad, mournful occasion… terrible… terrible for the country.

The acting was good, terrific, but fooled nobody.

Don't believe the long faces. Forget the funereal oratory. They love Jan. 6, and always will… a date that will live in gladness for all time thanks to the crazies who stormed the Capitol in Trump's name. As Biden read the Megillah of evidence against Trump, did you hear graggers go off throughout Democrat strongholds each time Biden mentioned Trump's name? I did.

(Yes, I know he only referred to him as the previous president.)

Even the COVID face-coverings could not hide the smirks.

In Trump they found their Haman and in Jan. 6 they found their Purim.

Hang him they will each time that date comes around and each day in between because hissing, booing, jeering, hating Trump is all they've got.

Without Trump to bash they'd have no reason to get up in the morning.

In fact, they should thank him. What a favor he did them when after four successful years in office, he unleashed that mob.

I fault Trump for putting his legions in a terrible fix. He had us at hello and thereafter, but the goodbye was awful. This can't be what he intended.

But now we must all suffer the media's smugness, self-

---

* Originally published in *Arutz Sheva* English site (israelnationalnews.com).

righteousness and *schadenfreude*.

Due to an inexplicable, self-destructive, impulse, Jan. 6 is his legacy… and not the wonders Trump did for America through secure borders and energy independence.

Nor… if they can help it… will he be remembered for doing something that no one else ever did.

He blessed Israel and made the entire world safer by introducing, through the Abraham Accords, a huge step towards peace in the Middle East.

Instead of gratitude, he's got Jan. 6 and Biden ripping him apart… Biden suddenly sounding like Churchill not in taking on China, but in taking on Trump.

The network boys and girls swooned. They pronounced it the best speech Biden ever gave… for being so furious, hard-hitting, spiteful and mean-spirited, as only he can deliver.

No doubt his speechwriters asked him which speech he wanted for that day… the Biden who unites or the Biden who divides the nation.

The speech that unites was missing from the files; it had been used only during the campaign, when bets were taken as to whether you can really fool all the people all the time.

Yes, you can.

Trump is a menace to Democracy, and it is poetry when Biden and Kamala accuse all Republicans of being insurrectionists.

Most festive of all, about Jan. 6, is that it gave cover to the Dems and their own crazies and assorted scoundrels, who far outnumber the loons found in any GOP dugout.

Who remembers the Dem sanctioned riots of 2020 when city after city went up in flames, robbery, murder, arson, dubbed "mostly peaceful?"

Except for the *New York Post*, and *Fox News*, who knew or cared that Joe's travelling companion, son Hunter, was allegedly on the take, Joe denying apparent complicity?

The Jan. 6 rioters… those found guilty… deserve what they get. There is no excuse for the lawlessness that they did.

But that was one day.

Yet everyday people like AOC, Rashida Tlaib and Ilhan Omar sit in Congress as LAWMAKERS.

The President's "Not My Problem" Approach to Leadership

***Jan. 5, 2022 – He must long for the days when talk was enough. Tough luck, America.**

In the 1972 film, *The Candidate*, Robert Redford utters a zinger of a last line. He plays the part of Bill McKay, a far-left California Democrat running for US Senate.

To succeed, as I recall the movie, he must unseat the popular GOP incumbent, and being desperate and so far behind in the polls, McKay/Redford makes promises that are sure to solve every problem in the nation and the world. Finally, after a bruising campaign, he wins, amazing everyone, including himself.

Following all the hurrahs, he has a private moment, and laments, "What do we do now?"

Fast-forward and you wonder if Joe Biden had the same kick in the gut reaction when it dawned on him that he'd won the presidency.

What does he do now, when a lifetime in politics only excelled him in the art of being there?

Too bad for him, and worse for us, that after the shouting it's time to produce, and it's time to make good on all those promises.

He must long for the days when talk was enough… and Joe talked all right. Yes, when he becomes president, he'll fix everything.

Now he is president and he's fixed nothing and rather than accept responsibility and take action Mr. Can-Do suddenly shifts to, "Who Me? Not my problem."

Or, as one Hollywood mogul used to say… include me out.

First… how this works… is blame Trump for everything. But that's gotten old.

What new, and what's news, is that Joe promised to shut down the virus. He had a plan, and during the campaign, trust me, he said, and as I approximate his comments – "My plan will succeed where

* Originally published in *Arutz Sheva* English site (israelnationalnews.com).

Trump's failed."

"Just vote for me and watch," …and now? Now the virus is worse than ever, and whereas for a time he said, "be patient, I'm working on it," … well, something snapped.

Last week, Mr. Trust Me opted for a different approach, saying that the solution is beyond his reach so do not look to him for answers… a watershed switch in leadership.

So, "Tough luck, America. You're on your own. Figure it out for yourselves, and stop asking pesky questions."

"Did you really expect me to work miracles? Even the Israelis are having a tough time with this, and they split the Red Sea."

On nearly everything else, Mr. Hands-on has become Mr. Hands-off… and so it goes with his answer for inflation…

"Well, what do you want me to do about it? I only work here, and get off my lawn."

So too, the terrible spike in crime throughout the nation, happening in mostly Democrat states and cities. Like New York.

"Too bad, but those are regional and local issues, and something should be done. But why ask me? I'm in Delaware most of the time."

About anti-Semitism sweeping the land…

"Shame. But I leave that in the good hands of Congress to solve."

Ilhan Omar!

"Ask me something easy. Like Afghanistan. I got us out of there, didn't I?"

True, but what about the thousands you left behind?

"They didn't move fast enough to catch the last plane. Not my fault. You snooze, you lose. Next, you'll be blaming me for the supply chain crisis."

As a matter of fact…

"Talk to Pete Buttigieg about that, when he's not on his honeymoon. That's his department. I'm busy running a country."

So, what about the border crisis that's swamping the country. Millions of unknowns are drifting in.

"I gave that over to Kamala to solve that problem, and she did."

But she didn't.

"Talk to her, if you can find her, and she'll explain everything, as only she can. I'm not the person to see about that, or anything else."

No Afterglow From Gantz's Meeting With Abbas

***Jan. 2, 2022 – Did Gantz know he was being played? What's it all about?**

Obviously, the charm offensive didn't work. Abbas spat on the hospitality and left the reception frothing at the mouth.

It began just last week or so, with congratulations all around. What was the big deal?

Benny Gantz, Israel's Defense Minister, had extended the welcome mat to PA chairman Mahmoud Abbas even so far as inviting him to his home. For the personal touch.

Nobody saw the snake in the carpet?

Indeed, Putin and Biden and other leaders around the world, even some within Israel, were effusively in support of Gantz's gesture… so full of warmth, love, peace.

What's wrong with peace? Nothing… if both sides want it.

Did Gantz know he was being played? He cannot have expected his extended hand to be met with such a blistering tirade, a rant running on with blood libel followed by blood libel.

"Ethnic cleansing," says he, Abbas, the man who pays his people to murder Israelis.

All that only hours after Gantz's come-on-a my house, I'm-a gonna give you candy.

What's it all about?

Abbas, the old pro at terror-diplomacy, is still smarting at being ignored all those years during the Trump era.

How it galled when one (mostly Sunni) Arab country after another, the UAE, Sudan, Morocco, Bahrain, all signed on for peace/nominalization with Israel, leaving the PA out in the cold.

For once, a Domino-effect that favored Israel.

---

* Originally published in *Arutz Sheva* English site (israelnationalnews.com).

All Abbas could do was watch from the sidelines as his dream of a united Arab front against Israel collapsed so suddenly and so spectacularly.

All those years of terror from the PA, the PLO, Fatah, Hamas... and Israel still lives... still thrives... and, with new Arab friends.

Abbas had been outmaneuvered. He did not see that coming.

Now it's different. No more Trump. Now it's Biden in the White House, and it's time to play Biden when your name is Mahmoud Abbas and the game is Israel.

Nothing big so far, but for Abbas, the signs are to his liking.

The Biden administration keeps dangling a US embassy for Arabs in East Jerusalem as one sign that it has cooled for the Israelis and warmed for the Arabs.

Abbas will take that for starters.

His outburst was studiously purposeful. To the world, he wants its attention. To the Israelis, it's a warning that he can make trouble, anytime, anywhere.

This time, he is certain, Washington will take his side.

He can make up stories about Israeli interference on the Temple Mount, knowing how well this sells.

Together with Hamas, he can stage confrontations that yield headlines that blast the Jewish State to an audience of willing readers.

This too, global anti-Semitism, has him emboldened.

The spike in anti-Semitism, troubling for Jews and good people everywhere, is a boon for this warlord terrorist, Mahmoud Abbas.

Between a more pliant DC, and a part of the world feasting on Jew-hatred, he's got a one-two-punch that he figures for a knockout.

Israeli leaders need to be prepared for what's coming, and going soft appears to be a mistaken strategy.

Whatever Benny Gantz had planned... it backfired... terribly.

This should be a lesson learned... all over again.

Accusing Netanyahu of Betraying Trump – Ridiculous!

***Dec. 26, 2021 – They accuse Netanyahu of being stubborn and difficult not only against Trump, but previous presidents too. He was never a pushover.**

According to the headlines, Trump is not happy with his former buddy Netanyahu… says Netanyahu is ungrateful for what he, Trump, did for Israel.

We covered the first cracks in the relationship right about here, but more keeps happening.

Let's first understand that both men, Trump and Netanyahu, were strong leaders. Each man did what he had to do… Trump for America, Netanyahu for Israel.

They were bound to clash. In this, there is no right or wrong.

Well, that's how I see it, but among columnists, the sophisticates, I appear to be in the minority. Whatever the dispute between the two, I call it even.

The sophisticates say Netanyahu is guilty for… everything! To collar Bibi, they'll go back to the beginning of time to find an imperfection.

To start with the most ludicrous accusation of all, they say that Jewish American support for Israel is at an all-time low… and guess whose fault that is. Netanyahu, of course.

To believe that, you were born yesterday. Otherwise, you are aware that there is nothing new under this sun, either.

You are also aware that alarmists and doomsayers have always been with us… with "facts" and "statistics."

In fact, and through ebb and flow, Jewish support for Israel has been at an "all-time low" for years, decades, centuries, even going back to the days of the Hebrew Bible.

---

* Originally published in *Arutz Sheva* English site (israelnationalnews.com).

That's how far back this goes, and most Hebrews, the rabbis tell us, chose to remain in the fleshpots of Egypt, rather than follow Moses to the Promised Land.

Netanyahu can't be asked to do more than Moses, not when so many American Jews are assimilated, their Zionism proportionately diluted.

Not when so many American Jews are Liberal, and will likely favor a weak-in-the-knees Democrat and never a strong-handed Republican, such as Netanyahu… or Trump.

Paradoxically, most American Jews do support Israel, in varying degrees. So, this is complicated, and to fault Netanyahu for what's happening in America is a stretch.

But stretch they do, my fellow columnists.

They say that Netanyahu betrayed Trump over Trump's Deal of the Century. Not so, unless they're talking about Netanyahu's stiff-arm over Jared Kushner's Part Two.

Part One was glorious. There, through Trump, the United States recognized Israel's legitimate rights over the Golan Heights, moved the US Embassy to Jerusalem, and then, more icing on the cake… the Abraham Accords… followed by smiles and handshakes all around; Trump and Netanyahu the best of pals.

But Part Two was sobering, Trump saying, "Now it's time to make the Palestinians happy."

Too happy, for Netanyahu… as this proposal almost took it all back, over land, prisoners and sovereignty; the two-state-solution smacking Netanyahu in the face all over again.

So, justifiably, Netanyahu said I'll take all of Part One; Kushner's Part Two, not so much… and for that, they're calling Netanyahu ungrateful.

As for me, I'll take "ungrateful" when grateful means jeopardizing the safety of my country, whether Israel or the USA.

Then they accuse Netanyahu of being stubborn and difficult not only against Trump, but against previous US presidents as well.

For nobody was he a pushover.

True, in no White House was he "popular."

Maybe it's because they too demanded and expected concession after concession, some of it or all of it to Israel's detriment.

Preceding Netanyahu, Israel had a number of prime ministers who were willing to give the other side nearly everything it wanted, including the kitchen sink, Jerusalem.

They were very popular.

For me, I'll take unpopular, and stubborn, and difficult, if it means unyielding for the safety, security, and sovereignty of the Jewish State.

Soft on Crime Politicians in A Panic

***Dec. 23, 2021 – Soft on crime leaders… now they're sorry for their catastrophic mistakes. Quite a reversal.**

They didn't know? You knew and I knew that if you decrease law enforcement, you automatically increase crime.

I can't think of anything more obvious, but then, I am not a Democrat politician, neither mayor, nor DA. But if I were, I'd likely be as far out as the rest of them, who can't do the math, which is the law of proportion, evidenced on every street corner where criminals rush in to replace the cop who's been defunded.

Any wonder that 12 major cities in the US experienced record-level homicides in 2021? I'm not surprised. You're not surprised. The politicians are amazed.

They can't figure out what went wrong. They reduced or eliminated jail, bail and the police, and rather than gratitude, a crime wave is what they got.

Can they really be that witless… as to have expected a different outcome?

Among the first to answer that question was Philadelphia DA Larry Krasner, who said crime wave? What crime wave? There is no crime wave. No crisis. I did nothing wrong. Go Eagles.

Then the fact that Philly leads the nation in homicides… 500-plus and counting… leading Krasner to humbly apologize for being so obtuse.

Then the mayor himself, Jim Kenney… some remember him doing a jig when Philadelphia was declared a sanctuary city… Kenney we find in the doldrums of reality.

The splash of truth comes even to high-end Liberals, and so from Kenney's lips, we get the political quote of the year, as follows – "It's terrible every morning to get up and have to go look at the numbers and then look at the news and see the stories. It's just crazy. It's just crazy and this needs to stop."

---

* Originally published in *Arutz Sheva* English site (israelnationalnews.com).

Is this trending? Yes, even snoozing Liberals in uber soft-on-crime San Francisco are coming around to meet the real world… the world of snatch and grab hooliganism.

Months ago, Mayor London Breed was perfectly pleased to cut $120 million from San Francisco's law enforcement budget, and now listen to her – She vows, "To end the reign of criminals who are destroying our city."

Quite a reversal that, and you can only wonder what time of the night she woke up in a sweat to realize her terrible blunder.

In Blue State America they're waking up one at a time haunted by the inconsolable refrain… "Dear Lord. What have I done!"

Indulgent Liberal Lori Lightfoot, mayor of Chicago, is having more than a comeuppance. She's in a panic.

She's calling on federal troops to save Chicago. The rate of theft, plunder, rape and murder is beyond anything she can control.

She's pleading for help… AFTER she proposed an $80 million cut from Chicago's police budget.

Different story now. Altogether different, as now she says, "We can't continue to endure the level of violence we are now experiencing."

For New Yorkers, it was good riddance di Blasio. Enter, law and order, Eric Adams, a former cop.

It's good that here and there Liberals in power are waking up… but has anything really been learned?

Spielberg's *West Side Story* – Good Art, Bad Politics

***Dec. 19, 2021 – For Spielberg and Kushner, Israelis never get a break, even in a movie, while *West Side Story* is replete with their radical liberalism.**

Spielberg's remake of *West Side Story*… well deserved applause and jeers.

They don't make 'em like they used to… or, maybe they do.

The critics are divided over Steven Spielberg's remake of the 1961 *West Side Story*, which back then captured 10 Oscars, including Best Picture.

Top that? Give Spielberg his due. He was game, and willing to give it a try, supported by a budget of 100 million dollars… and now playing in theatres everywhere.

For some, even most reviewers, yes, it was worth all that, and for any doubters out there… "those wonderful people out in the dark," (Norma Desmond), we are ecstatically assured that Spielberg has not lost his touch, but that he has indeed surpassed the 1961 classic, so what's stopping you from buying a ticket?

Alas, so far the movie is tanking at the box office, for reasons nobody can figure out. Perhaps COVID and the few bad reviews are keeping people away.

Can it be politics, and that only Democrats will go watch anything directed by Spielberg and written by Tony Kushner? Both are flaming Liberals.

If that's what's happening… politics bleeding into art and entertainment… then guilty we are for succumbing to our baser instincts.

But so are director Spielberg and his screenwriter Tony Kushner.

They too are guilty and they don't get off claiming artistic immunity, not when they're so loudly in your face in the service of radical Liberalism… as when Spielberg chose the Spanish dialogue in the film

* Originally published in *Arutz Sheva* English site (israelnationalnews.com).

to run along without subtitles because, he said, he did not want the English to have power over the Spanish.

That's a political decision, not an artistic decision, and what shameful pandering this is, and it comes with a price – lousy box office.

The play should be the thing, and we should be allowed to appreciate the music without political interference.

For example, I'd rather know Kushner the artist, and not Kushner the authority on politics and world events, as when he tells *Yale Israel Review*, the following – "Israel was founded in a program that, if you really want to be blunt about it, was ethnic cleansing, and that today is behaving abominably towards the Palestinian people."

So now let me be blunt about it, which is to say that Kushner has it all backwards, and that in tolerant/freedom-loving Israel he and his husband can speak and behave freely.

In Gaza they'd be tossed off tall buildings.

By a margin of 90 percent, Jerusalem's Arabs say they prefer Israeli rule instead of being governed by the Palestinian Authority.

That, for some, is an inconvenient truth.

Maybe Spielberg chose the right project, but the wrong writer.

From *West Side Story*, it included the song *Somewhere*.

Leonard Bernstein composed the music; Stephen Sondheim wrote the words, for the 1957 stage play.

Two artistic geniuses writing about a NYC turf war, but the yearning is entirely Jewish, whether straight up or subliminal... and the message still rings for a Jewish homeland.

Through *Schindler's List* and his Holocaust Foundation, Spielberg can be counted on to speak well of Jews dead and buried.

But Jews living lively in the open air of Israel... these make trouble and cause him a problem. Likewise, Kushner, and so together, in 2005, they gave us a movie that mendaciously equates the victim with the murderer, in yet another example of Jews suffering from Stockholm Syndrome.

In *Munich*, directed by Spielberg, co-written by Kushner, they took the oldest scenario in the world... good guys versus bad guys... and turned it into bad guys versus bad guys.

Or maybe it's Kushner who all alone imposes his prejudices within Spielberg's films.

In some minds, evil and good weigh about the same… possibly the tragedy of our times.

The movie was ostensibly based on the actual 1972 massacre at the Munich Summer Olympics, when PLO terrorists murdered 11 Israeli Olympians in an atrocity that shocked the world.

For about five minutes.

The Israelis never forgot. They sent undercover agents around the world to track and eliminate the killers.

In bygone Hollywood they would be directed by John Ford and played by Gary Cooper, the strong silent hero that can be counted on to take care of business.

In the hands of Spielberg and Kushner, *Munich* is full of words, more than half of them given to the killers who are scripted, by Kushner, to eloquently justify their bloodlust.

So for Spielberg and Kushner, the Israelis never get a break, even in a movie. The most they can count on is moral equivalence.

Now Kushner says his views on Israel have been mischaracterized. How so? We all speak the same English. He says, "I want the state of Israel to continue to exist."

Gee, thanks.

Such breaking news I will immediately pass along to my relatives in Israel… that it's okay for them to stay. Tony Kushner says so.

But keep the bags packed in case he changes his mind.

As for Spielberg, there is no joy, no *schadenfreude*, for this particular box office failure. I am sure he feels he deserves better for all the toil and expectation.

Join the club.

Tough Luck for the Jewish Couple Booted Off A Plane

***Dec. 6, 2021 – No one stood up for them. What's happening to us?**

A Jewish couple has been traumatized on a plane

The question is… what would you do if faced with a situation like this; whereby a Jewish couple were allegedly booted off a plane over a Tallit.

I say allegedly because we only know what we read in the papers.

So according to the *New York Post*… by far the best newspaper in the land… Roberto and Elana Birman were on an American Airlines flight returning to Brooklyn from a stay in Miami.

Roberto is 76, Elana is 71, and from the looks of them, downhome Yiddishe people, and not exactly Bonnie and Clyde.

Nor is it likely that people bolt their doors and hide the children when the couple, married 52 years, stroll by, because, who knows, Mr. Birman might be packing a Tallit.

We pick up the story as a flight attendant, making her usual pre-takeoff rounds on Flight 322… and behold, a Tallit.

The sacred shawl, as per usual, was secured in a plastic bag, and there it was, in the overhead bin, above Mr. Birman… bothering nobody.

Except a flight attendant.

As I imagine the conversation…

"Sir, does this belong to you?"

"Yes."

"What is it?"

"It's a Tallit."

"A what?"

"A prayer shawl that is holy to me and my people."

"Well it has to be taken down and placed underfoot."

"But that would be sacrilege."

---

* Originally published in *Arutz Sheva* English site (israelnationalnews.com).

"Rules are rules."

To quote Mr. Birman, "She was screaming at me and pointing her finger."

We can imagine the horror when a figure of authority takes that attitude. Reasoning doesn't help. Makes it worse.

Some people you just can't reach.

Some people have it in for you from scratch.

We know it when facing hearts of stone at the motor vehicle bureau, and other places where they get to lord it over you.

We all know the feeling when someone dislikes you over nothing you said or did, quite the opposite of love at first sight, but there it is.

Does it have to be anti-Semitism? Could be. But it can also be the new incivility and coarseness that has overtaken the United States.

On this flight, Mr. and Mrs. Birman must have felt selected. They must have felt they were still in anti-Semitic Argentina, from where they left in 1985.

Next, we read that the pilot shows up, says nothing, but moments later the Birmans are escorted off the plane.

"The humiliation," says Mrs. Birman.

They've taken legal action against the airline. We await its side of the story.

But how's this for apathy? From Mrs. Birman, we hear, "Nobody defended us."

So it appears that of the fellow passengers, no one came through in the clutch. No one stood up to declare, "This isn't right."

What's happening to us?

Too bad, we now say under such circumstances, of persons who need our help. Tough luck. None of my business.

People on the same plane become neighbors. They become a community. A community sticks together. Neighbors support one another.

In America, quite so… once upon a time.

Is Kyle the Best We've Got for A Hero?

***Dec. 1, 2021 – To say that he is not guilty is one thing, but to use an act of Congress to stamp him a hero is something else.**

Apparently, we are short on heroes in this country when the pickings come down to Michelle Obama, Kamala Harris, Pete Buttigieg, even Kyle Rittenhouse.

If that's the best we've got, no doubt about it, we are a nation in steep decline.

Heroes are made to lift our spirits, but Michelle, Kamala and Pete… that's who the Democrats are proposing and projecting for leadership come 2024.

Pete Buttigieg, in case you hadn't heard from him in a while, is our Secretary of Transportation, who, la di da, took off two months paternity leave during the height of the supply chain crisis.

Two full months, absent on the job, while the shelves kept getting emptier. Transportation secretary and yet he couldn't transport himself to where the supply glitch was happening.

Just so you know priorities as practiced by the current administration.

Joe didn't think to phone him, "Hey, Pete, maybe take a half day from the babysitting to check this out?"

Then again, did any of the generals tell Joe, "Yo, Joe, ya think you should evacuate the civilians first, before you evacuate the troops?"

Anyway, Michele, Kamala and Pete, such are their champions. Those are their best and their wisest for the future, even after they punk'd us Joe Biden.

Joe wasn't punishment enough.

So far as who's batter up for the next round of elections, Republicans are sensibly playing it close to the vest. Obviously, whoever they choose will get trounced by the media.

So, the later the better, before all hell, and Adam Schiff, breaks loose.

---

* Originally published in *Arutz Sheva* English site (israelnationalnews.com).

But now is the time, apparently, for Kyle Rittenhouse to strut his stuff to fill the role of a hero, though still not sure for which party.

He takes pictures with Trump, then says he supports BLM. He also keeps ready for his close-ups on Network TV.

Fame is good!

Whichever way.

After all, he is still a kid, only 18. No rush.

But Georgia GOP Rep. Marjorie Taylor Greene thinks the time is right, to proclaim the teenager a savior.

So she has introduced a bill to award Rittenhouse the Congressional Gold Medal… for protecting Kenosha, Wisconsin, during the BLM riot, August 25, 2020.

I believe that's the highest honor for a civilian.

I also believe that this is so wrong, and I'm the writer who supported the kid, vehemently, throughout his trial.

What exactly did he do that is so terrific, and through what daring and selfless acts does he rate so much widespread praise, if only from the right?

It was the right thing for the jury to find him not guilty on all counts. He killed two people, but, they ruled, it was self-defense.

I cheered the verdict.

But even then, to be honest, I wasn't cool with the notion of a 17-year-old showing up with an AR-15 to take on the bad guys like Alan Ladd in *Shane*. Or like Clint Eastwood in any movie.

Something about that…

To say that he is not guilty is one thing, but to use an act of Congress to stamp him a hero is something else. Maybe he'll fill into the role, some day. Maybe not.

We can do better, even as we hunger for someone with true leadership qualities to save us from this leaderless purgatory.

Heroes are rare. This kid is still much too common. Likewise the others.

Richard Gere Et Al, Thanks for the Reminder to Bless Israel

***Nov. 24, 2021 – Richard Gere and more than 100 other movie notables signed a letter not to bless, but to curse the precious land and its holy people.**

Surely, I am as guilty as the next person about taking Israel for granted. We forget the miracle, that there she stands, for all of us, risen from the ashes, a Biblical dream come true.

So obsessed by politics, we forget what Israel means for our glory, our tradition, our safety, and our deliverance from the hands of our enemies, who, to this day, hate us without cause.

So here they come again, Richard Gere and more than 100 other movie notables to sign a letter not to bless, but to curse the precious land and its holy people.

You heard this before? Yes… once a year they come to remind us that it ain't over… the world's oldest hatred still lives, even among the fancy people.

You would think to be rich and famous would keep them busy counting their money and their luck, but no, as throughout history, there is always time for the Jews.

What is it this time? It is about… well… the Palestinian Arabs, and how lovely they are compared to the Israelis.

Fortunate for them to have the Palestinian Arabs as their darlings.

Otherwise they would have to look themselves in the mirror and admit that it is a mindless, brutish ancient grudge that motivates and enrages them.

Big question. Where would they be without Israel… to blame?

Bigger question. Where would we be without Israel… to cherish?

The precise grievance, contained in a letter sent out to the world, runs something like this… apartheid, occupation, settler-colonialism… but without the music.

---

* Originally published in *Arutz Sheva* English site (israelnationalnews.com).

If you need the details, here is a sample, but I don't need details, because so far as plain hatred, like Justice Potter Stewart said about obscenity, "I know it when I see it."

No need to explain or elaborate over something that stares you in the face.

You know it when you see it, smell it, taste it, and feel it when it comes knocking at your door.

People like that…. Gere and fellow kvetches, Susan Sarandon, Julie Christie, Mark Ruffalo… it only encourages them and empowers them and justifies them if you try to reason with them.

I never try.

It is hopeless and useless and thankless and they've got all the answers anyway derived from Julius Streicher and their focus groups.

I remind myself what it was like before modern-day Israel, when, in my day, they had no complaints. Nothing specific. No Palestinians around anywhere.

Not when or where I grew up.

No Palestinians in sight, except that in that sacred place in the Middle East, before 1948, people who lived there were systematically called Palestinian… among them the Jews.

Like David ben Gurion, referred to in the press, even at the *BBC* and in *The New York Times*, as "the Palestinian leader of the Jewish population." Look it up.

So, growing up in those days, they did not intellectualize their grievance, nor specify their complaint.

You were Jewish and that was enough.

Enough to call you "kike" and "Juif," up and down Saint Laurent Boulevard, as they marched with swastikas and howls to smash the shops and burn the Jews.

Yes, Montreal. But it could have been anywhere. Mordecai Richler tells about it in *Barney's Version*, and I tell it in *Escape from Mount Moriah*.

There was no use talking, and there was no time explaining, not when they trapped you, to and from school, home, and synagogue.

You learned how to fight because it was literally do or die and because there is no reasoning with a baseball bat aimed at your head.

They usually came at you about a hundred at a time… gangs of 100 against one. To them, a fair fight.

That was then. Richard Gere and his gang of 100. That is now. Same thing. Only the names change.

One other change; finally, blessedly, this is beyond their reach – "Am Yisroel Chai."

It Didn't Start With Kyle Rittenhouse, Nor Will It End in Kenosha

***Nov. 21, 2021 – Media tried and failed to convict Kyle Rittenhouse, and now, after the verdict, which way America?**

Finally, after three agonizing weeks, the verdict is in, on a trial and a televised courtroom drama that had the nation riveted, though in a sense, it is the nation that's still on trial.

Will there be more bloodshed?

Going back to last summer, the mobs who came to punish Kenosha, Wisconsin after a police shooting, knew they were in the right place at the right time to get a green light for bedlam.

From earlier riots in Minneapolis, Portland, Kansas City and Seattle, they learned that guilt-ridden, or terrified, or simply yellow governors and mayors would make no moves to stop them, until plenty of damage had been done, or until the point was made, mission accomplished – whiteness is the root of all evil.

From out of the 1960s came word, let it Burn, Baby, Burn.

As Downtown Kenosha was going up in flames last August, 17-year-old Kyle Rittenhouse arrived with an AR-15 rifle to help restore order, or to make things worse.

(True. They don't make teenagers like they used to.)

Was he part of the solution, or part of the problem? Was he guilty or not guilty for firing at three "demonstrators," two of whom were killed by his bullets?

Was it murder or self-defense?

Today, Friday, Nov. 19, the jury found him not guilty on all charges.

So that's the end of that story. If only it were so.

Rittenhouse's prosecutors kept arguing that the "demonstrators" were "only" targeting property. They had a right to do this, without intervention, because property, such as cars, homes, shops, synagogues,

---

* Originally published in *Arutz Sheva* English site (israelnationalnews.com).

churches, schools, hospitals, libraries, books, are lifeless, inanimate entities and therefore of no consequence.

Nothing there, they say, that deserves protecting.

That's how Rittenhouse became anathema to the Left. He came to interrupt a riot in progress.

How rude!

The streets should be safe not for the law-abiding, but for the mobs.

That pretty much sums it up for the Left. It has been their Soviet/Mao view for some time that property is valueless and individualistic, if you know your Marx and Lenin.

Or Bernie Sanders.

Nobody, it goes, is entitled to own anything. That is communism 101, but the thugs on the streets, tossing Molotov cocktails, need nothing so theoretical.

Any excuse will do, rain or shine.

My friend Kuana Bell once explained why they seldom are out rioting when it rains. That's because the downpour would ruin their coiffure.

These days, many in the media say property is racist… the same media that, by use of consistent bad vibes, tried and convicted the kid before they knew the facts.

Rittenhouse, they said (without evidence) is a white supremacist.

Property, they say, is white privilege.

So, prepare for more violence in our streets because we know how one thing leads to another; how vandalism against property begets brutality against people.

Only human life, they say, is worthy of our blood, sweat and tears… theirs especially.

Others, like myself, would contend that property is life… case by case. We can begin with your car and home, without which you have no life.

For slow learners, for example Biden voters, I will unpack all this later. For the rest, there is only the obvious…

Such as a Torah Scroll, parchment that lives and breathes, and for which there is nothing more sacred. It is life itself.

Kristallnacht targeted property, as a preview. We know how that ended, and we know the damage to lives and livelihood when, from

Gaza, Hamas sends incendiary kites and balloons into Israel for the purpose of turning that good earth into properties of waste and scorched land.

Rudy Giuliani (Mayor of NYC, 1994, 2001), changed everything when he introduced the "broken windows" initiative which got tough against small and property crime.

The idea was that policing small crimes… turnstile hoppers… windshield wiper intruders… creates a culture of law and order that sends a ripple effect to discourage serious crime.

It worked. NYC then was safer and cleaner than it had been maybe ever.

These days is there anyone like that to step up? Or is that asking too much?

US Jews:
Rise and Shine for Jerusalem

***Nov. 15, 2021 – Jewish Americans, what company do you want to keep? Woke-ism is the enemy of civilization. Support Israel.**

The Biden administration's feverish rush to re-open a US consulate in Jerusalem ought to alarm American Jews for a least five reasons --

One: There already is a US Embassy in Jerusalem. It is the official one; the one that attests to Jerusalem as the undivided capital of Israel.

Why then another such office, in the Palestinian Arab sector, except to divide the Holy City?

Two: Jerusalem has been in our prayers for more than 3,000 years, since King David founded it as sacred, sovereign and indivisible.

Three: A divided Jerusalem weakens Israel and invites the doubters, and the accusers, and the deniers to keep dreaming of Israel's demise.

Unless you are one of them… a Liberal do-or-die… who on earth would want to be an accomplice with that brand of scoffers?

Alas, another vote for Biden or his Party, puts you in that category.

Four: A weakened Israel threatens American security. To this day, America counts on Israel's intel brains and military muscle to serve as the reliable, steady hand in a region known for unstable rulers and murderously chaotic regimes. Iran has designs against both Israel and the United States.

Israel stands as the seasoned and ready battleship in these stormy waters.

Five: Team Biden's emerging policy towards Israel is similar to its policy for America… intended, in each case, to scrap history and rewrite it for the Woke/Progressive cause.

For America, their scam is racism. For Israel, their big con is colonialism, or apartheid, or everything else they can invent.

---

* Originally published in *Arutz Sheva* English site (israelnationalnews.com).

That is where Biden comes in, as a satisfied customer of the Woke/Progressive far left agenda. He is all in. What the Squad peddles, he buys.

No wonder, then, to be watching the Biden administration cold-shoulder Israel as it warms to the PA, Fatah, and yes, even Hamas.

Awarding them a foothold toward a divided Jerusalem is what a Woke president will do. It is what a Woke party, the Democrats, will celebrate.

But Jewish Americans… is this the company they want to keep?

The Woke philosophy, which sneers at tradition and tramples everything that is noble about our Judeo/Christian system, is being roundly rejected by the American people.

The polls say so, and the election results of last week reveal a nation disgusted with the can of worms for sale by the far left.

If Woke-ism means Down with Everything, which it does, Americans aren't interested in anything so far removed from Mom, baseball and apple pie.

Woke activists… it is being recognized… are the termites of civilization.

Jewish Americans should take note that the rest of the country is okay with good old-fashioned patriotism, and this includes love and support for Israel.

This would be a perfect time for American Jews to show strength and resolve for Israel.

A good place to start is to make some noise against that Palestinian Arab eyesore, such as those plans for a US consulate in Jerusalem.

We need to get this right. The rest of the country is watching.

It Gets Personal When Migrants Are Rewarded $450,000

***Nov. 10, 2021 – True, a $450,000 jackpot awaits illegals into the US.**

Frankly, I do not remember my family receiving nearly half a million dollars when they arrived here as refugees from the Holocaust.

Land of opportunity, yes, thank goodness, but no goldene medina (golden land of paradise) awaited them, nor the others who somehow got around FDR's quota.

Upon arrival, the work had just begun, and for most, making it in America came only through the sweat of your brow.

But under Joe Biden, migrant families coming here illegally are to be compensated $450,000 if, during the Trump Administration, they were separated at the border.

So, the streets are paved with gold after all, but for border scofflaws.

The more the better as Biden and company purposefully invite the traffic that will eventually turn America into Honduras.

Israel has its own story about the influx of illegal immigrants, among them Sudanese and Eritrean, a flood of which can be harmful to the Jewishness of the nation.

In the United States, most illegals are airlifted and dumped throughout the country without being checked as possible health risks to themselves or their new neighbors, who never expected them or asked for them, and most are not "children," as we are told to believe, but grown-ups, the majority of them men.

They keep coming, illegally, and those from the past who obeyed the laws and played by the rules are perplexed by the disparity from one group of newcomers to another.

My group were called greenhorns. Not a compliment, and not the worst of the situation.

---

* Originally published in *Arutz Sheva* English site (israelnationalnews.com).

Recall the scene in *Godfather Part 2*, where Vito Corleone arrives as a child at Ellis Island and after being examined is placed in a cell to recover, or, be sent back, due to some health defect that was found in the boy. That was not fiction but fact for the many who had made it this far, and as for me, I was in the same type of cell after it was discovered that I'd had Scarlet fever.

In those days, citizenship was prized. You were lucky to get in, and luckier if they let you stay.

The process took years, and there were always documents to fill out, schedules to meet, and appointments to keep (as it was for my parents).

As it turned out, one mistake from all the paperwork and you had to start all over again… years of waiting in the wrong line.

Everything had to be exact.

Even at the point at arriving in America, there were still harrowing obstacles.

After weathering German patrols on the high seas, The Serpa Pinto, the ship of hope, arrived in Philadelphia, but not to stay. Passengers were to be moved along to Canada.

FDR did not want us, and neither did Mackenzie King. Canada's message for the Jews fleeing Hitler was, "None is too many."

But a deal was in the works, and Canada it would be. Second best will do. But not so fast.

A slim wooden board serving as a plank was placed between the ship and a bus; the bus then leading to a Montreal-bound train. Read this for the memoir of it all.

But first… walking the plank.

Some, in horror, saw it as trap, a trick, a test meant to be failed.

In fact, an announcement was made, blared loudly, to warn against breaking the law, which would be "setting foot on American soil."

Setting foot on American soil was meant literally and was forbidden in the strictest terms. Life and death hung in the balance.

Even an accidental slip would cause you to be arrested and sent back. Armed soldiers, rifles drawn, were keeping watch.

Nothing came easy…

The Media Slipped Up in Virginia – and Youngkin Outsmarted Them

***Nov. 7, 2021 – From print to broadcast, too much power, it surely seems, is in the hands of the wrong people. But Virginia leads us to hope.**

Media can't handle the truth.

Hope for the nation came last Tuesday when voters chose Republican Glenn Youngkin over Democrat Terry McAuliffe for the governorship of Virginia.

According to the odds-makers, this was not supposed to happen. But it did, and it has got Dems throughout the country alarmed, as they foresee a red trend.

The sobering began the morning after the results were in.

After years of Progressive drunkenness, *The New York Times* staggered out of bed with no choice but to notice that it was "a rough night for Democrats."

That was followed by another moment of clarity; the paper assessing the setback as a "grim immediate future" for the Democrat Party.

But never grim enough, some might say, for a Party that welcomes America haters and Israel deniers the likes of AOC, Ilhan Omar and Rashida Tlaib.

The Party, wrote the *Times*, after a second cup of coffee, will have to reconsider its priorities if it hopes to retain its grip on Congress and the White House.

How long can such sobriety last?

Not long.

Hours later, along comes lefty columnist Charles M. Blow to view the damage to his party as, aha… "White Racist Anxiety Strikes Again."

---

* Originally published in *Arutz Sheva* English site (israelnationalnews.com).

So that is the answer. For everything. For liberals, it is the race card or bust.

No epiphany likewise for the wild and crazy people at *CNN* and *MSNBC*.

They managed their sorrow by finding no flaws within their woke-ism, which finds 70 percent of Americans saying the country under Biden is headed in the wrong direction.

Instead, the inconsolable talking heads pointed fingers at "white supremacists," a category into which we are all bunched together, the entire country.

One anguished commentator at *MSNBC*, Joy Reed, referred to all Republicans as not only racist, but also "dangerous"... failing to explain how and why.

From print to broadcast, too much power, it surely seems, is in the hands of the wrong people.

Some, we suppose, dabble in actual journalism, which was once a highly respected profession, until it became populated by activists determined to "make the world a better place."

Well, is it?

Not nearly so within a newsroom system that ruthlessly permits one point of view only. What used to be called dissent... well, try it, and see what happens.

Many of these bellyachers are mere entertainers, personalities not bright enough to memorize lines for a David Mamet stage play, but talented enough to go about spouting political slogans.

Do not underestimate them. They can, and do, sway public opinion through their snap, malicious judgments.

How much anti-Semitism now making the rounds can we trace back to the potency of their tongues!

The shame of it is that, in the guise of journalists they cannot be voted out of office. No term limits for them.

They cannot be removed even if they are wrong about everything.

Yet we feel their influence every day.

It was the media apparatus which brings us to this juncture... to name only empty supermarket shelves, pain at the pump, a migrant invasion, the inglorious retreat from Afghanistan.

Together, falsehood after falsehood, they concocted scheme after scheme to bring down President Trump.

By use of the same manipulations they built for us a golden calf to worship named Joe Biden.

They stuck us with the worst president in American history, and about that they still have no shame.

They slipped up in Virginia. Or, Glenn Youngkin outsmarted them. He made the rights of parents the issue against his Woke-loving opponent.

Down with Critical Race Theory. Up with moms and dads. So ran his message, persuasively.

He used their tools, the camera and the microphone, to make his case a winner.

So, it can be done.

It must be done, to keep us safe from a news media complex that has turned so harmful.

Moms, Dads, and Other "Domestic Terrorists"

***Nov. 1, 2021 – The White House may think Israel should not call out PFLP NGOs, but then the US is where parents are called "domestic terrorists."**

Something is rotten in the state of our schools when parents are termed "domestic terrorists" for objecting to what's being taught to their kids.

Something else is wrong when Israel, for the sake of its national security, targets and classifies six "humanitarian" groups as actually being terrorist entities… but then must suffer the indignity of being lectured by the Biden Administration for acting on its own, without first checking in with Antony Blinken at the State Department.

Since when did Israel become the lesser partner in this relationship? More on that in a minute, as meanwhile…

In too many cases, throughout the country, the American young are being fed woke/leftist pabulum, such as Critical Race Theory, which actually promotes hatred between the races.

Parents complained. They showed up at school board meetings to register their disapproval. They thought they were in a free country. Promptly, the National School Boards Association told parents to shut up and mind their own business, or else there is going to be trouble. "Our kids ARE our business," responded the parents… and there WAS trouble.

In a snap, the FBI was called in to monitor school board meetings, with a special eye on parents who speak too loudly… hence, they must be domestic terrorists.

A bit much, that, even for the school board association, which tagged them as such, yes, moms and dads, domestic terrorists.

Sorry, they said. After the outcry. They went too far, they admitted… and, we are told, the FBI is hands off.

---

* Originally published in *Arutz Sheva* English site (israelnationalnews.com).

But the chill remains… likewise the stigma.

What's this got to do with Israel? America decides for itself who gets to be named a terrorist, domestic or foreign…. from parents, to mention the absurdity of leftist fantasies, to PLFP, the Popular Front for the Liberation of Palestine, to name a clear and present danger to both the United States and Israel.

The United States designated the PLFP a terrorist organization back in 1997… along with nearly 100 other such groups… and never asked Israel for permission.

Israel, through defense minister Benny Gantz, a week ago designated six of the PLFP satellite groups as terrorist organizations.

Sounds reasonable. Few doubt Israel's capacity to know its intel.

Nobody, it seems, is saying that Israel got it wrong, only that Israel failed to meet the protocol of alerting Team Biden of what was up.

Sounds like nitpicking, to me.

Sounds like Team Biden is out to get Israel any way it can. Feigning hurt feelings is one way, so that Team Bennett/Lapid is off to Washington on bended knee.

So sorry we forgot who's boss, Mr. Blinken.

Another means to remind Israel who's boss, is to keep Israel guessing on what day Biden will be totally committed to disunify the Jewish holy city by re-opening the US consulate in East Jerusalem. (Please don't tell me that Israel must consent for this to happen. Against both the United States and Israel, fanatical Democrats carry the big stick.)

Then, to demonstrate to the Israelis that there's a new sheriff in the White House, and in the State Department, any plan to build in the "settlements," must get Washington's approval.

That is no way for one sovereign nation to talk to another sovereign nation.

There is talk that Gantz forgot to tell his own government about the action he was taking against the dirty half-dozen.

That's not good, and, some say, failure like that positions the entire Israeli government as positively amateurish.

Maybe. But neither Gantz, nor Bennett, nor Lapid picked up from Afghanistan and left multitudes behind.

That was Amateur Joe who did that, because that is what he does, to everybody, everywhere, and of Joe Biden, people say that he is [also] abandoning Israel.

Good guess, Leroy.

Snakes On A Train – Philadelphia Style

***Oct. 23, 2021 – City of Brotherly Love? – not quite.**

According to reports, help came from nowhere, until it was too late. A woman was being raped on a Philadelphia commuter train and fellow passengers did nothing.

Correction: Yes. They did something. They used their smartphones to take videos. That is all they did. Only later, after the assault, a transit officer called police.

But the damage was done, to the woman, the town, the country, the mayor, Jim Kenney, the president, Joe Biden.

The story made headlines and continues to disgust and dismay.

We should not be surprised when a single incident, just one, but so brutish, captures our attention.

Where are we headed? Can we look ourselves in the mirror, truly, and recognize ourselves as heirs to Judeo/Christian values?

Rather, expect apathy, when police officers are maligned for their service, and calls persist to have law enforcement defunded altogether. Expect lawlessness when bloody riots are termed peaceful protests. Mix all that with open borders, persons we don't know flooding in with the consent of the government, and watch us go slouching towards Sodom and Gomorrah.

Count on no neighborly mercies when Critical Race Theory is being campaigned in the schools to foster hatred between the races.

When historical monuments are toppled and historical books are withdrawn from the curriculum, be prepared for a generation of know-nothing, do-nothing heretics.

People will say… come on, so far as apathy, it's no worse today than it ever was.

Partly true. It happened in 1964 when Kitty Genovese, a 28-year-old bar manager, was assaulted outside her apartment building in Queens, New York. The story goes that 38 neighbors or bystanders

---

* Originally published in *Arutz Sheva* English site (israelnationalnews.com).

saw it but did nothing. The newspapers picked it up, sensationally, as symptomatic of a town, and country, turned abrasive, callous and pitiless.

Later came the fact-checking that placed the number of do-nothing onlookers at fewer than 38. But in fact, a woman was murderously attacked in the open and people did nothing.

The uproar turned national and psychological.

They called it the "Bystander Effect," which proposed that the greater the number of bystanders, the less likely anyone of them will intervene.

Soon after, Good Samaritan laws were passed in New York State and elsewhere, this, to encourage people to help victims without fear of litigation.

The Genovese incident, it is believed, motived the creation of the 911 emergency system.

Two weeks ago in Philadelphia, short of physical intervention, 911 would have been the number to call.

Somehow, those dunces on the train considered themselves men and women of action through the act of snapping videos of a rape in progress.

Next step for them would be getting the "likes" on social media.

What more can you expect from a generation for whom nothing is real, and life is a "virtual" experience?

Actual real-life events mystify them and force them to scurry to their tech devices. Maddeningly self-absorbed, they freeze and go blank when faced with real-time decisions.

Books about life not so much, but movies about life they know, through cartoons.

Their fathers and mothers were the heroes of United Airlines Flight 93, September 11, 2001… when it was do or die against Islamist hijackers… and they did, and they died.

Their grandfathers stormed the beaches and took no videos or selfies.

Combat Photographers like Joe Rosenthal, who snapped the iconic Raising the Flag on Iwo Jima, were of a different breed.

Those were images of triumph, pride and patriotism.

Nothing like that in Philly.

Who Stole the Abraham Accords?

***Oct. 19, 2021 – Why are the Abraham Accords out in the cold? What's not to like about them?**

It appears that the Biden administration is getting ready to re-open a US Consulate in Jerusalem as a means to bring the Palestinian Arabs back into the big picture.

This is not good news. Because it is old news.

In the past, before Trump shut it down, 2019, the US Consulate General (not to be confused with today's actual US Embassy) somehow became de facto Palestinian headquarters.

Intended to serve the Arab sector and Jews, American personnel looked aside as the Palestinian Authority began staffing the place with Palestinian Arabs who ran it as a separate capital.

Israel shrugged. Better to have them shuffling papers than hurling Molotov Cocktails.

To Jews and Arabs alike they had the means to do municipal business… even to issue passports… and sometimes front door or back door, world dignitaries came to pay respect.

So, there it was… by some measure a divided Jerusalem, anathema, and contrary to the fact that Jerusalem, all of it, is absolutely the unified capital of Israel.

Back to the future… are we?

Or is it that some people will never warm to Israel until the Palestinian Arabs are frolicking happy campers?

Although, even the Palestinian Arabs themselves are in no rush for too many favors, even from Biden. They're okay being miserable.

Being miserable is what they count on to give them the edge against the Israelis. Griping is their default position.

"You are here by mistake," to quote Knesset Member Bezalel Smotrich sizing up the situation.

But Biden wants his turn playing master diplomat. He wants to fix what ain't broke. It is his specialty.

---

* Originally published in *Arutz Sheva* English site (israelnationalnews.com).

We know that he is prepared to go to extremes to undo whatever Trump did. Trump got the Palestinian Arabs to sit quietly in the corner sucking their thumbs. Hardly a peep out of them for four years, and not much talk about a two-state solution, either. Then he shut down the PLO office in DC, and then he turned off the spigot of funds to the PA.

Proof, by the way, that the power of the American presidency is immense.

After that, with Netanyahu as partner, he did the impossible.

For years, decades, centuries, it was an historical imperative that there can never be peace between Arabs and Jews.

Since modern Israel's founding, it was received wisdom that the Arab World would always be at war with Israel… even with Egypt coming around, and halfway so Jordan.

"Then I'll tell you," says Ibrahim Hassan to Joshua Kane in this masterwork. "On the surface, for the sake of Arab unity, my country is in a perpetual state of war with Israel… However."

However, things change.

The Arab League's Three No's of Khartoum from 1967, ran as, no peace with Israel, no recognition of Israel, no negotiations with Israel.

Two years ago, Trump got all three done as yes to peace, yes to recognition, and yes to negotiations with four Arab countries… the UAE, Sudan, Bahrain, Morocco.

They said it couldn't be done. But it was done, against all odds, and with no interference or approval from the Palestinian Arabs. They were unnecessary. They had no say.

This we know as The Abraham Accords, a diplomatic breakthrough that is astonishing.

You'd think there'd still be dancing over this achievement… fireworks, parades… lofty speeches from leaders around the world. Rather, it seems to have gone missing.

Where's the Nobel Peace Prize? Arafat and Rabin shared it in 1994 while Arafat's Arabs were still murdering Rabin's Jews. ("Sacrifices for peace," per Rabin/Peres.)

No shots were fired when in 2020 Trump did the impossible together with Netanyahu.

Instead, the reaction varies from ho-hum, to whispers, to no big deal.

What's not to like about the Abraham Accords? What's not to like about peace?

The Europeans don't like it because it came from America. Biden's America doesn't like it because it came from Trump.

Israel's ruling coalition pretends not to notice it, because it came from Netanyahu.

To further spite Trump and ingratiate himself with either Abbas, Mahmoud or Monsour, Biden can't undo it – can he?

Writer Sally Rooney – Anti-Semite of the Month

***Oct, 14, 2021 – It is necessary to share what came, to me at least, upon reading the news about Sally Rooney.**

We've been reading about the Irish writer Sally Rooney who's been making a splash for her alleged refusal to have her latest novel in the hands of an Israeli publisher.

Even that part is confusing, which we'll get to in a minute.

She's 30. She focuses on millennial angst, and her books… two previous and now this latest one… are all bestsellers, translated and sold around the world, including Israel.

Not so, however, for her latest, *Beautiful World, Where Are You*, for which she wants Hebrew excluded. No Hebrew for her, suddenly. Or so it appeared when the scandal first broke.

Now, apparently, somebody got it all wrong. Now she says that she has no objection to Hebrew, only Israel. She wants no Israeli publisher.

Why? For all the usual leftist reasons… even though most Israeli publishers are leftists.

Either way, here's a millennial who's had an anti-Semitic epiphany, and we wonder if this is where it's going for millennials.

If so, it is necessary to share what came, to me at least, upon reading the news about Sally Rooney.

For some reason, or for obvious reasons, flashback-style, I remembered a gray-haired lively-looking woman who got to talking with me at the train station in Atlantic City.

There was immediate kinship when she cited my book of memoirs, and then said she also had a story hard to believe, but true.

In Berlin, before the war, she'd been a hospital nurse.

"Then the Nazis came."

She was fired, as were all Jewish doctors and nurses. But before she left, in one day she saw enough.

---

* Originally published in *Arutz Sheva* English site (israelnationalnews.com).

"The German nurses came, and what they did was – one by one they grabbed Jewish newborns by the ankles, and smashed their heads against the walls. Nurses!"

Sally Rooney, I conclude, would have been such a nurse. On the topic of Jewish survival, we mince no words.

Writers Ezra Pound, Celine, Roald Dahl, T.S. Eliot, Thomas Wolfe, William Faulkner and others would have been such doctors.

This is the company Rooney chose, the dark side of literature, and no amount of "social justice" sophistry can "make a crooked thing straight." (Ecclesiastes.)

Rooney's high-minded aversion to Israel's defensive actions against Hamas, against Hamas' firing 10,000 rockets from Gaza, can only mean she prefers dead Israelis.

Is this millennial? Is this Irish? Is this nurture? Is this nature? Pick any one or all. For Rooney, a daughter of Ireland, she likely drank her animosity from mother's milk.

Shouldn't a novelist be prided for original thinking, rather than dish views so derivative?

Of all the countries in the world, she chooses Israel to boycott, the country that supports equal rights for all its citizens.

The Palestinian Arab Cause has never been about that, but only about wiping Israel off the map ever since Grand Mufti Haj Amin el Husseini schemed with Hitler.

Sally Rooney should know this if she is to be taken seriously… and she should know that activist writers are boring, especially when they choose the wrong side.

For the big-time literary anti-Semites as mentioned, Israel was far from their minds, and for some, modern Israel had yet to be born.

What was their beef?

No, it wasn't about Israel. It was never about Israel. It was always against Jews everywhere and elsewhere that they bore a smoldering grudge.

You too, Sally Rooney.

Today, we remember them with regrets… and even their finest works come with an asterisk. Knut Hamsun's remarkable *Hunger* case in point.

This is not good company to keep, Sally Rooney. What a waste.

Liberals Want Your Kids

***Oct. 11, 2021 – And you thought only the PA, the Palestinian Authority, teaches hatred to its young as a good thing.**

Liberals want your kids.

They want your daughters to grow up like Alexandria Ocasio-Cortez, and your sons like Bernie Sanders.

That's why they're pushing CRT… Critical Race Theory… in the schools, beginning with toddlers.

A cockeyed theory like this is what comes from a generation that's had it too good for too long.

The sum of their proposition is that we are in a cycle of never-ending strife between the races. White People are inherently and incurably racist; Black People are hopelessly and perpetually marginalized victims. Nikole Hannah-Jones elaborated on that in *The New York Times*, tabbed as "The 1619 Project," and that is what they are teaching in a school system near you.

It is their bible, their religion for which all of us… namely our kids… are expected to bend the knee.

This is not Jewish, nor Christian, rather Liberalism uber alles… and you thought only the PA, the Palestinian Authority teaches hatred to its young as a good thing.

When Liberals speak of Unity… Biden ran on this… they mean, let us all be miserable together. Appropriately, the US ranks way down on the worldwide happiness index.

Brother, can you spare a smile?

Israel usually ranks among the top ten. Israelis are happy with what they've got… a nation at home, at last.

Who's the happy person? The person who is satisfied with his or her portion, say the Sages.

For ingratitude, there is Liberal America.

---

* Originally published in *Arutz Sheva* English site (israelnationalnews.com).

Here they are asking neighbor to snitch against neighbor, should the mom and dad next door be critical of the leftist pabulum being served.

Parents… we don't know exactly how many… but plenty… are furious.

So they've been converging on school board meetings coast to coast to stop the CRT brainwashing. The protests have been heated.

So heated that if, as a parent, you complain too much, or too emotionally, or too logically, you could be considered a threat to national security.

That includes moms… who've been reduced by the Left as nothing more than "birthing persons." (No, I am not kidding.)

Back in my day, school board meetings were mostly routine. Largely about budgets. Hardly anyone showed up.

That was before they tried to separate momma bears from her cubs.

So the teachers' unions are worried about the safety of their teachers; parents are worried that their kids are being used as laboratory experiments.

Okay, but is this any reason to bring in the FBI? Attorney General Merrick Garland has done just that, so that any parent who dissents above a certain decibel could be labelled a domestic terrorist, subject to arrest, by the FBI. If this sounds positively Mao, then you are catching on to where Biden and his people are taking us.

Welcome to the revolution nobody asked for or wanted.

So far, so far as we know, there have been no actual arrests of moms and dads who exercise their rights to free speech, but that is beside the point.

"They want to silence any act of lawful dissent," a parent told me. "Knowing the FBI is on your case has a terrible chilling effect."

Parents who voted Democrat are not exempt; only collectively at fault for what they wrought.

From another parent. "Since when is it wrong… a crime… to speak your mind in America?"

Apparently, since Biden and company run the show. Simply put, they want your kids. Parents have no say.

Moms and dads… be quiet, behave, or else…

A neighbor who came here after the Soviet Union was dissolved, and has grandkids in the school system, says, "I never thought I'd see this day. Not in America."

She goes on... "Back there, we didn't need to be told to keep our opinions to ourselves. We knew we were being watched. By the Secret Police."

Around here, it's no secret. We know what they want. They want everything, one child at a time.

Like Tucker, I Am Tired of Being Right

***Oct. 5, 2021 – I agree with him so much that it hurts. It hurts because we lost.**

So Tucker Carlson, I notice, is in the news. Seems that the ADL's Jonathan Greenblatt wants him fired… for being critical of Jews?

Not at all.

Haitians… migrants… illegals… the ADL is sympathetic with more coming in. Tucker wants less.

Tucker is worried about the influx, and that at this rate, America as we know it will be deluged out of existence.

I agree with Tucker, and find it odd that an organization, the ADL, that was founded to protect Jews, instead runs cover for groups that are none of its business.

Nor is it proper or polite or decent for Greenblatt to call for Tucker to be fired from *Fox News* over a disagreement. It is disgusting… but par for Liberal hysteria.

Does this mean we're in the clear? We have it made? We are safe? There's no more anti-Semitism? There is plenty. Let Greenblatt explain why he is so busy kissing up elsewhere.

Or like-minded Geraldo, who says the migrants need our support because unlike the Jews, "they have no friends, rabbis, or fixers."

To which I responded, "So where were they, you dumb klutz, for the Six Million who perished?"

Onward, I agree with Tucker about losing America over open borders.

But now I have to admit that I have not been watching Tucker. Been months since I've tuned him in and it is not because I disagree with him and his politics.

Just the opposite. I agree with him too much. I agree with him so much that it hurts.

It hurts because we lost.

---

* Originally published in *Arutz Sheva* English site (israelnationalnews.com).

A headline over a recent Op-ed in *The New York Times* gushes like this – "Cheer up, Liberals, you have the America you wanted."

Well ain't that the truth!

Even with Trump in office, doubly so now with Biden, Liberals have been on a warpath to erase everything that might offend somebody, somewhere, anywhere.

Alas, they have succeeded.

On this day, the Cleveland Indians are no more. Cleveland, yes. But Indians, no more. (Don't you feel safer now?)

Liberals have censored our free speech and opinions, defaced our books, statues, schools, monuments, streets, products wholesale and retail, movies, culture and history.

Often enough, Tucker is brilliant, but nothing he said or did was enough, or is enough, to stop the carnage.

Watching Tucker and some of the others on *Fox News*, you find yourself nodding in agreement, thinking yes, yes, yes, but saying… so what?

We lost.

Must quickly add… thank goodness we have *Fox News* otherwise it is all media wasteland.

Over the months and years, through Tucker, and Hannity, and Laura Ingraham, and Mark Levin, we were assured that justice would be done. Just hang in and watch the cesspool that colluded against Trump and against truth and against the American people being shackled and marched off to jail. The *Fox News* Team is on the case.

They were good. They are good. But not good enough. (Good ratings, but for Cable; nothing that can compete with the falsehoods from *CBS*, *NBC*, or *ABC*.)

Hillary hasn't been locked up, despite everything we know. We know the Russia Hoax to bring down Trump was largely her doing.

Comey, Clapper, Brennan and other parts of the dirty dozens walk free, write books, give lectures, while Republicans like Paul Manafort, go directly to jail.

For years now, Prosecutor John Durham was expected to shed light on the Russia Hoax. Finally, he has indicted a few people. What will happen to them? Nothing.

Against Democrats, it seldom sticks.

That's because Democrats are in it for keeps. They will always protect their own, and clobber anyone who dissents. Dissenters are termed racists or domestic terrorists.

Democrats know how to play this game. Republicans need to sharpen up and learn it quick.

Kamala, and A Cavalcade of Dunces

***Oct. 1, 2021 – They have the power to lord it over our lives… yet without the benefit of knowledge or wisdom.**

Does anybody know anything?

When asked to reveal why some movies succeed and others fail, screenwriter par excellence William Goldman explained that there is no formula.

Often, it is plain dumb luck. Or, as he put it – "Nobody knows anything."

Everyone in the entertainment business, particularly in Hollywood, knows that to be true, and anyone paying attention to the news can only conclude that the people who run our lives from Washington, DC, don't know anything, either. Hollywood is fiction. So no worries. But these DC types are fact, real people.

They have the power to lord it over our lives… yet without the benefit of knowledge or wisdom. Often, there is no choice except to call them a cavalcade of dunces.

Speaking of which… can you believe Kamala Harris is vice-president of the United States? She got the job even though she was the least popular of all the 2020 Democrat candidates.

She scored the lowest on the likability scale, so, given Biden's habit to do everything backwards, maybe that is why he picked her to be his running mate.

Turned out to be Contrary Joe's first poke in the eye against Americans.

Then, seeing that she knows nothing or cares nothing about our Border, he chose her to serve as our Immigration Czar.

We are still waiting for her to do anything about the flood of migrants… except giggle. That's her style when she gets stumped, which is often.

---

* Originally published in *Arutz Sheva* English site (israelnationalnews.com).

Nor does this chic grooving out of California Dreamin' know anything about foreign affairs. On Israel, she is either flatly prejudiced or plainly ignorant.

When a student at George Mason University accused Israel of "ethnic genocide," here was Kamala's chance to feature some worldly smarts and set the record straight.

"No," she could have snapped back. "On equal rights for all, Israel is a light unto the nations."

Instead, going Progressive all the way, she sided with the student, saying, "Your truth cannot be suppressed." (She ought to read this from Melanie Phillips.)

Disappointing… but predictable… given the absurdities we've come to expect from her and the other masters of our universe.

For example, our generals.

There they were, the top guns from the Pentagon sitting before committees in the Senate and House to answer for the catastrophe that became Biden's Afghanistan.

Who got it so wrong, this exit that left our men and women behind… and cost the lives of 13 members of America's military at the height of the chaotic evacuation?

They tried to get Biden off the hook, but grudgingly had to admit that the "Big Guy" failed to heed their advice, which was to leave 2,500 of our troops in place.

What they could not say was that Biden acted recklessly and thoughtlessly and that here was a commander in chief totally and dangerously unfit.

How about their own failures?

Failure?

Nobody failed. According to Defense Secretary Lloyd Austin, Chairman of the Joint Chiefs of Staff Gen. Mark Milley, and Gen. Kenneth McKenzie, stuff happened.

The operation was a logistical success, they said, but a strategic failure.

Translation: The surgery was a success, too bad the patient died.

That way, nobody is at fault. Nobody pays.

Life goes on…one blunder at a time.

AOC and the Squad's Type-A Anti-Semitism

***Sep. 26, 2021 – A pogrom in the American House of Representatives.**

A pogrom in the House?

Who knew that the debate over re-funding Israel's Iron Dome would turn out to be a gut-wrenching emotional experience?

Who knew there'd be a debate at all?

Usually, these things are automatic. When it comes to partnering with our greatest ally in the region on matters of security, it's a done deal.

Israel's security is thereby buttressed as well as ours.

The Iron Dome, which was designed in Israel, by the way, is likewise being used by the United States as a proven way to thwart incoming rockets and missiles.

So why the tears?

Like baseball, there's no crying in the House of Representatives. Never used to be. Not supposed to be. Or so we thought.

Along comes Alexandra Ocasio-Cortez to shed bitter tears after the measure was finally passed in Israel's favor, as if it's personal.

Obviously, it is.

For some people, it keeps them up at night, feeling miserable, the thought of Jews living happily and safely in their own land.

Whatever is good for the Jewish people, is bad for them, and ruins their day.

This is not your ordinary or casual country-club Jew-hatred. This is the real deal. This is Type-A, hi-octane anti-Semitism.

This is pogrom, Vichy, Wannsee Conference Judeophobia.

Many of us lived through that, so we know the sound, the taste and the smell.

---

* Originally published in *Arutz Sheva* English site (israelnationalnews.com).

So AOC cried when the bill passed, 420-9, after she failed to swing enough House Dems to her side to scuttle the measure. She needed to be consoled. Poor baby.

We all knew someone like that in high school… the brat who knew how to call attention to herself by staging a tantrum.

No doubt AOC was soothed by some other members of the squad, the likes of Rashida Tlaib (D-Ramallah) and Ilhan Omar (D-Somalia) who must have assured her it ain't over.

"Don't worry. We'll get 'em next time."

They surely consider this a trial-run… and they nearly got it to work. They got Israel stymied the first time around the House.

They lost round two, but proved that they mean business.

That is something to consider, as a warning, if you care for the well-being of Israel, and the United States.

There are more votes to come, and these squad sisters are young, and they are being replenished by like-minded socialist/progressives.

There's more coming with a grudge like these Mean Girls, especially from Muslim countries, and they too may be counted on to legislate from one-track minds.

There's some comfort that we've got them crying.

Let's keep it that way.

Open Borders, Eyes Shut

***Sep. 22, 2021 – Survey proves US is a divided country. This is not your grandfather's America anymore.**

Apparently, Joe Biden can keep on doing what he's doing, since enough people are happy with his leadership.

A *Fox News* Survey says so… says that 45 percent find him to be a "strong leader." True, 53 percent believe otherwise, but that only means America still has a pulse.

We ain't done yet.

But it's getting close, and that figure of 45 percent suggests that some 150 million Americans are cheering for Calamity Joe, as all of us together are being driven over a cliff.

Who are these guys? Who are these people, nearly half the country, who find no imperfection in a president who so far, from Afghanistan to our Border, has done everything wrong?

These people are 1, utterly clueless, 2, fanatically Liberal, or, 3, aren't even Americans in the first place.

I say this with eyes on the Southern Border where at the moment thousands of migrants have washed into Texas and built themselves a shanty town under a bridge.

They do not need to be vaccinated for COVID or for any other diseases. You do. They don't. This is so due to Biden Logic we have come to expect.

Just as we have come to expect his spokesperson Jen Psaki to becloud this and every other issue through double-speak. Open borders? Nothing there Team Biden can see.

Despite assurances that the intruders will be sent back… well that is not how it works. Most, unvetted, will stay and be distributed throughout the land, likely to a school district near you.

The Israelis know this story from their own migrant crisis, where, due to the incursion, crime and disease are rampant through parts of south Tel Aviv.

---

* Originally published in *Arutz Sheva* English site (israelnationalnews.com).

Then there's the fact of Israeli sovereignty and the threat of losing the Jewishness over the Land should the nation be swamped from gate-crashers.

Here, for this latest influx into Texas, largely Haitians, the number we are being given is 15,000… all that over a period of a day or two.

But in the weeks and months since Biden has been in office, the number of illegals marching in, and staying, has been tabulated to be in excess of two million.

(Legal refugees, like your folks and mine, often waited five-plus years in order to secure the proper papers.)

They've been arriving at 200,000 a month. Since Biden flung open the Border. The number could be higher. That's the point. We just don't know.

We know nothing about these invaders… except this…

Soon, they will be voting… as Democrats.

So now you get the general idea. Demographics is the name of this game, and the game will be played out only after all 50 states are turned blue.

Now we get the picture as to why Democrat leaders want multitudes voting without IDs.

At this rate, Donald J. Trump may be the last of a kind, a Republican president.

That has been the plan all along, to overwhelm the country with instantaneous Democrats, coming in, unchecked, from anywhere and everywhere.

But even before Biden came along, waves of illegals kept coming in, in numbers, over the decades, that vary between 20 million and 50 million.

Nobody knows.

Yet here they are and we do not know to what degree they have reshaped the cultural and political landscape of the country.

Then this… in the midst of Biden's blunder, thousands of unvetted Afghans got on the last planes leaving Kabul to make themselves at home in the United States.

Welcome, I suppose, but please drop your systemic anti-Semitism, because more of that we don't need.

Nor will we need more slanderous anti-Israel voices in Congress once you get elected. The Squad is enough.

Americans… what's left of us... we certainly are a generous people… generous to a fault.

Overall, if you think this is not your grandfather's country anymore, welcome to the consensus.

Holocaust Survivors Deserve More Than This

***Sep. 12, 2021 – Afghan refugees being resettled in the US will surely benefit from Jewish generosity. Holocaust survivors are starving.**

I wasn't ready for this, an item telling us that 179,000 Holocaust Survivors live in Israel, but 40,000 of them, 25 percent, live in poverty.

How can this be… I mean about the poverty? Obviously, help coming from various sources is not enough… so are there no children, no grandchildren?

Now this… some 80,000 Holocaust Survivors live in the United States and… and a third of them live in poverty.

This too should not be.

Recently, I read where a particular Jewish group in the US raised millions for Haiti. How nice. Next, surely, Afghanistan.

Afghan refugees being resettled here by the hundreds of thousands will surely benefit from Jewish generosity. Bringing into our neighborhoods the clash of civilizations amounts to lessons unlearned. Biden is chipping in billions from the government.

The newcomers won't miss a meal.

Survivor Jews go starving.

Coming to America, Jewish Holocaust refugees never got the red carpet treatment.

Through various memorials and moments of silence we do pay tribute to this Holocaust generation… these, The Last of the Just… if you recall Andre Schwarz Bart's book of remembrance… but food on the table ought to come first for the living. This is a precious people who merit our love and respect.

Next, their stories.

If only someone will listen. They have so much wisdom to share from actual experience.

---

* Originally published in *Arutz Sheva* English site (israelnationalnews.com).

Harrowing, yes. All the more reason attention must be paid.

Time is short. They won't be around forever.

I have been asked to help write their stories and when I was younger I did what I could, but now… who has the strength?

Having a story to tell, but no means to tell it… this too is poverty.

A man visited me a few days before Rosh Hashana. He asked me for help to write his story, perhaps in the simple style in which I wrote my memoir.

Shouldn't take long, he said… one three-page vignette after another.

So happens that it took me 20 years to get mine done. Simple writing is the hardest to do.

His story begins when… *Sophie's Choice*… he sent his parents on a transport to Auschwitz. The Nazis were famous for such tricks.

They would say to the child, one bus leaves for freedom, the other for the camps. Naturally, he pointed to freedom, unaware at the moment that both were headed in the same direction.

He has not gotten over the guilt.

The guilt, this too is famous, as Survivor's Guilt… a syndrome in which people feel guilty for no reason. There is nothing they did wrong.

My friend Al suffered from this. He alone was spared when he went playing with some friends and got back home to find his entire family slaughtered by Ukraine Nazis.

In America, he became a success, but never successful enough to stop feeling guilty… every day.

This is not necessarily typical. In fact, there is nothing typical about any Survivor story. All are different. All are unique. All need to be told.

All need to be heard before it's too late.

Fellow Jews who have it made might consider offering a helping hand to their brothers and sisters… if there is anything left over after Haiti.

It is not only for the Haitians and the Afghans where the need is burning.

Joe Biden's Next Blunder – Jerusalem

***Sep. 15, 2021 – Biden has set his sights on Jerusalem so far as his next blunder following Afghanistan.**

You are probably wondering what comes next for the man who's done everything wrong since he became president.

Wait no more. Biden has set his sights on Jerusalem so far as his next blunder following Afghanistan.

Biden is prepared to fix everything that ain't broke.

Robert Gates, defense secretary under Obama, put it like this: "Biden has been wrong on nearly every major foreign policy and national security issue over the past four decades."

Say this about that, he is consistent, and to remain consistently wrong, Biden seems determined to reopen the US special consulate in Jerusalem.

(That is totally separate from the US Embassy in Jerusalem.)

Trump had the consulate shut down, largely because he was clear-eyed and knew that it was designated to do business with the PA—terrorists.

That has never been a bother to Biden and fellow Democrat lawmakers, who view the term terrorist differently from Monday to Thursday.

Accordingly, the Taliban are now people we trust, and the Palestinian Authority are Israel's partners in peace… among other such fantasies.

Re-opening the consulate amounts to a reward for terrorism… terrorism aimed specifically against Jews through the Palestinian Authority's Martyrs Fund.

"Pay to Slay," in other words, or, "Kill Jews, Get Rich." There is nothing like this anywhere else in the civilized world.

The Taylor Force Act was supposed to put an end to this barbarism. No such luck when Jewish blood is so appetizing to Mahmoud Abbas and his gangs.

---

* Originally published in *Arutz Sheva* English site (israelnationalnews.com).

You'd think an end to this practice would come first, that is, before any talk about a US consulate in Jerusalem, yet Biden, Blinken, etc. are raring to go forward with this blight.

Regardless.

Perhaps they forget, or need to be reminded, that Israel is a sovereign nation, and Jerusalem is its capital… been so for 3,000 years.

The Palestinian Arabs have no legitimate claim.

The return of the US consulate, however, would let them pretend that they share the capital. Step one, in their minds, to taking it over completely.

The Palestinian Arabs, successfully pushed aside by Trump, don't need much to place themselves back into the big picture. Nobody does it better.

Are the Abraham Accords still safe from Biden's wrecking ball?

From day one, Biden has been on a spree to savage all of Trump's accomplishments. So we can't be sure about anything… nothing that he touches.

For the terrorists among the Palestinian Arabs, however, in Biden they see someone they can work with handily, being the un-Trump.

Biden, after all, cut and ran and gave up Afghanistan to the jihadists…. people of the same family as the PA.

That is surely a signal to Ramallah and Gaza that here is a man always ready to give up old friends in order to make a separate peace.

The Outrages Keep Coming

***Sep. 3, 2021 – We're supposed to believe abandoned Americans chose to stay. Who would want to trade downtown Kabul for New York anyway?**

Men dressed in American military fatigues are now beheading men and raping women. Only they are not Americans. They are Taliban, wearing G.I. uniforms Biden left behind to facilitate his disgraceful exit from Afghanistan.

American regimentals have always signified courage, comfort, decency and mercy. Still do. But now this!

(Only the Israeli uniform commands the same respect.)

Then this – American military equipment worth more than $85 Billion was given up to the Taliban on Biden's rush to accommodate his surrender, and as if to illustrate how quick and how steep our decline, the terrorists are parading around on our tanks and Humvees in ways to leave no doubt that they won, we lost, badly.

How bad?

The mockery is both the perception and the reality for the rest of the world to gloat at our shame.

As for our generals, where was a Patton when we needed one?

Also this – USA military service dogs have been left behind in cages to starve or to be tortured by the terrorists, thanks to Biden.

Thanks to Biden, hundreds of Americans have been left behind… Sen. Lindsey Graham suggests thousands… to become amusements for the world's most depraved Jihadists.

You would not know this if you listen to Biden himself and to his highest-level spokespersons. In a language nobody believes or really understands, it is so full of Beltway evasiveness, baloney and gobbledygook… they shrug off the stranded Americans as dispensable. Tough luck, if you missed the boat.

Their briefings mirror Abbott and Costello's "Who's on First."

"Only" a few didn't make it out, they say in guv-speak.

---

* Originally published in *Arutz Sheva* English site (israelnationalnews.com).

Is any life Only?

The mission, they say, has switched from military to diplomacy. There is nothing reassuring about that.

To further rub it in, Biden says many were given chances to leave, but chose to stay. He provides no evidence for this.

We are supposed to take him at his word, this Biden who had promised to get everybody out.

We are supposed to believe that nine times they were phoned and warned to leave… but no, they preferred to stay behind.

That is both comedy and tragedy. Tragedy for the real lives in jeopardy; comedy for the joke that ANYONE would choose to stay in the hell on earth that is Afghanistan.

Who needs New York when you've got beautiful downtown Kabul?

The crisis, it appears to me, rests on the belief, on the part of the Liberal Elite, that we the people are children who can be served whatever pabulum they choose.

They think we're stupid. They think we'll buy anything they're selling.

They could be right, considering the choice we made to serve as our president.

Yes, I Miss Donald Trump

***Aug. 31, 2021 – Biden was a calamity waiting to happen, and it happened. We were right all along about Trump being the president we needed.**

I miss the days of Donald Trump.

Those were the days, not so long ago, when our friends trusted us and our enemies feared us. The nations gave heed when Trump spoke because they knew he meant business.

Not so under Biden.

So far as people being left behind, stranded, now that we're gone from Afghanistan as of this writing, August 30, some might quip, it's Biden's way of saying, "So long, suckers."

Our troops served honorably. Our leaders chose disgrace.

Trump also intended to leave… but not that way.

Trump was the real deal, a strong leader, a champion for America First. He secured our southern border.

He made us energy independent. He strengthened our military.

He started no wars. He cut down Iran. He got both the EU and UN to bend his way.

Legal refugees only.

He silenced the Palestinian Arab terrorists, and brought forth the Abraham Accords, which was a light at the end of the tunnel between Israel and four Arab neighbors.

Forget most of that on Biden's watch.

Trump did much more than all that, but you'd hardly know it because the Democrats, the people who put Joe Biden in office, were so busy tearing him apart.

They spent his entire four years going after him for anything, everything. Russia… Russia… Russia.

The House had no time for the nation's concerns, because Trump was its only concern.

---

* Originally published in *Arutz Sheva* English site (israelnationalnews.com).

David Remnick's *The New Yorker* magazine kept asking, and hoping, and dreaming, "Will this be the knockout punch?"

Yet they found no wrong, but still went after him. Suddenly, Ukraine. What did he do? He made a phone call. So let's impeach him again.

Again and again and again.

Anyone associated with Trump found himself being bullied, and even arrested. Paul Manafort was placed in solitary confinement.

That's how medieval it was at the time… a time when good people… Trump people were being muzzled, battered and shamed. You wore a MAGA hat at your peril.

Up to the election, Trump voters became hip to the scene and chose silence when canvassed. They did not need the grief.

But the harassment kept coming.

If Trump was your man… in those days when America turned medieval… you must be racist.

In that way they lorded it over us.

They were glib all right. They had all the answers, namely Joe Biden, so shut up, and be happy.

Don't you dare be contrary. Don't even think about mentioning Biden's lack of fitness, open to anyone who chooses to see… a man so utterly lacking.

Pay no attention… they warned… to the person he chose for vice president. She can't be all that bad. Can she?

Yet that is what they gave us to lead the greatest, most powerful nation on earth.

The grieving mother of a Marine killed in Kabul says, "Biden voters" killed her son.

Biden voters – but we all bear the burden and pay the price.

Beginning with Biden, the dumbing down has been so steep that we had our generals saluting Taliban terrorists.

Who knew it would come to this… the folly that is Afghanistan? We did. We did not know it would be Afghanistan.

We knew it would come from somewhere… yes, the knockout punch that would stagger Joe Biden and bring America to its knees.

Biden was a calamity waiting to happen, and it happened.

They can shame us no more. We were right all along. They were wrong.

In Trump we had the perfect president for our times. We miss him.

Say it loud.

For Israel, It's A Different Biden, Perhaps

***Aug. 29, 2021 – The meetings with PM Bennett went well, though it is too early in the game to know if Biden can be trusted should Israel find itself in crisis.**

It was not the best of times for an Israeli leader to meet the American president.

President Biden was in the midst of turmoil for his mishandling of the withdrawal from Afghanistan.

Biden was being scorched here and around the world for his failure to stand by our commitments.

"Can any friend ever trust the United States again?" So ran the headlines.

Along comes Israeli Prime Minister Naftali Bennett, representing America's best friend in the Middle East. It was to be a routine visit.

How would Biden botch this one?

Well, he didn't. So far. The meetings went well, though it is too early in the game to know if Biden could be trusted should Israel find itself in crisis and in need of US moral support.

We will always remember Biden's Afghanistan.

Or… in Bogie terms… we'll always have Afghanistan.

Nor will we forget Obama, who had no time, no patience, no affection for the Jewish State. Through it all, Biden was vice president; Netanyahu was prime minister.

So this is a different time, a partly different cast, and Biden has a chance to prove he is his own man. Or that he is a man, period.

Bennett left satisfied. "Biden loves Israel," he declared.

That could be true. It was true of old-time Liberals. Biden used to be one of them, but then he turned Woke.

Can he be turning back again to embrace the Old Time Religion?

Then about Israel… what's not to love?

---

* Originally published in *Arutz Sheva* English site (israelnationalnews.com).

What is there to say except that Israel is not Afghanistan, thank G-d.

How glaring the difference between a failed Muslim state and a successful Jewish State. How wide the gap between a thriving democracy, which is Israel, and a repressive tribe versus tribe Islamist regime, which is Afghanistan. No wonder Biden was glad to meet Bennett even, or especially, at this tough time. What a relief!

What a pleasure to meet a leader who is not needy, not here for a handout, only a handshake, and whose nation has not plunged the United States down a 20-year quagmire.

Vive la difference?

Thousands of US troops fought and died for the Islamic regime of Afghanistan. Not even a single US soldier or marine was ever asked to fight Israel's battles.

Nor has Israel sought or received anything remotely close to the trillions of dollars the United States wasted on Afghanistan.

Leaders come and go. This much is indelible – our common heritage based on the Hebrew Bible.

That's enough to keep us safe as partners against the unsteady hand of any US president.

Now They Tell Us Biden is Unfit. Now?

***Aug. 23, 2021 – It is now the consensus that Biden does not know where he is, what he is, or what he's doing. The media sold him to us, spare us their regrets.**

Who's sorry now?

Just about all of them throughout the media who used their immense powers of persuasion to unseat Trump and then to foist Joe Biden into the White House. That's who.

Now they're sorry.

Back then they colluded to sell us damaged goods. They lied. They cheated. They coerced.

Biden, they insisted, shall be your president.

Who says so? We do… *The New York Times* along with the rest of the media, print and broadcast.

All were in it together to give American voters no choice. Seldom, if ever, has any candidate been so fully manufactured, as was Biden.

For four years plus, they smeared Trump while cleansing Biden. To know the truth, that Biden is a corrupt, mediocre, empty suit unfit for any office would be for us to figure out – when?

When it was too late.

Now that he's got everything wrong about Afghanistan, the same media that romanced Biden have now turned against him.

They have no choice now that it is so obvious that Biden is so roundly pathetic.

Even his staunchest supporters, like Joe Scarborough, are on to the fact that they erred terribly. Biden was always nothing more than a small-time Delaware politician.

Being that, he was also a big-time opportunist, and so, rather than stick to his convictions, if he ever had any, he chose to run and serve as a gopher for the radical left.

He'd be their man for the hysterias of global warming and systemic racism.

---

* Originally published in *Arutz Sheva* English site (israelnationalnews.com).

That made him the perfect candidate… but now, as president, when it counts, it is a different story. Names are being taken. Legacies are being built. Every action is scrutinized.

So soon, but Biden's name is already firmly tarnished. Someday, by the numbers, we will know how many people he left behind and at the whims of the Taliban and ISIS.

Preceding presidents were also wrong on Afghanistan. But for the sloppy and deadly exit, that is all on Biden. He owns this.

It is now the consensus, across the board, that Biden does not know where he is, what he is, or what he's doing.

He orders out the military from Afghanistan… forgetting, oops, the civilians left behind. So now the military has to go back in again… with this caveat.

Due to the hasty retreat, not our generals, but the Taliban run the show. Our generals? They're just taking orders, we suppose, from their commander in chief who, from the looks of it, is so foggy, he most likely emerged from another nap. This is not a president who inspires trust or confidence from generals or the general public.

So yes, Biden is the disaster many of us saw coming. But we don't run the newspapers or the networks.

David Remnick runs *The New Yorker* magazine and this was the headline he used when Trump won the 2016 Election – "An American Tragedy."

How does that swallow now in 2021?

Or maybe *The New Yorker* was some four/five years too early with that estimation and had the wrong guy.

They all had the wrong guy.

The Selling of Joe Biden was entirely media fixed. Hunter's follies, which implicated both the son, Hunter, and father, Joe, is a story of corruption at the highest levels, and which the *New York Post* carried fact for unrivaled fact, but never reached the Establishment Media… too hot to handle for Joe's sake… and for telling the truth, *Twitter* banned the *Post* altogether.

So they covered for Joe from miscue to miscue, until he finally made a decision so awful that it could not be covered up.

Time has expired to keep blaming Trump. Biden gave it a shot, nice try, but even that tanked. Even the roll-over media now wanted Joe to man-up.

Spare me their regrets.

We are stuck with him and the damage has been done.

But never should we buy anything that they're selling.

US Racism and Israeli Apartheid – Telling It Like It Is

***Jul. 18, 2021 – If you go out, say to the hospital, in the US and Israel, you can decide for yourself. Is this racism, is this apartheid?**

Racism in America? Apartheid in Israel? No way.

If you go to the hospital for tests or for a stay, or for an emergency, you will wonder what those Progressive "Woke" people are talking about.

They keep talking about racism, even worse, systemic racism.

Nowhere is that in the America that I know.

The shame of it, by the way, the pity of it, is that we should even be writing or talking about race when for decades the goings have been good.

We thought we had this thing licked.

Over the years, we did not obsess over the color of a person's skin… whether electing Obama for president, or worshipping Oprah for television, or Michael Jordan for sports.

Of recent vintage, no American has been more beloved than Muhammad Ali.

Nothing is perfect, but everything's been okay in America… until the Woke people came along to have us hyperventilating on race.

It is always something with Liberals. They need a cause. They need a cause to stay in business and to keep the money flowing.

Any cause will do, and it is better for them, much more satisfying and lucrative for them, when it's got us choosing sides and hating one another.

Somewhere, someone at one of their meetings got up and said, "Hey, we already did gender. Why not do race next?" Excellent choice, and so it has been, and has been working.

But not when I went to the hospital for those tests.

---

* Originally published in *Arutz Sheva* English site (israelnationalnews.com).

Of the doctors, nurses and technicians, there was only the business to be done, with no thought between them or among the patients about race.

Was I supposed to be shocked and amazed that everything went along so smoothly and professionally?

I suppose so. After all, half the staffers were Black, the other half White, and even Biden keeps saying it is hopeless and useless.

Systemic racism is everywhere… he says… they say.

Too bad they weren't there with me, to find no sign of it… nope. No clash of personalities. Rather, Blacks and Whites were on the same team.

They bonded as teammates as we've been bonding everywhere throughout the nation.

Some at the hospital were tall, some were short, so another cause soon to come against height inequality. Wait for it. Height Supremacy. Systemic Height Privilege.

Similarly, those who cry apartheid against Israel should have been there with me when I was hospitalized in Haifa.

There were Israelis everywhere among the doctors and nurses, and also there were Arabs, equally so among the patients.

Surprising? Not so. In Israel they do not know what you are talking about if you mention apartheid.

Working together over there is just "another day at the office." Literally so.

Somebody needs to tell the Leftists about all this. Never mind. The facts will only confuse them and deprive them of their cause.

Are Olympic Ingrates Strictly An American Thing?

***Jul. 8, 2021 – Olympic participants dishonoring their own flag and anthem – does anyone else do this besides American ingrates?**

The story, from *Google*, begins like this: "Gwen Berry, who specializes in the hammer throw, protested the anthem last Saturday as she accepted bronze at the U.S. Olympic track and field trials. During the event, held in Eugene, Oregon, Berry turned her back to the flag and draped a T-shirt over her head that read, 'Activist Athlete.'"

We say "begins" because we do not know how it will end for the Tokyo Olympics, which get underway July 23.

At that time, and for weeks thereafter, the whole world will be watching. Who will be the first to win the gold? Who will be the first to snub flag and anthem?

We do not know for sure about the gold. But as for snubbing the anthem, the smart money says USA.

Maybe it will be Gwen Berry all over again, if she gets that far against tougher competition. Or maybe it will be a repeat of the black power salute at the 1968 Mexico City Olympics.

Or maybe it will be the USA's women's soccer team, where a few of them, at a warm-up against Mexico, July 5, seemed to act petulantly at the playing of the anthem.

Or maybe not.

They just wanted the game to begin and had no patience for ceremonies, and for that reason the few, or many, of them, if you ask me, acted without due respect… slouching instead of standing tall and proud. Frankly, they looked put-upon and miserable, as if celebrating America was too much of a chore.

Maybe they were just bored. America, you know, big deal.

It is an attitude, some might say, that comes when people have it too good, too easy, and so get too jaded, too spoiled.

Otherwise, pride in the country you represent is taken to be auto

* Originally published in *Arutz Sheva* English site (israelnationalnews.com).

matic. It is the same all over. The Israelis, for example, differ heatedly on politics, but count on them to put all that aside hoisting the Star of David. Yes, the "Palestinians" will also be there, and have been there, at all the Olympics since 1996, even though they are not a nation. But they do get around.

Never to forget, however, the 1972 Munich Olympics, where 11 members of the Israeli Olympic team were murdered by Palestinian Arab terrorists… aka, the Munich Massacre.

Back in the USA, well, not exactly, so far as pride for country. Ingratitude appears to have replaced patriotism.

Going public to the world with family gossip is less than protesting, and more like snotty tale-bearing.

"Activist Athlete" at the Olympics is a contradiction in terms, and ordinarily strangers do not want to know your troubles but griping is all we do these days, home and abroad.

For certain, most USA Olympians in Tokyo will do fine as patriotic ambassadors, but then, what about those who can't resist dishing the dirt from back home?

They will have an entire world to hear their grievances, as "activist athletes," and the question is… is this an American thing?

Seems so.

Apparently, for public events, such as the Olympics, only Americans have complaints, which they are eager to share, to bring attention to surely a just cause.

At least for that individual or team.

You would think that America, the place millions run to for freedom and opportunity, is the only nation on earth that suffers from imperfections.

You would think that the rest of the world is perfect.

That's because for the rest of the world, flag and anthem are sacred. That goes even for countries where seldom is there freedom or opportunity.

But watch them as they clasp hands and sing their hearts out for their own anthems. Lower Slobbovia ain't much, they could be thinking… but it is home.

What then, about this land of plenty, this land that so many love… but still, somehow, produces so many ingrates?

Ilhan Omar Needs to Answer for the Stabbing of Boston Rabbi

***Jul. 4, 2021 – Omar feels comfortable enough to lash out against Jews again and again, with that Mean Girl smirk, because no one stops her.**

Words matter. Words have consequences. Except for some.

Every couple of weeks or so, Rep. Ilhan Omar goes off with some remark hateful to the Jewish people. First, the nasty comment… which is heard around the world, by the way.

Yes, anti-Semitism travels with the baggage of centuries.

Next, comes the "clarification," which clarifies nothing, and only makes it worse…. for Jews everywhere.

Earlier, we wrote it here, like this: "So, we the people at the forefront of science, medicine, commerce, literature, music, radio, television, warfare (Hyman Rickover, the father of the nuclear submarine), the creators of Hollywood and Broadway… these people now find themselves in a different and less tolerant America all because some twerp from Somalia says 'boo.'"

So it was when Omar sat with *CNN*'s Jake Tapper to "clarify" her latest smug, self-satisfied stink-bomb.

Now what's her beef? Her Jewish colleagues in the House "haven't been partners in justice."

This means nothing, of course, especially coming from an ingrate who has equated the United States and Israel with the Taliban and Hamas… and then talks "justice."

But it meant something, perhaps, to a man who stabbed a rabbi in Boston during the same news cycle.

The rabbi is recovering and the alleged assailant has been caught.

But that is not the point. One… will Omar be taken to account for her words that create or contribute to a climate of bigotry and intolerance?

---

* Originally published in *Arutz Sheva* English site (israelnationalnews.com).

We'll be waiting.

The larger question is whether the country is still safe after the influx arriving from particular Muslim countries.

Again, from the earlier column – "But a new generation is upon us; people who know nothing or care nothing about our Judeo/Christian values, and they keep coming, and are beginning to get elected."

In other words, it can be said that Omar and her AOC crew give diversity a bad name.

Also that we knew sororities like this in high school, Mean Girls who could emasculate an entire cafeteria… and now… now an entire country.

We cannot say with certainty that from DC to Boston one thing led to another, but we can quote King Solomon, saying, "Death and life are in the power of the tongue."

Imagine, then, the power of that tongue when it lashes out against Jews from within the government, yes, the House of Representatives.

That gives it the stamp of frightful authority.

Yet Omar feels comfortable enough to do it again and again, with that smirk, because there is no one to stop her.

Nancy Pelosi is "satisfied" with this week's Omar "clarification" as she was with last week's clarification, and so it will be next week.

Omar and her squad sisters know exactly what they are doing. In the works is their plan to make American Jews feel unsafe and unwanted.

That would be Plan A.

We hate to think what they have in mind for Plan B… though what happened in Boston could be a sample.

Can Baseball Save America?

***Jun. 29, 2021 – We can use a lift, and there is no better place to start than at the ballpark.**

Bottom of the ninth. Yankees down by a run. One man on base. Up steps Aaron Judge. The crowd freezes in anticipation. Kids stop slurping their ice creams, their eyes fixed imploringly on the batter, who was built for these moments, and who delivers on his promise more often than not when he is going good… even as near as yesterday. But not today.

Mighty Aaron Judge has struck out.

But "there's no crying in baseball" – from the Tom Hanks 1992 movie *A League of their Own*.

That's the thing about baseball; it's a game of promise, hope and redemption, which can come at any time, the next batter, the next inning, the next game.

That is all we ask out of life.

From out of Brooklyn came the never-give-up expression "wait till next year." The Brooklyn Dodgers fielded some great teams in the 1940s and 1950s.

Alas… the damn Yankees.

The Brooklyn Dodgers lost to those Yankees four times in nine years, in one World Series after another… 1947, 1949, 1952, 1953. (Robinson joined April 15, 1947.)

But then came that "next year," 1955. Riding a classic Johnny Podres performance from the mound, the Brooklyn Dodgers did the impossible.

But that's the thing about baseball. Nothing is impossible.

Yes, 1955, finally, the Brooklyn Dodgers beat the Yankees in seven games… for the Brooklyn Dodgers, the likes of Jackie Robinson. Duke Snider, Pee Wee Reese.

For the Yankees… Mickey Mantle, Yogi Berra, Whitey Ford.

---

* Originally published in *Arutz Sheva* English site (israelnationalnews.com).

Sometimes a person gets one chance to rise and shine, only one moment, one year to achieve everlasting glory, and so it was with Johnny Podres, who was never top stuff, until 1955, when he rose to the occasion, pitching a complete game shutout against the lords of baseball.

Two years later, Walter O'Malley moved the Dodgers out of Brooklyn and into LA, and everywhere in Brooklyn, it still hurts.

In Brooklyn, people never say the LA Dodgers. For them, and most New Yorkers, such a team does not exist. At best, it's "that team in LA."

To this day, the Dodgers will always be Brooklyn, and that's the thing about baseball. It is a game of tradition.

You do not mess with tradition. The folks who owned the Cincinnati Reds in the 1950s changed the team name to Redlegs in 1953 to avoid being mistaken for communists.

To heck with that they said in 1960. "We were the Reds before they were the Reds," they wisely acknowledged, and moved the name back to the Reds.

So it had been since 1881, when (with a few variations of the name) the Reds were baseball's first professional team.

Every year since then, it seems, experts come along to say that baseball won't last. There are so many other distractions, especially for the young.

But there is only one national pastime, and that is baseball. Nothing says America so much as baseball. FDR insisted on a full schedule even after Pearl Harbor.

The nation, he declared, needed the game for morale.

The game endured, even with rosters depleted after hundreds of major leaguers joined the WW2 fight, among them Bob Feller, Hank Greenberg, and Ted Williams.

Morale, indeed. So too for the present, for a nation stumbling in the dark. We can use a lift, and there is no better place to start than at the ballpark.

There remains something magical about Opening Day, and every day when the game is being played somewhere, everywhere in America, from the sandlots to the stadiums.

There is something special, something uniquely American, about the crisp sound of a bat hitting a ball that is being sent 400 feet into the bleachers.

Memories are still made of Ted Williams' swing, and of Willie Mays' over-the-shoulders catch.

Ask any son or daughter what it was like tossing ball with Dad in the backyard; what memories he shared, what nostalgia he instilled.

Baseball is a game of nostalgia. We remember it to remind us when times were good, so as not to fret when times turn bad. Like today.

So even today, the fans are back, the stadiums are getting packed. Listen to the Silent Majority roar gladly and argue heatedly… but about balls and strikes.

Maybe now is the time for Tom Hanks to say, "There's no politics in baseball."

Regrets, Anyone?

***Jun. 27, 2021 – Among the 85 million who picked Biden, any regrets? Are they happy, or disappointed?**

So far, there has not been much, by way of surveys, about voters who chose Joe Biden, and whether they would do it again.

If *The New York Times* and the networks are any measure, the honeymoon is still ongoing. No complaints. Only praise. Biden can do no wrong.

In the *Times*, for example, you will find not a single editorial or Op-ed critical of him. Of course, none dare. Ask Bari Weiss.

Nearly every headline is worshipful. Don't blame Joe. It is the media that can't be trusted to provide us with a square accounting of Biden's performance, warts and all.

Such an analysis would be helpful for we the people, and for Biden himself. Otherwise, how do we know what needs to be fixed?

Even in North Korea the leader gets approval only at 99.9. Just to make it appear legit. Can Biden be so absolutely perfect? He'd be the first.

To find out, let's try a survey that would go something like this –

One: That Keystone XL Pipeline that brought Canadian energy into the United States, are you happy that Joe stopped the flow through his first executive order? This was one of many executive orders intended to cancel out Trump's policies one by one. You saw this coming, and the thousands of jobs that were lost? Are you prepared for pain at the pump?

Two: But a pipeline from Russia into Germany, Biden okays. We lose, Russia wins. Or so it would appear. Is this satisfactory? Wasn't it Trump who was supposed to be sweet on Russia?

Three: Should you wonder why Putin sends Biden back home with an A-plus report card, praising him to the skies?

---

* Originally published in *Arutz Sheva* English site (israelnationalnews.com).

Four: Does it make you feel good that this administration is doing everything it can to please the mullahs of Iran so far as the Nuke Deal? Some call it shameful groveling.

Five: Cozying up to Iran destabilizes the entire Middle East… Arabs as well as Israelis… so did this enter your mind when you cast your vote?

Six: Are you thrilled that under this administration, Palestinian Arab terror groups are being re-funded and therefore rearmed?

Incidentally, throughout the years, Biden has been a friend of the Jewish State. Pray that he may still be so, and manages to resist the hecklers of the Left, who have taken over his party.

Seven: Are you happy about the de-fund the police movement? Is this what you wanted? Have you considered who you would call when you need help at home or the highway?

Eight: Are you okay with your party's proposed legislation that would let anybody vote, no ID required? Or should this sacred right be reserved for proven citizens only?

Nine: Are you pleased that the southern border is now open for everybody? This means criminals, drug traffickers… everybody! Are Kamala and Joe themselves the "root cause" of the invasion?

Ten: Are you familiar with Critical Race Theory? This teaches that all white people are oppressors and all black people are oppressed, and it is being taught to kids all across the country. The result is a climate of suspicion and a cycle of perpetual antagonism. Would you ever vote for something like this? Well, actually, you did.

Eleven: Is it okay that your 10-year-old daughter must share the same public bathroom with a man dressed as a woman?

Twelve: Do you feel safe and secure knowing that Kamala Harris is your vice president?

Did I miss anything?

Ilhan Omar is A Wakeup Call for American Jews

***Jun. 13, 2021 – A new generation is upon us; people who know and care nothing about Judeo/Christian values. They keep coming and are getting elected.**

Voting "Democrat" with both hands, as American Jews tend to do, is what gets you Ilhan Omar.

The temptation is to shake these people, who vote 78 percent Democrat no matter what, to get them to wake up.

Someone needs to remind them that FDR (never a friend anyway) and Harry Truman have left the building.

If the House were in the hands of the GOP, at least Omar would not be sitting on the House Foreign Relations Committee.

She would also more likely be censured for her monthly anti-Semitic outbursts. Smart cookie. She times it and then sits back and laughs.

She knows exactly the reaction that's coming. There will be calls to condemn her. Prominent Jews, some of them, will express their indignation.

Jews don't riot. Jews write letters to the editor.

All that she knows, and on mischief like this she is smarter than all of us put together. She enjoys the tumult she ignites.

Next, she "sets the record straight." No apology, but only an "explanation" that mentions her aversion to all forms of bigotry.

Pure gobbledygook, but good enough to pacify the suckers.

The pattern continues when her squad sisters rally to her defense and cry Islamophobia; which cleverly renders them all untouchables, and cynically positions Omar as the victim.

They've got it all figured out, and meantime the anti-Semitism hangs in the air.

---

* Originally published in *Arutz Sheva* English site (israelnationalnews.com).

The latest figures on anti-Semitism we all know… up, up, and up. Jews are being targeted every which way, in print, broadcast, social media, and on the streets.

Jews are being advised to pocket their yarmulkes.

So, we the people at the forefront of science, medicine, commerce, literature, music, radio, television, warfare (Hyman Rickover, the father of the nuclear submarine), the creators of Hollywood and Broadway…these people now find themselves in a different and less tolerant America all because some twerp from Somalia says "boo."

That's enough to make us feel less comfortable, and to wonder… is this how it starts?

Holocaust survivors will say, yes, this is how it starts.

It doesn't take much. All it takes is one false accusation, or one blood libel to unleash the whirlwind, and I need say no more than Dreyfus in France and Leo Frank in America.

So it can happen here, and it does happen here, and American Jews managed, but this time, can it happen here in the worst possible way?

The generations I grew with and who knew America as Sinatra told it in *The House I Live In*, would not even whisper the possibility. Here? Never.

We can still say that when we consider the Judeo/Christian values that kept us together under the same fellowship and flag.

But a new generation is upon us; people who know nothing or care nothing about our Judeo/Christian values, and they keep coming, and are beginning to get elected.

Some bring with them the prejudices they were raised with in the old country, and when enough of them gain power, this stops being the country we once knew.

What can we do?

Stop voting for them!

Will Netanyahu Be Allowed A Dignified Exit? At Least That?

***Jun. 9, 2021 – We know that from the start, for both Trump and Netanyahu, it's been baseless hatred that had them snared and got them removed.**

So we read that Naftali Bennett, incoming Israeli prime minister, by hook or by crook, wants to create a law that would prevent Netanyahu from ever running again, for any office.

Same deal here in the United States, against Trump. Charges are being drawn up against him to keep him busy from one courtroom to another for the next hundred years.

They don't want you defeated. They want you destroyed.

Back here, there already is a law, unwritten and unspoken, but clearly understood among the media – Trump's name is never to be mentioned, unless, of course, detrimentally.

What did he do that is so terrible? During his four years, there was no quagmire. No wars. Only peace. He made us energy independent. He secured our borders.

Together with Netanyahu, he scored a peace deal with four Arab states.

Anathema is his reward.

Recently, I asked someone, what hurts? What did Trump do to make you hate him so much?

The answer I get, always, is Charlottesville, the Capitol riot, and that he's a racist. Okay, besides the Woke language, specifics, please.

What did he do so harmful to you and the nation?

They never come up with anything solid. Ditto when it comes to Netanyahu after you ask his detractors to name what ails them about him.

Surely to the Left he was too Right, and to the Right he was too Left, but for 12 years he served the nation honorably. He got it ranked as a powerhouse among the nations.

---

* Originally published in *Arutz Sheva* English site (israelnationalnews.com).

He championed the Zionist cause. He never gave away or offered away the house, as did some of his predecessors.

All that during the era of Obama, when a lesser man than Netanyahu would have buckled under the heavy hand of a hostile US administration. Bibi gave as good as he got.

That in itself is worthy of a pat on the back… instead of a kick in the back on his way out the door.

Saying that, I can already hear the groans, and the nitpicking, with no regard for the big picture.

What about this, they will say,… and what about that… and what about the corruption charges against him?

To which I say, and what about the corruption charges against Trump… that never seem to pan out… but keep on coming… just to keep him tangled up?

How is it different for Netanyahu, when we know that from the start, for both Trump and Netanyahu, it's been baseless hatred that had them snared and got them removed?

I have not heard the Democrats mention any policy differences between themselves and Trump… only that Trump must be defeated because he is Trump.

Yes, Joe Biden is undoing everything Trump did. But that is not for policy. That is for spite.

The "Anyone but Trump" movement got started even before he got nominated… and never let up to this day and onward.

I cannot pinpoint the exact moment when the "Anyone but Bibi" movement got started, only that it became awfully shrill day by day.

Nor have I heard Bennett's specific differences with Netanyahu, on policy… only that "Netanyahu must go." Apparently, that is policy enough.

Or politics too much.

I did hear him say that it is time to "end the chaos" … which maybe he started?

If our treatment of Trump is any measure, Netanyahu should expect no parades for a job well done. He should expect continued character assassination.

The laurels will have to come from future historians whose eyes are clear and not clouded by baseless animosity.

Rebuild Gaza? Why?

***Jun. 3, 2021 – Just like that, overnight, it's a different America, a country that now tolerates the PLO flag hoisted from DC to Jerusalem.**

I hate to say I told you so, but it came about pretty much, no, exactly, as I predicted while the latest Gaza War was getting underway.

In the column titled "Here's the Gaza War coverage you can expect," published May 18, I opened with the following – "Foremost, the media will report on 'the children' who were killed… never mind that those children are used by Hamas as fodder and human shields."

That was the focus all right, the Gaza children, and what makes me so smart?

Nothing, except the wisdom of experience, and a nose for news that comes from years in one newsroom after another that, in time, sharpens your instincts, and teaches you to expect no surprises.

In the newsroom, you are always waiting for the other shoe to drop. Wait a while, and it does. Any minute it could come. That is why you kept a "hole" on the front page… for late breaking.

So again, Hamas starts a war, which lasts 11 days, and stops when the terrorists get what they wanted.

They wanted *The New York Times*.

They got *The New York Times*.

Simplistic, this analysis?

Possibly, but I have read all the experts, and they are certainly correct to name it a trial run for Iran, and all of it designed among Iran, Hezbollah, Fatah, the PA, and the PLO.

They were all in it together.

I will also add that the Gazans were so bloated with missiles… some 30,000 we are told… that they had to get rid of some of them somehow.

What better way than to dump them on Israel, until the next batch, courtesy of Iran?

---

* Originally published in *Arutz Sheva* English site (israelnationalnews.com).

All that, all that expertise makes sense, but not enough for this ink stained news hawk. I saw it from the beginning, the middle, and the end as a quest for the hearts and minds of the American people. Then the timing. Trump out, Biden in. Just like that, overnight, it's a different America.

It's a country that now tolerates the PLO flag hoisted from DC to Jerusalem. So the terrorists knew they were halfway there when the real purpose was to isolate Israel through PR.

They would wage this as a public relations war, knowing that as before, it would be about the children. Their own children. That they use as grist.

But which the media will always play in their favor, as victims, against Israel, to be played as aggressors.

Did it work as it did in Gaza Wars before… 2008-9/2012/2014? This time around, 2021, even better.

They got all the networks. As before. As always.

In unison the networks opened and closed with angry Gazans weeping over their children, with no correspondent on hand to explain that, truly, they were murdered by Hamas.

Chalk that one up as a win for the terrorists.

But that wasn't enough. The prize, the jackpot, would be *The New York Times*, which calls the shots for the entire news media, and shapes public opinion as no other.

Would *The New York Times* give them the blood libel that they wanted?

Yes, indeed. On May 28, the paper had a front page hole to fill and filled it, nearly top to bottom, with a photo gallery of Gaza children victimized by Israel, so the images and copy would have you believe… then doubled down with the heart-catching headline, "They were just children."

So maybe Hamas murdered them by putting them in harm's way, as is their habit?

The New York Times would rather you not think about that possibility.

Rather, you should focus your blame strictly, squarely and entirely on Israel, as would any reliable *Times* reader and good Democrat.

Speaking of Democrats, they now want Gaza reconstructed.
Rebuilt again, and again, and again, and again?
Will anything be different this time?
Will we never learn?

Let Us Now Praise Bill Maher

***Jun. 1, 2021 – How many viewers see Israel in a different light after watching his show last week?**

Bill Maher at his best – "Hamas' negotiating position is, you all die."

One clip here, another one here, and you will find Maher roundly critical of the media, and in full support of Israel.

This gets a nine-point Wow. Ten points when he tells his audience, "Israel did not steal anybody's land." Then adds that the Jews have been in Israel for centuries.

We've been waiting for a breakaway hero from among the stale political entertainers. Never thought it would be this guy. Bill Maher? Yes, Bill Maher.

You never know.

Where's this been during the hatefest?

Due to Israel's chutzpah to defend itself, the sleeping giant of Jew-hatred was reawakened, led by *The New York Times*, a paper that prints only the news fit for Hamas.

Says Maher, "It was frustrating for me that there was no one on Liberal Media to defend Israel, really. We're kind of one-sided on this issue."

On moral equivalency and the Palestinian Arabs getting the better of it, Maher goes straight to the facts: "Hamas' charter says they just want to wipe out Israel."

You know this. I know this. But do they know this, the people who know nothing?

But at last.

A voice in the wilderness… au contraire to John Oliver and Trevor Noah, who have already taken and wasted their best shots, and never saw Maher coming.

Do not underestimate Maher's influence.

---

* Originally published in *Arutz Sheva* English site (israelnationalnews.com).

He comes from the Lenny Bruce school of merciless pinpoint satire… as we knew it in the 1960s.

That's the kind of funny that hurts for being so true.

Maher reaches the young, the uninformed, and the misinformed, and his message infiltrates even mindless Liberals.

He is a Liberal himself, but not that kind; the kind stuck in the mud of political correctness.

Maher can swing either way, as he has done since 2003, weekly, on HBO. His zingers can be confounding, as when he said the 9/11 hijackers were not cowards.

At the same time, he can be highly critical of Islam… to the amazement and chagrin of his Liberal guests and audience.

Maher is one of those rare Liberals – maddeningly but refreshingly unpredictable.

Those are his people. Liberals. So he speaks their language. They understand him, and they believe him, and they trust him.

So when he takes a position at odds with their orthodoxies, attention must be paid. How many viewers see Israel in a different light after watching his show last week?

How many no longer trust the media, nor believe Palestinian Arab propaganda after he scorched them both with biting wit?

How many with their minds shut had their eyes opened?

I'd say plenty, and I have never been a fan.

Over the years, some of us on the Conservative side tuned him out. Perhaps too fast? The liberties he took at our expense was just too much.

I'm still no fan, but got to say, all is forgiven, after coming through like this… in this climate… when all around us is anti-Semitism.

We have a saying, "In a place where there are no men, be a man."

Along came Bill Maher.

Here is What "Peace" Looks Like for the Jewish State

***May 23, 2021 – Israel is at war every day. Even when hundreds of rockets become thousands, it counts as news only when Israel fights back.**

When thousands of rockets are launched at Israel… this means war.

But when "only" hundreds of rockets go crashing into Israel… everybody relax. This means peace.

Or in the language of the Left – in either case, those would be "mostly peaceful" missiles, just as "mostly peaceful" protesters burned down American cities one after another.

In Portland and Seattle, the good folks won't go near downtown for fear of the mostly peaceful mobs.

The mobs have set up their own country there and elsewhere for the sake of equality and diversity, the result being a state within a state.

Why then, here it is, in our own backyard, a "two-state solution?"

So how has that been working out? Violence, lawlessness, chaos and misery all around, which brings us to Gaza, and 2005, when Prime Minister Ariel Sharon thought he had it figured out how best to achieve peace and security with the Palestinian Arabs. He'd give them Gaza. If things worked out, Gaza would be utopia.

To make it happen, first things first. The Jews living there, happy and prosperous, would have to be removed, by force, if necessary.

It was necessary.

"Why should we go anywhere?" asked the Israelis of Gush Katif/Gaza. "This is our home."

Too bad, said Sharon. For reasons of equality and diversity, no Jews allowed… and on August 26, all Jews were removed from the region, resisters beaten.

The Palestinian Authority moved in, invited, guns blazing, and

---

* Originally published in *Arutz Sheva* English site (israelnationalnews.com).

then destroyed everything of value the Israelis had left behind… miles of state-of-the-art agriculture, plus schools, hospitals and synagogues, of course… bulldozed. Dayan surrendered the Temple Mount, flash-point number one since 1948, and Gaza, flashpoint number two, was Sharon's doing.

In both cases, how the Palestinian Arabs say thank you.

The PA held on for a while, but were no match for Hamas, which moved in (2007) and took over Gaza with even bigger guns… and it's been raining rockets on Israel ever since.

People notice Gaza Wars only when they are prime time. Previous to this one, 2021, there was 2008-2009, 2012, and 2014, all the result of Hamas firing thousands of rockets into Israel, and spiking world-wide anti-Semitism nearly as much as today. Hardly anyone gives a damn what happens before and after, when it is routine for Hamas to send in its rockets at a rate of, say, 200 a week.

Every week.

For 14 years.

Some people do notice. Those would be the million and a half Israelis who live on the border with Gaza… and live half their lives in bomb shelters.

That rates no coverage even below the fold.

To them, the media, it is tranquil.

Nor does the world pay attention when Fatah and the PA summon their people to commit murder; congratulates them, honors them, and pays them when they do.

That gets no mention from the bleeding-heart networks… and not a word from Bernie Sanders and the Squad.

Cleverly, when it gets too quiet, Mahmoud Abbas stirs things up on the Temple Mount. When Israeli police are called in to quell the rioting, Abbas gets his wish.

The nations perk up… and blame the police… and a new round of riots gets fueled.

We haven't mentioned Hezbollah armed to the teeth, and Iran raring to go with genocidal intent.

Nor have we mentioned balloon and kite terrorism, another regular feature from Hamas, saved for the weekends.

From one place to another, Israel is at war every day.

But it only counts as news when Israel fights back.

Otherwise, it is peaceful in Israel. Except to the Jews who live there.

Israel's Two Wars – The Jihadists and the Media

***May 19, 2021 – We are expected to believe that Hamas, famous for hiding behind women and children, would never use an *Associated Press* building in Gaza as cover for its terrorist operations.**

If that doozy is not enough, here's another one…

We are expected to believe that the *AP* would never share office space with Hamas… like that building the IDF toppled to thwart Hamas from further deadly mischief.

Shocked… SHOCKED… says the *AP* at the inference that it knew anything.

The Israelis have already provided proof that indeed the two, *AP* and Hamas, were neighbors. Nevertheless, *AP*'s bosses are indignant.

They want a war crimes probe, even though the Israelis made sure the building was first evacuated.

Perhaps they protest too much?

In war and peace, the media have seldom played fair, have always chosen sides, and never to Israel's benefit.

The PR War automatically favors the terrorists… and here's how, "To put things in perspective, Honest Reporting readers should recall the words of Fayad Abu Shamala, *BBC*'s correspondent in Gaza for the past 10 years, who spoke at a Hamas rally in Gaza, as follows – 'Journalists and media organizations are waging the campaign shoulder to shoulder together with the Palestinian people.'"

The research was done by Daniel Seaman, Israel's press officer at one time, who exposed the following as well – "Terrorist leader Marwan Barghouti used to call reporters and inform them what was going to happen. Then they filmed only the Israeli response."

Also… "Those producers advised Barghouti how to get the Palestinian response across better."

---

* Originally published in *Arutz Sheva* English site (israelnationalnews.com).

Then… "Seaman discovered that Palestinians who work with the media attend a course in media manipulation at Birzeit University, and exercise control over information flow. The Palestinians let the foreign journalists understand: if you don't work with our people, we will sever contact with you, you won't have access to information, and you won't get interviews."

So spare us the righteous indignation, whether from the *BBC*, the *AP*, or any of the rest who "fight shoulder to shoulder together with the Palestinian people," towards the annihilation of the Jewish people. We know your cause, and as it is today, so it was yesterday and through the ages. Nothing new under the sun.

Or maybe there is.

Who foresaw this day – when the United States Congress would become a forum for anti-Semitic agitation, harangues galore… specifically in the House.

More specifically by the Democrats.

Then explicitly Reps AOC, Rashida Tlaib and Ilhan Omar… who, through hereditary grudge, miss no chance to falsify, fabricate, incite, deceive in order to slander the Jewish State.

Tune in, and you wouldn't know this is America. This can't have come here, you say. But it did.

Of Ilhan Omar – some might ask, how does such a tiny woman get such a deep male voice… as if it's someone else really talking? Spooky, some might say.

Of those who voted for her and the others… what were they thinking?

Of the anti-Semitic riots throughout Europe, it's what you get with Merkel and her open borders.

Of the *AP*. Yes. There should be a probe. Let's find out how deep it goes between the *AP* and Hamas.

Here's the Gaza War Coverage You Can Expect

***May 16, 2021 – That the other side started it and that they turn their civilians into human shields will hardly ever be mentioned.**

Here's the coverage you can expect as the Guardian of the Wall war continues:

Foremost, the media will report on "the children" who were killed… never mind that those children are used by Hamas as fodder and human shields.

In *The New York Times*, *CNN* and the *BBC*, there will be a picture of an elderly Gaza woman weeping in front of a home that was ostensibly destroyed by the Israelis.

They won't tell you that more than half the time, Hamas misfires, accidentally and on purpose, in order to get the picture… or that the picture was professionally staged.

Former Israeli press office secretary Daniel Seaman has already fully explained how the media and the Jihadists cooperate and coordinate.

They will provide a Hamas/PA spokesperson to rant about the "disproportionate" Israeli response.

The reporter, for *CBS*, *NBC*, *ABC*, *NPR*, *PBS*, through ignorance or through prejudice, will make no attempt to square the story towards Israel's right to defend itself against an unprovoked attack – starting with Fatah riots in and around Jerusalem, arson, acts of random assaults against civilian Jews anywhere and everywhere, followed by thousands of Hamas rockets fired from Gaza.

That the other side started it will hardly ever be mentioned.

Nor will any reporter ask… why? What did Israel do to deserve this?

The answer is that the Israelis can do nothing to satisfy the Palestinian Arabs.

---

* Originally published in *Arutz Sheva* English site (israelnationalnews.com).

This war, like all their other wars, goes forward with one purpose in mind, the total annihilation of the Jewish People.

In a word – genocide.

Khartoum's Three No's still motivate them (following their defeat in 1967) – no peace with Israel, no recognition of Israel, no negotiations with Israel.

Deals are useless.

Nikki Haley is gone from the UN Security Council. "We'll be taking names," she said, of any country that noisily objects to Trump's decision to move the US Embassy to Jerusalem.

Expect nothing so direct from Biden's UN ambassador, Linda Thomas-Greenfield, who, by the way, supports Critical Race Theory, and believes that America is inherently racist.

Expect her to feel the same way about Israel. At best, she will adapt moral equivalency and demand an end of hostilities from "both sides."

Don't expect the media to remember that only last week or so, her boss delivered $250 million to Mahmoud Abbas of the PA/Fatah/PLO.

How many deadly rockets did that buy for Hamas… now landing in Tel Aviv?

Expect UN Secretary General Antonio Guterres to insist on an immediate ceasefire, and a continued "peace process" toward a "two-state solution."

In fact, he has already done so, forgetting that Gaza was handed over to the Palestinian Arabs to be a model for a two-state solution… but Hamas is what you get.

You also get the terrorist group Islamic Jihad, plus the terrorist regime of Iran, which supplies the newly sophisticated long-range weapons.

Expect Liberals… including Jewish Liberals… to cry that the Palestinian Arabs need our support to lead a better life.

Let them explain where the money goes… the billions from around the world each year… for better roads, better schools and better hospitals?

Or does the money go for better rockets… stockpiled to the hilt and stuffed to the gills.

How many tunnels do they build instead of libraries?

Expect Leftist professional Jew-haters like Trevor Noah and Mark Ruffalo and Roger Waters to decry this as an unfair fight due to Israel's superior might, as if Marquis of Queensberry rules apply when for Israel what's at stake is life or death. The gloves are off when Hamas terrorists are merely the shock troops for Iran.

Expect the networks to play up AOC and her squad of terrorism loyalists, Tlaib and Omar and Pressley – unintentionally showcasing the Democrats as a Party of anti-Semites.

In a New York Minute, urged on by AOC, leading mayoral candidate for NYC, Andrew Yang, a Democrat, flipped from Israel friend to Israel foe.

Expect no one to come to Israel's aid except the mighty IDF.

You Know Philip Roth, But Do You Know Blake Bailey?

***May 7, 2021 – Cancelling Bailey's book is a hanging without a trial, and with that, all our heads are in the same noose.**

Writer Blake Bailey spent 10 years working on the authorized biography of Philip Roth. Finally, weeks ago, it was published, to much acclaim.

Cynthia Ozick… the gold standard… was ecstatic.

Days later it was condemned and terminated by the publisher, W.W. Norton. Book and author, cancelled.

Something happened.

After the best of times for an author, came the worst, when Bailey, highly regarded biographer as well for Richard Yates and John Cheever, found himself accused of being a sexual predator, of grooming 8th grade students, and even of rape – all of which he denies. Objecting to the publisher's quick hook are dozens of literary luminaries. To no avail.

This is a hanging without a trial, they say, and with that, all our heads are in the same noose. Agreed.

(Others judge and fault Bailey instantly, because this is the year for it, 2021.)

Plus, guilty or innocent, a book ought to live on its own merits, not the author's. Dostoevsky was an anti-Semite. Are we to quit reading him?

The shelves are full books and plays… good ones, even great ones… written by individuals less than stellar.

I have my own list, starting with Shakespeare and Thomas Wolfe and Knute Hansen and Celine.

But I particularly like it when Mordecai Richler names them in his novel, *Barney's Version* – Lewis Carroll, he writes, "beloved by generations of children, wasn't the guy you wanted to babysit your ten-year-

* Originally published in *Arutz Sheva* English site (israelnationalnews.com).

old daughter." Onward to others flawed in different ways – Simenon, Odets, Malraux, Frost, Mencken, T.S. Eliot… and more, of course, who should never be cancelled but were no saints.

Treachery and lechery were everywhere. Fame was the honey.

Nor was Philip Roth so perfect, either. Which is partly the point. By banning Blake Bailey's biography of Roth, we are being deprived of the full picture about a novelist that the mavens refer to as the most important writer of our times – and this is where I come in to disagree. Weeks ago, on *PBS*, they said the same thing about Hemingway.

It depends who's in season.

Towering above them all… according to the luminaries… is Saul Bellow. I didn't care much for him, either, I call him a kvetch.

Everything he covers in *Herzog* … his most popular… I'd heard from the old-timers on the steps of 5050 Saint Urbain Street, Montreal.

Roth himself offers Bellow the top spot; the highest respect. Figures. Both wrote as Jews but sold their Jewishness with an asterisk.

Their views on Israel were Zionism Lite.

They spread their superficial Yiddishkeit as if it were expertise… and therefore served as false witnesses.

To be fair, I never gave either of them a chance, and since this is about Roth, I must say as a kid born in Toulouse, France, a month after Hitler invaded, I could never identify, nor sympathize, with a writer born in Newark, New Jersey. He was born and raised in America …. the place my family ran towards, the Gestapo at their heels, from 1940 to 1945, finally arriving in Montreal (later the United States) destitute. What's his beef?

Roth is said to have been an angry writer. It's what gave him his juice. Good. A writer needs this. Yet angry about what, except the usual things. Turned down for the Prom?

I know. He goes much deeper.

Perhaps an anti-Semite in the schoolyard?

Deeper than that, too. Sure.

But all of it happening in America. Not Europe, where the French Underground up in the Pyrenees stuffed cotton in my mouth so that I shouldn't make a sound and give us all away.

To real Nazis.

My memoir *Escape from Mount Moriah* will have to rescue me if any of this sounds like a gripe.

Because I only intend to distinguish Roth's world from a world where so many were forced to flee their homes and for years remain trapped in Barcelona with false papers… so that at any moment we could be snatched up and put away as escaped Jews from Vichy. Meanwhile, Roth's world was Newark.

Which can sound awfully Ozzie and Harriet to anyone peeking in from the outside.

Neither father nor mother in Spain could speak Spanish and the other giveaway was that a man and a woman with only two children could not possibly be Catholic.

(Thanks to my sister Sarah for that and so much more information.)

My first impression of America, arriving at Penn Station, NYC, was to behold a country where people did not have to whisper.

For me, the word for America has always been… gratitude.

No wonder, then, that I could never take Roth seriously… not his books… and certainly not his anger… and nobody ever says, "We'll always have Newark."

But given the reviews, I would like to know more about Philip Roth. I want to be corrected. He may truly be the best. Enough people say so.

Too bad about Blake Bailey. Really, the book ought to be set free.

Roth deserves another chance. We all do.

Stiff-Necked Israeli Politicians

***May 4, 2021 – I won't mention the players who hold all the cards... because I don't know them well enough... but must say their behavior is childish and churlish.**

My neighbor asked me who is running Israel these days. Is Benjamin Netanyahu still prime minister?

Yes, I said. Of course, he is.

But didn't he lose the most recent election?

He didn't really lose. He simply didn't win... in what is fast-becoming tradition. Israel's semi-annual election process.

I don't understand.

Who does?

Yes, I agreed, it is complicated, and it got no better, for either of us, and that ended that, when I started to explain that Israel operates on something like a 40-Party System.

That's like 40 years wandering in the wilderness, politically speaking.

Instantly, our USA Two-Party System sounds much better. Except look what it got us. Biden.

Go explain the Israeli system, which is full of traps, so much so that some in the headlines are prepared to hook up with an Islamist terrorist party in order to win the premiership.

You need 61 seats in the Knesset.

Easy. Snap, and a right-wing government is in place again, today, if the three right-wing players, together with their 70-plus seats, dropped their grudge against Netanyahu.

But they won't.

In Israel, politics is personal. Come to think of it, so it is in America. But we are so far gone that only a miracle can put us back together again.

But the Israelis are THIS CLOSE if only they'd get their act together.

---

* Originally published in *Arutz Sheva* English site (israelnationalnews.com).

We are taught that the Second Temple was destroyed partly because of squabbling, vendettas and baseless hatred among ourselves.

Sound familiar?

I won't mention the players who hold all the cards... because I don't know them well enough... but must say their behavior is childish and churlish.

Their personal beefs, mostly against Netanyahu, come first, above what's good for the country.

It is like the Jew in a new town who built himself two synagogues because he won't go into THAT one.

Both G-d and Moses called us a stiff-necked people.

For sure, that... in politics.

Are these wannabes aware how lucky they are to be given the chance to do what's right for so patient and so great a nation? Apparently not. Not so far. Every man for himself.

This politician won't play ball with that one, and that one won't play ball with this one – and "if Rubin is in, I'm out."

It was like that in Ben Hecht's day, when in NYC he called for a meeting to save the Jews of Europe and it fell apart on account of petty grievances.

Déjà vu all over again.

Our excuse in the United States is that as a civilization we haven't been around that long.

Israel has been around since time immemorial... plenty of time to figure this one out, you'd think.

The Mobs

***Apr. 25, 2021 – Mob tactics have taken over America and in Jerusalem, they listen and they watch and they learn.**

The mobs have taken over the country.

This much we have learned – the radical Left and their mobs will never be satisfied.

They got what they wanted, Officer Derek Chauvin guilty on all counts for the killing of George Floyd, and America breathed a sigh of relief.

It's over. Justice was done. Everybody can go home now.

Can we please get back to normal?

Not so fast. Not at all. The verdict against the Minneapolis policeman did not appease the mobs who were gathered coast to coast, nor did it pacify the race hustlers within their ranks.

They continued to erupt, howling that it's not over. Chauvin was a start. The revolution has just begun and won't end until all law enforcement is discredited, defunded and dismantled.

The streets remained restless. Al Sharpton and Rep. Rashida Tlaib and their fellow travelers, Biden himself, rushed for the cameras to remind Americans that we are all racists, still.

The mobs picked up the chant, and went wild particularly here in NYC.

What do they want? What do they really want? Do they know? Do we know? Nobody knows.

We only know that mindless destruction of people and property has the nod of approval from the Democrat Party. Rioting is a proper form of expression, now in America.

The talking heads say that protesting is as American as apple pie. But every day?

The message? Get used to it America. This now is NORMAL.

Indeed, it is. Every day now is the same. America waits and won

* Originally published in *Arutz Sheva* English site (israelnationalnews.com).

ders… where and when will the next incident take place?

We can be sure something will happen. It usually does when police risk their own lives whenever they answer a call, notably in inner-city neighborhoods.

Often they have a split second to make a life and death decision, as happened in Columbus, Ohio, the other day.

The cop arrived at the scene of a knifing in progress… one Black teenager against another. The one armed, and ready to strike, the other, helpless.

There was no time to waste. No time to debate. No time to think. Act, or do nothing. The cop acted. Instinct and training kicked in. He shot and brought down the assailant.

The cop saved a life, and now? Now there is plenty of time to debate.

It is not the nattering nabobs who were on the spot and compelled to face a harrowing moment of truth.

They are now all over the airwaves with plenty of time to think this through, safely, comfortably and smugly judgmental.

It was the cop who had to decide who shall live and who shall die… in a fraction of a second.

NBC Nightly News and others played down the fact that the attacker was wielding a knife, thus a hero cop is turned into a villain.

The media says so. So it must be true… and now they are rioting in Columbus.

But where next?

What stores will have to be boarded up and which citizens will have to barricade themselves in fear of reprisal after the next incident?

Will it be safe to walk, to drive, to dine?

The nation waits, and the mobs? They are always waiting, always ready.

This is now routine. This is how America lives…. awaiting nervously tomorrow's eruption.

Now mob tactics have moved to Jerusalem. They listen and they watch and they learn.

Among the terrorists, if it's okay in America, it must be worth a try in Israel.

This depends upon how law enforcement reacts. The Israelis… there is nothing they can learn from us.

Maybe we can learn from them. If they act promptly, decisively, and wisely to keep their citizens safe from leftist-approved lawlessness.

Woke Dollars for Terrorists

***Apr. 11, 2021 – To me, and to others who remember America before it got lost, woke means, "The cancelation of everything we hold sacred."**

Joe Biden's rush to replenish the Palestinian Arabs with millions of dollars should not be taken as a slap in the face to the Israelis, necessarily.

It is simply Joe being Woke.

I hate that word. Rattles my teeth and hurts my ears. But it's all you hear these days.

So, I looked it up, and officially it means, "Alert to injustice, especially as to racism."

That is not what it means to me. To me, and to others who remember America before it got lost, woke means, "The cancelation of everything we hold sacred."

Or the obliteration of everything we value… our past (warts and all), our traditions, our religions, books, movies, music, family, country, Johnny Carson, and even our mothers-in-law.

All gone, so far as reverence, in the presence of woke.

I mention Johnny Carson only as counterpoint to the no-talent generics who've taken over the Late-Night airwaves. Jimmy Kimmel?

All of them are woke, of course, and typify a country gone bland and humorless, and ready to point fingers at you, you, and you. No hero is forgiven. No statue is safe.

However, the Palestinian Authority erects statues to its heroes, namely, people who have committed murder… against Jews.

More than statues, the PA and Hamas name schools, streets, their children and their holidays in homage to their terrorists… preferably those who've done it through suicide.

They run a death cult… first in their schools.

On top of that, they pay to slay. This is a system that rewards "martyred" terrorists and their families with hefty sums of cash.

---

* Originally published in *Arutz Sheva* English site (israelnationalnews.com).

Pay to Slay is an operation utterly barbaric and medieval. It has no place in the civilized world. Yet it persists throughout the Palestinian Authority.

That's been the case ever since the Oslo Accords, when the PLO/PA were legitimized, and recognized as Israel's "peace partners."

That special brand of terror persists even in the face of the Taylor Force Act, which was intended to halt the thriving business of harming Jews for profit.

Trump said they don't need American money to keep that business going… and he cut the funds.

Enter the Biden administration and its gang of woke worshippers.

Now that they are in charge, all that money is going back to Mahmoud Abbas and company. He shares their way of thinking… de-fund the police, and to heck with law and order.

Plus, rule number one among woke enthusiasts – hate your own country, and despise the men and women who built it up. Call them racists.

So the money is coming. Something like $75 million into one pocket, and $290 million into another pocket of Israel's sworn enemies.

Nothing personal against the Israelis, necessarily.

It's just that they don't share the woke philosophy.

They believe in law and order. They love their country. They believe in build, baby, build. Their philosophy is to "choose life."

The PA, on the other hand, to which most of the money is going, even if it's through UNRWA, is a perfect fit for Team Biden.

Woke means destroy everything sacred.

Hunter and How the Left Rescues Its Scoundrels

***Apr. 6, 2021 – You just leave it to Big Media to come bail you out and rehab your good or bad name. After all, Liberals are all in it together.**

Hunter Biden needed a hug. He wouldn't get it from the *New York Post*. That's who exposed the sordid details about him.

The *Post* ran it front page, how Hunter got rich allegedly sponging millions from China and Ukraine just by showing up with his father, then VP Joe Biden.

"Influence peddling," wrote the *Post*, about shady deals that may, or may not, have corrupted the future president himself.

This was a big story, so big that the 2020 Election hung in the balance. So big that if it ran in *The New York Times*, the Pulitzer Prize would have been automatic.

Instead, it ran in the *New York Post*… and only the *New York Post*. Soon picked up by *Fox News*, but only *Fox News*.

The rest of the media along with Big Tech suppressed it, so most of the country was kept in the dark about something that could have changed everything.

That was back in October, when the election could still have gone either way. People were still making up their minds.

Jack Dorsey at *Twitter* now says it was a mistake to have muzzled the *Post*'s Hunter story… now, after the damage. Clever, how these types work this yo-yo of damage and regret.

Today, we learn, that some 47 percent never heard of Hunter's follies… not until now… when it's too late… and that one out of five would not have voted for Biden had they been briefed.

The fix was in, and never before had the media so deliberately cooked an election. They were all in on it together.

Slowly now, the truth is starting to trickle out, thanks to Hunter himself, who cannot seem to stay out of trouble… in and out with

---

* Originally published in *Arutz Sheva* English site (israelnationalnews.com).

drugs and relationships.

He's been quiet all these months, but he's got a book to sell, so he's a player again, but where to play his game of catch-me-if-you-can?

Where to go pitching his brand new two million dollar book?

Certainly not *Fox News*, and definitely not the *New York Post*.

They might ask tough questions. They might not buy his evasive answers. They might not fall for his act of being just a boy… and boys will be boys.

He is 51 years old, for crying out loud.

But here is where he can pull it off, on *CBS* and the other mainstream channels… and here is how we learn the way it works between the two different Americas.

If they catch you being corrupt in the few conservative news outlets, the *NY Post*/*Fox News*, you wait it out.

You leave it to Big Media to come bail you out and rehab your good or bad name.

Just another case of Liberals all in it together.

Come to Big Media. Big Momma will make everything good.

So, Hunter's first stop, on the road to rehab his reputation, was with reporter Tracy Smith at *CBS Sunday Morning* where he was evasive about practically everything… everything pertinent.

The laptop that contained revealing emails about his business dealings… maybe it's his, maybe it isn't. He is not sure.

We are expected to believe this; a grown man, and he doesn't know.

The reporter, a grown woman, did not press him on this, as this would take us to Ukraine and China, and whether he walked off with a fortune from those places.

Did he, or didn't he? Well… it's complicated.

Best to leave that alone… and she did.

One more tiny detail… (from another show)… did his father share any of that loot? Dear Old Dad – never. Not a penny. Honest.

Back to the drugs then, and his struggles to kick the habit, poor boy, and this was how it was left, for America to sympathize with this desperate child… 51 years old.

In the end, the cameras caught him wiping his eyes… then, cue the tears.

That's how it's done.

Biden – A "Nice Guy"

***Apr. 4, 2021 – He certainly has made a career of it, if on no other quality worthy of leadership, and some might say he's nice to all the wrong people.**

Millions voted for Biden not because he's a smart guy, or an honest guy, or a tough guy. They chose him because he's a "nice guy."

They say so all the time. He says so himself. "I'm a nice guy," he says.

Most recently he said it in response to this question from a reporter – "Sir, the people coming over the border say you invited them because you're a nice guy."

Okay, it really wasn't a question. They ask no questions of Biden, except does he prefer chocolate or vanilla.

If it's not written down for him, he won't know the answer anyway. But about the border and the migrants he's letting in by the millions, why?

"Because I'm a nice guy."

For that he's quick on the draw. The media adore him for this. Finally, a nice guy. So whatever he says is good to go. Even when he lies, they lap it up.

So they report it as truth. It's worse than Jim Crow, he says, when people must show ID in order to vote. Amen, says the media.

"Nice guys finish last," is a quote attributed to baseball's Leo Durocher, who apparently did not know Joe Biden, nor how Biden finished first on a single merit so strictly mediocre.

He certainly has made a career of it, if on no other quality worthy of leadership, and some might say he's nice to all the wrong people.

The word is out that he's back to Obama's appeasement policy with Iran, as but one example of his preference of our enemies over our friends.

---

* Originally published in *Arutz Sheva* English site (israelnationalnews.com).

Specifically, everything Trump did, Biden is undoing… one executive order at a time… with no one to stop him. The media, certainly not.

The mullahs are sure to love this nice guy, as much as they hated Trump. Trump refused to play their game. So naturally, Biden is prepared to go all in.

How long, therefore, before Biden would start building bridges with the Palestinian Arabs, while burning bridges with Israel? Not long at all.

Already, Israel is being told that Judea and Samaria… the "West Bank" … are once again "occupied territory," and that Israel's security rests on the Trojan Horse of a two-state solution.

Money, Money, Money.

Trump said no more, so he cut off US funds to the PA, due to the fact that so much of those dollars were funding the terrorists within Fatah and the Palestinian Authority… and despite the Taylor Force Act, Israeli civilians were still liable to be hunted for fun and profit. Enough of this, said Trump.

Trump, you see, was not a nice guy.

Trump was a tough guy… so far as our enemies.

Biden is a nice guy.

To prove it, he is enriching the gluttonous PA with the same millions that Trump held back. Terrorism is back in business.

Biden did this.

Because Biden is such a nice guy.

We Don't Get No Respect

***Mar. 21, 2021 – A nation that has so much contempt for itself is always open to scorn, ridicule, and belittlement from the outside.**

First, to start a week of ignominies, Biden calls Putin a "killer."

Not smart, not diplomatic, from one world leader to another... each with 10,000 missiles directed from the one to the other.

Perhaps Biden forgot that he was live on-air, and when he speaks, people listen. So maybe he thought it was just between himself and George Stephanopoulos over at *ABC-TV*.

Two Democrats, you know, just chewing the fat, as pals do... and only about 20 million people listening in.

Not a chance that this might get back to Putin. That is, if you are Biden and your handlers keep you in seclusion.

The name calling wasn't even Biden's idea. It came from Stephanopoulos who asked Biden yes or no if Putin was a killer. Biden said yes. Loose lips from the leader of the Free World?

Or... a real possibility... maybe, at that moment, Biden forgot that he was President of the United States... that has been happening to him... and that a reckless utterance from such a person could start a war. There are days when Biden thinks Kamala Harris is president, and maybe between themselves he's right.

In any case, Putin wasn't pleased.

But rather than go to war, Putin challenged Biden to a debate.

Putin did so with a smirk, knowing that this world leader was no world beater on the debate stage, nor on the world stage.

It was a taunt, from the Russian, intended to humiliate the American president... and so another day to channel Rodney Dangerfield.

We don't get no respect.

Next, at around the same time, a delegation of Chinese officials met with Sec of State Antony Blinken and warned him against any lectures from America.

---

* Originally published in *Arutz Sheva* English site (israelnationalnews.com).

It's what you'd expect after people in China and around the world watch how we within the United States cancel each other out and rip ourselves apart. Thanks to the Left, we've become a nation of accusers and book burners. Every imperfection is magnified and no one is spared the horror of public shaming.

And it begins early.

Eight-year-old school children are being subjected to Critical Race Theory, which together with *The New York Times* Project 1619 teaches that we have always been and always will be racists.

No wonder we don't get no respect.

A nation that has so much contempt for itself is always open to scorn, ridicule, and belittlement from the outside.

Enemies laugh. Friends turn their heads from the embarrassing sight of our decline.

It wasn't like that just a few months ago, when we were told that we were the greatest, and we believed it, and the world believed it… or else.

Funny how everything changed literally overnight after Biden took the White House, and thereafter we became a laughingstock to the nations.

Then, perfect timing to symbolize our debasement.

Biden trips and falls, three times, climbing the ramp to Air Force One. The third time he fell flat on his face.

The picture… seen around the world… says it all.

Someone Else Did It First, Joe

***Mar. 14, 2021 – We expect nothing much from our politicians, so whatever their faults, we say good enough.**

I'm always grateful when some other publication does the research for me, as in the case of *Real Clear Politics*, in which I found the following – "It's also important to note that he's been accused of lifting entire sections of speeches from others for his own use without attribution. And of copying, almost word for word, policy platforms of other candidates.

"He's even been caught lying to voters about his academic record. Biden acknowledged that he had plagiarized during his time at Syracuse University Law School. The law school had him repeat a first-year class, after initially flunking him, for copying at least five pages from a published law review article."

It gets worse. That is why the article is titled, "Joe Biden's Plagiarism Problem."

The article then goes on to document nearly all the instances where and when Biden got caught cheating.

There is no choice, seems to me, except to call him a serial plagiarist.

Yet 81 million Americans did not flunk him. They voted for him. Did they not know? Or did they not care?

Either way, it's a problem. They voted him in through ignorance, or through cynicism.

Nobody, they would say, is perfect… and everybody deserves another chance.

But Joe has made a career out of second chances. He gets caught, but nothing sticks. He gets away with it, all that cribbing, and even rises up and up the political ladder.

Along the way, apparently nobody detected this character flaw that usually stops most such people from advancing.

Nobody stopped Joe all the way to the White House.

---

* Originally published in *Arutz Sheva* English site (israelnationalnews.com).

As we say here... luck is everything... and maybe that's just it with Joe.

He's lucky... an Inspector Clouseau type... a bumbling fool who does everything wrong but yet succeeds, gets his man, gets promoted, and gets the girl.

Or maybe it's not about Joe. It's about us. We have become jaded. We expect nothing much from our politicians, so whatever their faults, we say good enough.

It's like gamblers at the racetrack who can't win through handicapping, so they pick names or numbers for the luck of the draw... and sometimes it works out.

But until you put your money down, or put your vote in, you don't know what you're getting.

What did we get with Joe?

Anybody who watched his "address to the nation" the other night saw a slippery politician in action.

He said that through his leadership, America was first to get a grip on the pandemic and first to rollout the vaccines, but as the *New York Post* points out, no, it was Israel.

More than that, Joe took the credit all to himself as to getting the vaccines invented and produced, when actually the credit, all of it, belongs to Trump.

Yes, Trump got it done in record time through his Warp Speed initiative. But 81 million Americans will always believe it was Joe Biden.

Because he told them so, and because he has been so lucky... so far.

Gov. Cuomo, Caught Being Too Cute

***Mar. 10, 2021 – Cuomo wrote a book during the nursing home fiasco, modestly titled *Leadership Lessons from the COVID-19 Pandemic*. It boggles the mind.**

How's this for "the bigger they are, the harder they fall?"

For a time, he was the toast of the town, and country… and what a good-time-Charlie!

Now, New York's Gov. Andrew Cuomo can't get a laugh, or even a smile. People want him out, and no thanks for the memories, either.

Those were the days, only a few months ago, when the Cuomo Brothers, Andrew and *CNN* brother, Chris, exchanged banters that creeped out half of us, but delighted the other half of the nation, which would be the Left, which found their skit so cute and so adorable, and so right-on during these tough times of COVID.

They kept yukking it up on *CNN* and through it all, Andrew, the governor, became a TV Star, and among women, hot property.

He was getting offers from all over the country, and he wasn't shy about calling himself what he was… simply irresistible.

In a word, the cuteness was nauseating.

During all that time, people were dying. Elderly New Yorkers by the thousands were being sent to die of COVID inside crowded nursing homes, because?

Because Gov. Cuomo sent them there… among them war veterans and Holocaust Survivors.

That, while he assured the public that no one had a better hands-on grip on the situation than he did. He was forceful. Almost believable. Charmingly homespun.

Only the Israelis, his team suggested, were doing as good a job… and the pity of it is, to lose Cuomo is to lose a true friend of Israel. That's a paradox we can't escape.

---

* Originally published in *Arutz Sheva* English site (israelnationalnews.com).

Then it turned out that he had fudged the figures, so whatever the original number, of needless deaths, had to be nearly doubled… up to 15,000.

Cuomo, without evidence, blamed it all on Trump, which is what everybody did in those days when Trump was in office… only Cuomo did it better.

So, the media let him get away with it… learning from Hillary Clinton, perhaps… 7,000 deaths, or 15,000 – "what difference does it make?"

The difference… in attitude… came when a number of women, one at a time, accused Cuomo of sexual harassment.

Now people paid attention… and even the nursing home scandal came under renewed scrutiny… and then something else.

Gov. Cuomo wrote a book.

Well, okay. He must have written it much earlier, while all was quiet on the western front.

Actually, no. He wrote it during the nursing home fiasco, and it was about his peerless and heroic leadership during the worst days of COVID.

So, while all his efforts and all his powers should have been directed at saving lives… Cuomo was too busy for all that… instead, writing a book.

He got paid seven figures, it is reported. People died. He got rich… but the title, given what we know, is priceless for irony… *American Crisis: Leadership Lessons from the COVID-19 Pandemic.*

Leadership, he says. Lessons, he gives.

Seven figures? Not quite the starving writer suffering for his Art. Nor, as was said of Kerouac… "This isn't writing. This is typing."

First of all, where did Cuomo find the time? Ordinarily, a book takes two years, at the least, if it's really a book and not a con job, or a hoax.

Some may remember the Clifford Irving Hoax of 1972. After Watergate, it was the biggest scandal of the year, when Irving faked an autobiography of Howard Hughes.

He got 17 months in the slammer for making up a story.

Nothing like that for Cuomo, we imagine.

Two – how did Cuomo's publisher get conned? We read that they approached him… seeing in him the rise of a meteoric political star.

Three – how many readers got duped?

Four – Will Cuomo return the Advance? Or does he get to keep the money?

In the case of Clifford Irving, he had people, including publishers, fooled for years before the truth came out.

Apparently, people are easily conned, notably when the perfect con artist comes along.

The Upside of the ICC's Decision to Target Israel

***Mar. 8, 2021 – A reminder that in your political cocoon you may be Left, Right, Forever-Bibi, Never-Bibi, but to the wider world you are JEWISH.**

So while Israeli politicians were busy taking sides for the upcoming election, even changing sides and trading insults, something else happened.

From The Hague came word that the ICC… International Criminal Court… intended to go ahead with plans to probe Israel for "war crimes" during the 2014 Gaza War.

That's when the IDF guys had to go neighborhood to neighborhood, house to house, to face off against Palestinian Arab terrorists who were hiding themselves and their weapons and ammo inside homes, schools and mosques… and dared anyone to come in and try their luck on so much territory trip wired and booby-trapped. Sixty-seven Israeli soldiers were not lucky.

Some 500 were wounded.

Operation Protective Edge was Israel's answer to the barrage of Hamas rockets that terrorized Israel daily.

So in the eyes of the ICC judges, when the Israelis say enough is enough and start defending themselves, it's a war crime… or war crimes that merit scrutiny.

News of this came from out of nowhere. The ICC, which has no jurisdiction over Israel (nor the United States), is not a group that people think about too much.

It's not the kind of thing where people here or in Israel greet each other and, rather than talk baseball, ask, "Any word from the ICC lately?"

Or, rather than basketball, "Any news on what the ICC is up to these days?"

---

* Originally published in *Arutz Sheva* English site (israelnationalnews.com).

Or, "It's so quiet from The Hague lately. I wonder what's on tap."

Well, now we know… and if you ask me, good timing.

A swift kick in the pants is what this is… a reminder that in your political cocoon you may be Left, Right, Forever-Bibi, Never-Bibi, but to places in the wider world you are JEWISH.

That's all they know. That is all they care about… and not with kindness, necessarily.

As in The Hague, for example… which dropped this bombshell weeks before the March 23 elections, as if to add spice to the political squabbling underway.

Yet it appears that Political Israelis have sensibly retreated to their corners and declared a semi time-out in consideration of this threat from outside.

I'll take a chance to suggest that even radical leftists are not happy with the ICC. They too have kids in the IDF.

Birds do it, bees do it, people do it… we bicker within, but when a hostile outsider steps in, we close ranks… and woe to the intruder.

Up until a few days ago, the politicians had the stage on which they could call attention to the other guy's failures… the other party's shortcomings… and do so with rage and gusto.

You would think there is no other business.

But yes there is, after a voice is heard from The Hague, targeting all the people, regardless of party affiliation.

Jewish… that's your party.

We all know the story, that when we forget we are Jews, someone always comes along to remind us… and hopefully to reunite us.

Thank you, ICC.

Is the Two-State Solution An Anti-Semitic Whistle?

***Feb. 28, 2021 – During Trump's presidency, we seldom heard that refrain... two-state-solution... and it was a pleasure to have it gone like a bad tooth.**

Is it anti-Semitic to promote a two-state solution?

The calls for a two-state solution are already coming in fast and furious. No surprise, with Biden now in the White House, but disturbing just the same.

The news media got it started, and on cue comes Secretary of State Antony Blinken to say that only through a two-state solution can Israel have peace and security.

Guess he is not up on the latest.

Because it has seldom been as peaceful and secure as it is today, since the Palestinian Arabs were marginalized, and the Abraham Accords were signed happily without them.

So the Arab-Israeli conflict is no more as it was, but rather reduced mostly to Palestinian Arabs in active conflict, on their relentless terror campaign against the Jewish State.

They had no say when sitting at the table with Israel were the UAE, Bahrain, Sudan and Morocco, as proof that even among other Arabs the dawning arrived that the Palestinian Arabs were never the solution, but always the problem. Apparently, that is not good enough, or maybe too good, for people who can't stand the thought that Israel is moving along nicely as is.

These are people who pretend to know what's best, but are bothered by the fact that Israel exists, period. There is a word for them... anti-Semites.

They focus on Israel as if it is any of their business, and won't leave it alone whether it's an entire political party, the Democrats, or some two-bit comedian spewing Jew-hatred on SNL.

---

* Originally published in *Arutz Sheva* English site (israelnationalnews.com).

Happiness to them, persons like Blinken and his predecessor Kerry, is a Jewish State that becomes less and less Jewish and more and more Palestinian Arab.

Also radioed-in to the same frequency are types like Roger Waters and Peter Beinart.

That'll teach those Israelis to imagine they are home at last in the land of their Biblical fathers.

Throughout Trump's presidency, we seldom heard that refrain... two-state-solution... and a relief it was. It was a pleasure to have it gone like a bad tooth.

Now it's back in style because all the anti-Semites are back in style.

I don't use that term lightly.

I don't know about you, but as for me, that phrase... two-state solution... gives me the creeps and a case of the willies.

It sounds to me like the N-word sounds to a black person. It registers the same feel of disrespect, animosity, and hatred without cause.

It says that Jews... Israelis... are only half a people, and thus deserve only half a country.

That is pure racism.

It says that the Israelis are usurpers, only renting, while the Palestinian Arabs are the true owners.

That is pure bigotry.

It says that if the Jews wish to stay, they must do so as beggars, and so must give up Jerusalem to the Palestinian Arabs.

It says that the Jews may not thrive or expand the land until permission is granted from the United States... and the world.

It says that the Jews must always be ready to cut the heart out of their own land in order to implant a Palestinian state.

It says that the Jews must always be ready to be uprooted, as per Gaza, whenever the world says, do as we say.

It says that after 2,000 years of being scattered, and finally reaching their destination, the Jews ought to "go back where they came from" (which happens to be Israel).

It says that Jews are not masters of their own destiny.

All of that is pure anti-Semitism, and it is what I hear when I hear two-state solution, and it is my view that persons who use that term ought to be branded and shamed as anti-Semites.

That would be in keeping with the mood of our times, a time when people are so quick to express their sensitivities, except for Jews, who do not get to scream when they hurt.

Time to turn it on them.

Trump's Tax Records – The Latest Craze

***Feb. 24, 2021 – Anybody notice that a few days ago NASA landed a rover on Mars? What counts today is that they've got their hands on Trump's taxes.**

They simply won't let go, will they.

There is a sickness in the land and Trump Derangement Syndrome is its name.

They have tried everything else – next?

Now they are qvelling over the Supreme Court ruling that after years of peekaboo, finally permits his tax returns to be examined by New York prosecutors.

Why the thrills? That's right… it's how the Law got Al Capone.

They're dreaming that this will finally… finally what? What exactly do they want from this guy Trump? How many different ways can you skin a man alive?

What's in it for the rest of us if even they do find something amiss with his taxes? Nothing. Zero.

If they prove that he finagled, yeah, so? What's it got to do with the price of tomatoes… or the fact that kids can't go to school because of the pandemic.

Parents with kids underfoot as they try to make a living don't give a hoot about Trump's taxes, nor of the Dems fixation about it all, nor if they get their man or not.

Who cares!

Anybody notice that a few days ago NASA landed a rover on Mars? That kind of stuff used to get round the clock coverage. America cheered.

Now it gets a headline or two, and Dems cheer that they've got their hands on Trump's taxes. That's the big story.

---

* Originally published in *Arutz Sheva* English site (israelnationalnews.com).

Precisely what is the complaint? Why this pursuit when they got what they wanted. They got their guy to replace Trump in the White House.

Happy Days for them, but apparently not happy enough until they bloody up Trump.

Crimes and Misdemeanors?

What was his crime at getting us energy independent, and what was his misdemeanor doing what is right for Israel while stabilizing the Middle East?

No thanks, says Biden, whose bright idea is to undo it all, simply to deny Trump, and America, and Israel, the satisfaction.

America First? Not for Team Biden. Iran First, and the Palestinian Arabs a close second. Israel? Israel can sit by the phone and wait.

Not that Israel is starved for attention. She has her own priorities. She can also wait… and now especially with the Abraham Accords, she too can play hard-to-get. Thanks to Trump.

For his entire term as president they smeared Trump with the Russia hoax. Then again and again they tried impeachment, but failed to convict.

Trump, they hollered, was a Russian agent. Trump? Trump is as American as baseball and apple pie.

Maybe too American for them, and that's their problem with him. Or maybe too New York. That New York swagger. That New York bluntness… "Hey, I'm walking here." That New York sense of greatness… all the way from Babe Ruth. That New York brashness that shakes them up where small minds meet small towns.

His Damon Runyon wise-guy sense of humor… the kibitzing perfect for Katz's Deli… riled them. They couldn't figure him out, so they set out to ruin him.

The kibitzing they never got. Humor? At this moment in the life of America? Rather, check your privilege and be miserable.

He flopped whenever he tried to do Don Rickles… in front of that crowd of uptight journalists?

January 6 was indeed a mistake and a lapse of good judgment on Trump's part.

But the chase was on from the moment he stepped off that escalator and announced himself a candidate for president… and not as a saint.

Brings to mind Cornell Wilde in the movie *The Naked Prey*, where the headhunters let him loose for the sport of tracking him and hunting him down.

Is that what this is? Feels like it all right.

Your World, If Bill Gates Has It His Way

***Feb. 16, 2021 – If Big Brother Bill Gates ran your world... and maybe he will... you better worry about how to keep warm when it rains.**

Bill Gates was on *60 Minutes* explaining how with his billions and his Silicon partners he intends to create a clean new world, a world unsafe for oil, gas, and coal.

But safe for solar panels... plus sun and wind. We weren't told what happens if it rains.

Say 40 days and 40 nights?

According to Gates, who sounded like a would-be Big Brother, there is something inherently wrong with you if you don't panic about fossil fuels, pollution, and global warming.

(Though right now, baby, it's cold outside.)

Gates himself is in a state of alarm. He is also absolutely certain about his action. A man so sure of himself is cause for suspicion, that he may be shooting loaded dice.

Saving the planet is one thing, but as Bob Dylan has it in one of his ballads, "You're playing with my world."

As you can tell, I don't know much about this futuristic technology and found 99 percent of what Gates said way over my head. But I tried.

Seems that we'll have to start from scratch, if Gates has it his way. He has already spent billions on redesigning Creation, with more billions to come.

Everything must go. Think the Empire State Building. It would have to be torn down and rebuilt certainly not with bricks and mortar, but with soybeans, or something.

Same for your house and home.

Suppose you object? Too bad. The Masters of the Universe... the same ones who already control 60 percent of your lives, now want the rest.

---

* Originally published in *Arutz Sheva* English site (israelnationalnews.com).

You have no say.

Together with the government, they will decide what's good for you, and you will have no choice but to heed.

Bill Gates wasn't kidding. He's got big plans and because he's got big money, and you don't, it's his way or the highway… which will also have to be repaved to conform with his standards.

If all this sounds like AOC's Green New Deal… well it is. Out of the mouth of babes.

More than that, there is no time to waste… in case you think you can relax with a cup of coffee which was boiled over a gas oven.

You will have to hide that stove when they come. Your gas-guzzling car has already been impounded.

Don't even try. Gates and his police force know everything. Think of that Ray Bradbury movie, *Fahrenheit 451* where they came for your books.

The technology is now available to make this real. Can't hide.

No time to waste, says Gates, because doomsday is coming in about 10 years… if we don't change our wicked ways.

How does he know? His scientists tell him so. Other scientists say otherwise. But they don't have Masters of the Universe on their side, nor Gates' billions.

In fact, some say our air has never been cleaner. You won't see them on *60 Minutes*. Gates meanwhile made his case without being challenged.

The interviewer let him go on, and on, so I forget whether Gates, now a prophet, in the eyes of *CBS*, intends to makeover America only, or the rest of the world as well.

Suppose China won't buckle? Or does he own them, too? What good are our windmills against their factory smoke if they, and others, won't comply?

Will Gates have to buy truculent Mexico?

We've had prophets like this before… throughout history. Most end up being forcefully sedated and being taken away in white vans.

For all that, maybe Gates is right after all? But he's an alarmist, who says trust me with your lives, and that's a turn-off.

Plus, anything coming from Silicon Valley must be reserved for further reflection.

Those are people with too much money and too much time on their hands.

When Did the Palestinian Arabs Become the Good Guys?

***Feb. 10, 2021 – It is noted that you quote the Bible frequently, Mr. Biden, so you know to whom the Promised Land was given.**

Picking those people as your home team is like rooting for the Miller Gang against Gary Cooper in *High Noon*.

Israel is Gary Cooper. That's a pure fact to people who understand that the world is made up of two sorts, good guys and bad guys. Woe to him who gets them mixed up, Mr. Biden.

Of bad guys, in most books, the Grand Mufti of the 1930s/40s shared secrets with Hitler on how best to murder the Jews, and out of that grew the fiction of a "Palestinian People."

That's the side you choose?

Did they stop drowning puppies and kittens for sport?

Have they quit the business of slaying Jews for profit?

On what merits did they become so attractive?

Of the Hitler/Mufti tag-team, it's even in the movie *Exodus*, which was written by Dalton Trumbo, from Leon Uris' book, and Trumbo was no particular friend of Israel. Uris was.

The truth had to be told, even from a reluctant screenwriter, a good man, whose heart and typewriter were always with the oppressed, though sometimes he forgot which was which.

Typical of socialists and communists.

The *Exodus* movie came out in 1960. President John F. Kennedy saw it and said he liked it very much. He approved of the historical accuracy from both the book and the film.

The Jews were the heroes. There was no confusion about this. Not for JFK. What happened to you, Mr. Biden?

What happened to you and your Party, that within a generation lost the means to tell right from wrong, the sacred from the profane, heroes from villains?

---

* Originally published in *Arutz Sheva* English site (israelnationalnews.com).

Back then… once upon a time… Democrats were good guys.

Truman did right, and JFK consistently reaffirmed America's special relationship with the Jewish State.

Like you, he was Catholic. Our first as president. You are the second, and *The New York Times* named you our most religious president ever.

It is noted that you quote the Bible frequently.

Then you know that the Hebrews are the stars and the heroes of the Bible and that the Promised Land was promised to them alone.

Those weren't the Palestinians who received The Ten Commandments on Mount Sinai, first because they wouldn't know what to do with them, and second because there were no Palestinians then. Nor are there any today, except as a collection of people from different tribes and countries who gave themselves that name, around 1964… months later than the Beatles.

They've been nothing but trouble ever since, and not just for the Israelis. During the 1970s and 1980s, under Arafat, they turned their attention to Jordan and Lebanon.

After a thousand acts of terrorism… brother against brother, they left both places in shambles.

But their terrorism was always global, and the Munich Olympics Massacre is just one example of their blood-thirsty reach.

Over the decades the Israelis have made miles of concessions to them, in order to make peace with them, but so far as terrorism, they can't seem to kick the habit.

Their school books glorify murder. So it goes from one generation to the next… which is why Trump tucked them safely away.

Now you bring them back front and center, while you stiff-arm the Israelis, the good guys since Abraham, Moses and King David.

What Bible are you reading?

Israel Holds A Winning Hand Against Biden Onslaught

***Feb. 4, 2021 – Biden is going back to Obama's relations with Israel, but the Middle East has changed for good. He would do well to realize that.**

Since Biden has stacked his inner circle with ministers and consiglieri mostly hostile to Israel, we shouldn't be surprised at what's coming.

Some of.it has arrived already.

One of Biden's first phone calls was not to Benjamin Netanyahu, but to the Palestinian Authority to assure the boys that everything is back to normal, yes, as it was under Obama. This means the PLO eyesore, that is, the PLO office in DC is okay to reopen. The funds that Trump took away from the PA are being returned … the "two-state solution" is back on the table… and Abbas is back in the saddle.

Some days it is good to be a terrorist. Be patient, and await the American voters to vote low for the highest office.

Abbas, no doubt, expressed his gratitude, and both he and Biden agreed that Trump was terrible… but hey, happy days are here again.

Trump had consigned the Palestinian Arabs to the far corners of the earth. For four years, sucking their thumbs, hardly a peep out of them.

Result? The entire Middle East changed… for the better. Who knew that they were the problem? Trump knew.

The Taylor Force Act, it was understood, still prohibits murdering Jews for the money… but that could change if the Israelis don't behave.

So to what extent do Biden and his team intend to diminish Israel? Of Biden himself, this we know. The man has no idea what he is doing… but whatever, it is out of spite.

Trump wanted the Keystone XL Pipeline to flourish, Biden turns the spigots off and shuts it down.

---

* Originally published in *Arutz Sheva* English site (israelnationalnews.com).

Trump set limits and restrictions to immigration, Biden invites the stampede.

Trump supported Israel; Biden embraces the Palestinian Arabs.

Nearly all of Biden's executive orders share that trend and have that tone.

We can count on this… concessions, concessions, concessions… all on Israel. From the other side, nothing is expected, except promises, which they never keep.

There will be a summit, as there was for Camp David and Oslo, and Netanyahu (or whoever after March elections) will be imposed upon to shake hands with Abbas.

Lights. Camera. Action. Biden and Abbas beaming, the Israeli forcing a grim half-smile.

That is, if the Israelis fall for that trap all over again… which would be trip-wired by the same old arabists who got everything wrong before and now get still another chance with Biden.

Old maps will be dusted, new maps will be drawn, meticulously setting out how easily thousands of Israelis can be uprooted from here to there to implant a Palestinian state.

Yes, we see this coming. No doubt about it at all. The same old formulas from the same old hacks.

But it does not have to end the usual way if the Israelis remember their ace in the hole, four actually… The UAE, Morocco, Sudan, Bahrain.

These new allies give Israel a strong hand to play.

Biden's arabists can no longer support their central theme, that for there to be peace in the region, Israel must first come to terms with the Palestinian Arabs.

Otherwise no deal.

Now there is a deal… the Abraham Accords… and that's a winning hand against whatever tricks Biden and company have up their sleeves.

Further, they best tread carefully. America will soon need Arab oil again, since Biden suspended so much of our own drillings and pipelines.

It would pay to go gently toward Israel and her oil rich Arab friends.

Biden's War on Girls and Women

***Jan. 28, 2021 – If you think a 128-pound high school girl can bench-press the same weight as a 280-pound man, then you voted for Biden.**

Biden cancels women.

Boys and girls are different, and if I have to explain how, then what we've got here is "failure to communicate."

In Biden's world of the far left, sameness is the ideal.

Not so where I grew up. There, boys were to be admired for their muscles, girls and women for their virtuousness.

Boys were boys. Girls were girls. Life was much simpler, then. Around the breakfast table, we did not have to be reminded which was which. This was Mom. That was Dad. Easy.

Nor was there any chance that one day Dad would switch to become Mom.

So away we go to one of Biden's first acts upon entering the White House… which changes everything since Adam and Eve.

Through executive order, he decreed that men (claiming to be transgendered) must be allowed to compete with women in the world of sports.

He inked this so fast, as if this were a national emergency. Maybe it is, among one percent of the population. The rest liked things as they were.

You have to wonder who asked for this change that turns biology on its head, and ruins any chance of girls advancing through sports scholarships.

Astonishingly, Biden's cockeyed action entirely reverses the feminist movement and… wait for it… empowers men to the detriment of women.

Did we miss something?

Was there an uprising against girls going it alone? Did Soccer Moms go rioting because they wanted big burly boys on the same field

---

* Originally published in *Arutz Sheva* English site (israelnationalnews.com).

with their developing daughters? We hear otherwise. We hear people complaining that Biden was way off the beaten path to do what he did. It isn't American.

Nor is it Christian, and it certainly isn't Jewish to demand gender conformity. Just the opposite. Vive la difference.

It's in the Bible, in many places all about the virtues of separateness for the sanctity of the individual, the family, the home.

Like this in our daily liturgy. In the wilderness, Balaam is provoked to declare, in astonishment, "Ma Tovu" – "How goodly thy tents O Jacob; thy dwelling places O Israel." Sent to curse, he is impelled to bless the Israelites after seeing their encampments so perfectly arranged, apart, for the sake of modesty between men and women.

Biden must have missed that part, even after *The New York Times* called him the most religious president we've ever had.

More precisely, leave it to the Liberal religion to fix something that ain't broke.

Liberals are less intrusive when they play with their favorite toy… global warming. Why pick on gender, which is the business of science, not the government.

Where are the feminists? In one swoop they've been outmaneuvered. Into silence.

Truly, we have all been roped into Biden's vision, which is to embrace for the nation the picture of the man himself – mediocrity.

Under Biden, no more reaching for the stars, nor scaling new frontiers. That was the past, the daring-do that made us exceptional.

Biden, you see, is a "nice guy." He does not want us towering over the rest of the world. No more America First.

Not last, either.

But ordinary. The nation, like the man.

Hemingway Wouldn't Make the Cut Either, These Days

***Jan. 20, 2021 – Used to be, your book got rejected because of the writing or the subject. Now what counts is who you voted for.**

Sen. Josh Hawley made quite a splash with the news that his book… taking on Big Tech… was cancelled because he doesn't play well with others, namely Democrats.

So if that's the new normal, and apparently so it is all along the New York's publishers row… conservative writers will have to resort to Samizdat.

That's how the Refusenik mostly Jewish Russians did it back in the 1980s when they used mimeograph and fax machines to get the word out that they are stuck in a regime that wants them trapped and silenced. That is something we should never expect to be happening in America, but the surprises keep coming.

Hawley didn't give up a different way. He got lucky. Chicago's Regnery Publishing picked up his book.

That's the same book Simon and Schuster had turned down, for political, not literary reasons.

I know something about this. Simon and Schuster were the first to publish my (Jewish/Biblical themed) novel *Indecent Proposal*. The book sold big. Then the movie came out and because it differed substantially from the book (no Jews), it was decided by the powers that the book would have to suffer.

There'd be no more advertising nor distribution for the book, and I knew this from the hundreds of phone calls I got from friends and booksellers across the country.

"No doubt about it," reported an investigative journalist in LA, "your book has been banned. Off the shelves."

---

* Originally published in *Arutz Sheva* English site (israelnationalnews.com).

Then, to keep this short, it was back on the shelves, and sales zoomed once again (and happily now in the hands of Paul Rabinovitch at CCB Publishing.)

So I know the industry, and perhaps I can play the part of a secret-sharer. Used to be, your book got rejected because of the writing or the subject. Now what counts is who you voted for.

If you voted for Trump, consider yourself Indexed… as in, black-listed.

If this sounds positively medieval, well, back then if you voted wrong or were disobedient any other way, you faced the Inquisition for being in conflict with the Index of Forbidden Works.

You could face the death penalty.

Something like that happened to Salman Rushdie when he came out with *The Satanic Verses*, 1988, which the Ayatollah considered blasphemous and placed a bounty on Rushdie's head. Rushdie went into hiding. Booksellers hid the book. They wanted no troubles from the Islamic world.

Many of us in New York City went marching for Rushdie and for the freedom to write and publish.

We were a fired-up group, mostly writers and artists, and a few lawyers who threatened to sue bookstore owners who refused to stock Rushdie's book.

After Rushdie, who's next?

Around that time, everything in the book world changed. Publishing houses consolidated. So that 100 publishers became Four. That left writers with slim pickings.

Then bookstores started to fail. The big chains swallowed up the local bookstore, and then the chains themselves started downsizing.

Enter Amazon, with perhaps the biggest idea since Gutenberg… bookselling online. Who knew?

One day I got a phone call from an executive at this new company. Would I mind if they picked up for sale all my published works?

I wasn't sure. Brick and mortar bookstores were all we knew and trusted, and what is online anyway?

Would it last?

Finally, after a few more phone calls, I gave in.

Then I was asked if I had anything new in the works. Always. But I've only got 10 chapters so far, with 20 to go.

Would I be amenable to running it as a series, say one installment per week?

Well, Twain and Tolstoy did it like that, so okay.

This warning I gave them… in what was to be *The Bathsheba Deadline* …this thriller is entirely up on Israel and down on Iran's type of Islam… thinking here of Rushdie.

No problem, to Amazon's everlasting credit, and the book ran as a hit series for 30 weeks… later picked up in full by DayRay Literary Press, an imprint of CCB Publishing.

Would I be so lucky these days, with everyone so touchy? Would anyone? Could Hemingway make the cut?

I don't think so. Because a bounty is now upon all our heads, thanks to ayatollahs of our own making.

Pray for America

***Jan. 17, 2021 – Dear World, it is sufficient to know that we've got troubles, and when we've got troubles, you've got troubles.**

Hello, Dear World. We can use a prayer or two.

I know. It's usually the other way round. You turn to us for help, and usually we deliver.

But something happened and we – this great big fat superpower – find ourselves on our knees, and we can't get up.

Long story. The short of it is that we are being devoured by politics. The trouble started when the Democrats decided that every day is another day to hang Donald Trump.

They call it impeachment, but we know that for them, even that won't be enough. They are forming a posse to pursue him even after he is out the door.

The hunt is on and anyone who voted for him is prey. That makes us a dysfunctional family, and the ruckus keeps getting worse.

The noise you hear is coming mostly from the Democrats (though for all the good he did over four years, and plenty of it was very good, Trump does not get off the hook for that one bad day, Jan. 6). But for you, Dear World, it is sufficient to know that we've got troubles, and when we've got troubles, you've got troubles.

Who you gonna call when we're gone? Who comes running when you cry for help? We don't keep grudges, either. Ask Japan. Ask Germany. Ask Vietnam.

Say the word, and we show up.

According to the Council of Foreign Relations, "The United States is widely viewed as the leader in international disaster relief, providing aid in response to dozens of disasters in more than 50 countries every year." It's what you would expect from a country whose heritage is based on Judeo-Christian values.

So it is no surprise that the nations count on Israel as well for the same type of humanitarian generosity.

---

* Originally published in *Arutz Sheva* English site (israelnationalnews.com).

America needs no ships, tanks nor planes from anyone, nor soldiers willing to fight, nor doctors willing to heal. We are okay in that department.

But spare us your *schadenfreude*. We hear the whispers. We are aware of the snickers. Instead, a pat on the back during these hard times would be appreciated.

That would be for services rendered past, present… though the future, who knows? That's the point. We don't know what's coming now that everything is upside-down.

This we know. Iran is a player again, and China celebrates our miseries, as do, we are told, some others around the world, who say we had it coming.

They resent our Big Stick, and yet without that Big Stick Western Europe would be speaking German, and Eastern Europe would be speaking Russian.

Once we were near invincible, and now we are down in the dumps, but it would be a bad bet to count us out.

We shall return. Stick with us and stay tuned.

Four Years of Frustration Led to Storming the Capitol

***Jan. 7, 2021 – This outpouring of frustration was four years in the making, and no Trump supporter can be happy that it turned ugly. Not in our name.**

Of the protestors who breached the Capitol, this much we can say… they learned from the best… Antifa coupled with BLM.

But lesson learned. If they can do it, so can we, goes the message, and now watch us do to Biden what you did to Trump over the past four years.

Karma is coming.

Trump's supporters haven't forgotten, in no particular order:

- Rep. Maxine Waters urging Democrats to declare war on Trump and his supporters, as follows: "If you see anybody from that Cabinet in a restaurant, in a department store, at a gasoline station, you get out and you create a crowd and you push back on them and you tell them they're not welcome anymore, anywhere."

Prophetic. Since those words were spoken June 2018, no Trump supporter was safe anywhere.

- From *The New York Times* came the word that Trump was to be Resisted and belittled by all reporters and columnists. Trump was to be given no shade. He was to be hounded.

Likewise, throughout the media.

- Comedian Kathy Griffin took the hint and showed up with a plaster mock-up, which depicted President Trump's head dripping in blood.

No federal action was taken.

On the Late Shows, people laughed.

- On all the Late Shows, Trump was a nightly object of derision.

- Robert De Niro drew wild applause when he said, of the President, "I want to punch him in the face." (Some might call it treason.)

---

* Originally published in *Arutz Sheva* English site (israelnationalnews.com).

Every Awards show, New York to Hollywood, began and ended with poison-tipped yuks against Trump.

- The House of Representatives spent Trump's entire four years with that single objective, to punch him in the face, through Russia, Ukraine, and impeachment.

- Shady lawyers were given starring roles on *CNN* when they offered themselves as proof-positive witnesses to Trump's alleged wrongdoings, until they were caught lying.

- Women of questionable repute were brought forth to allege indiscretions. None were substantiated.

But worth a try. Something might stick.

- Rep. Schiff was everywhere, claiming to have absolute proof that Trump was a Russian agent. The goods never materialized.

- But the show must go on, and it did when Speaker Pelosi theatrically ripped up Trump's State of the Union address.

- Special Counsel Robert Mueller was handed the task to dig up any dirt he could on Trump. After a probe that lasted two years, and cost millions, zero. No bang for the buck.

- When it appeared that Trump's campaign for a second term might succeed, the Democrats sent in the goons.

-Throughout the country, they defaced statues, harassed pedestrians and motorists, burned down shops and destroyed entire neighborhoods.

The media saw nothing, heard nothing. Peaceful protests, they said.

We will see how peaceful it feels now that payback is coming and the shoe is on the other foot.

The Big Deal Over Alec Baldwin's "Spanish" Wife

***Jan. 6, 2021 – Today, through the gossip of social media, everybody is his own lawyer and prosecutor. And people want blood.**

Turns out that Alec Baldwin's Spanish wife Hilaria is not so Spanish after all. She is actually Hillary, plain white bred from Boston.

But since to make it in America, it pays to have an act, Hillary chose Spain as her heritage for that exotic touch.

Married to Alec (since 2012) and moving with the fast-crowd in Hollywood, a girl has to keep up.

Nobody wants to be ordinary. Everybody wants to be a contender.

Now, exposed, it's a "scandal" du jour that she would present herself as something she isn't. She and her husband are now being targeted and harassed as phonies. As if she committed the heist of the century. A crime that deserves hard labor. Americans really from Spain feel usurped, claiming it is skin off their back what she did.

Okay. She's been outed… but the story is much larger than Hillary Baldwin. The story is about how America has changed from an empathy culture to a cancel culture.

Nobody is safe.

Years ago we were known as a litigious nation. Lawyers everywhere for everything. Today, through the gossip of social media, everybody is his own lawyer and prosecutor.

People want blood. Through a thousand cuts, you will pay. Give the scoffers a taste and they will *Twitter* you out of your home, your family, your reputation.

In a flash, your good name becomes anathema.

Yes, Hillary Baldwin came from Boston… and what sin did she commit for wanting a new life, a different identity?

But that is exactly what America is all about… second chances, and it has never been anybody's business where you came from.

---

* Originally published in *Arutz Sheva* English site (israelnationalnews.com).

People took pride becoming something from nothing. Going from Rags to Riches has always been the crown of American Exceptionalism.

It's worked beautifully like that throughout the generations. So that all the men who created Hollywood took America at its word and left the shtetels, and then the tenements, to become tycoons. Samuel Goldfish became Samuel Goldwin. The others transformed themselves likewise, because this was America.

Is it still?

Well, they do tell us that gender is interchangeable, which means, we are told, that today you could be a man, and tomorrow you could be a woman.

Just say the word, and it's done.

There would have been no scandal if Hillary Baldwin had revealed herself as all of a sudden Harold, or Harry, and if so, there'd be congratulations.

Moreover, Alec and Harry Baldwin, a typical American couple, doing us all proud. If only Hillary had thought of this, rather than Spain.

Those two in Congress, Ilhan Omar and Rashida Tlaib… they've got it thought out perfectly, how to fib yourself into someone else's culture.

They have no bloodlines going back to slavery, nor have they a history of the Civil Rights Movement, and yet straight off the boat they call themselves African Americans.

That gives them cover and endowments reserved, you'd think, only for a true and unique class of people. Those who paid the price beginning with their ancestors in bondage.

Where is the scandal about that chutzpah?

It's 2021, and Still Waiting for Godot and Durham Report

***Jan. 1, 2021 – What happened to the Durham Report on the FBI's investigation of the Trump 2016 campaign? It was supposed to be a game changer.**

Promises… promises. A whole year's gone by and Godot still hasn't shown up, and no signs of John Durham, either.

If you know Beckett's play, well then you know how it ends. Two apparently luckless but hopeful characters, Vladimir and Estragon, keep waiting for Godot, who never arrives.

Never!

Curtains!

It's been like that, a Big Tease, a nation on edge, waiting for the Durham Report. We were all there for the excitement, the tension, the drama, which was supposed to change everything after Super Extra Special Counsel John Durham spilled the beans. For Conservatives and Trump enthusiasts, at last, the Deliverer.

Hannity has been waiting. Watching the calendar, and then the clock, with Trump, for this messianic figure to lower the boom.

But it seems like forever, believers and *Fox News* regulars kept saying, and it's getting late.

It's coming. It's coming.

When?

Tomorrow. Any day. Any minute. Be patient. Durham's got the goods. He's launched a worldwide investigation that will expose the Swamp, all the way up to Obama.

Wow. Just as we thought!

He will name names.

Naturally. Durham is known for his thoroughness.

He will prove conclusively with facts, pictures, charts, witnesses that the fix was in against Trump from Day One.

---

* Originally published in *Arutz Sheva* English site (israelnationalnews.com).

We all know this. Does he have it solid?

Don't worry. The Report is being finalized. Just a few more touches.

That's being conscientious all right.

Just a few more roads to travel, a few more appointments to keep.

Then?

Why then it's kaput for the Democrats. They will have been put to shame. Their laundry of Dirty Tricks will make all the headlines, and prove them unfit for any office.

Finally, and even *CNN* and even the rest of the media will go with the story?

Blockbuster news like this can't be suppressed. The truth always gets out.

I don't think so.

Leave it to John Durham. When he talks, people listen.

Thank you, John Durham. He Da Man. Then what happens.

Biden? No shot. Trump sails in, this time winning every state, handily. Both houses of Congress fall to the GOP, needless to say.

Just a second. For that to happen, shouldn't Mr. Durham get the goods out there BEFORE the election? Otherwise, what's the use?

Huh?

After the election it's too late, too late to make a difference, the wrong people in, the right people out, all because John Durham failed to deliver.

He will deliver.

We were promised on time. But here we are, 2021. Zip, and who cares anymore. The waiting's been done. For nothing.

That's the point. Now you are catching on.

What's he hiding?

Now that… that is the question.

Look At the Bright Side, They Say

***Dec. 30, 2020 – 'Chin up, please.' 'Smile.' 'Remember what the Rebbe said,' wrote readers. But Trump and Netanyahu were such a great team.**

Polite criticism is always welcome.

A reader (one of many along the same vein) writes, "Dear Mr. Engelhard. Why so gloomy? I have read three of your books… *Indecent Proposal*, *The Bathsheba Deadline*, and the memoir *Escape from Mount Moriah*, and they all end hopeful. So as to your most recent column, why the despair? Chin up, please. We need you. Remember what the Rebbe said."

Yes, the Rebbe said, Goornisht is farfallen… nothing is hopeless… or as Yogi Berra translated it, it ain't over till it's over.

"So, it's up to G-d to sort things out, right?"

Amen.

"Who would have thought that in so short a span, four, soon five, even six Arab countries would come around to make peace with Israel? Did you see this coming?"

Honestly, no. I am amazed. If only some of that normalization between Jew and Arab would rub off within the camp and stop the political heckling between Jew and Jew. Too often the political clouds obscure the glory that is Israel, the people and the Land. Every day someone else wants to bring down the government… check out Caroline Glick… and the world is watching, and wondering – now that they have, why spoil a good thing?

"There you go being negative again."

Maybe you've got the wrong address. Try Caroline's Complaint Department. She suffers terribly from being too clear-eyed and astute.

"With clear eyes, you would agree that miracles do happen."

Of course… but there are several types of miracles; Providence in a bang, or behind the scenes. It helps when the right person comes along. Moses, for example. Trump is no Moses… nobody is… but it

---

* Originally published in *Arutz Sheva* English site (israelnationalnews.com).

does appear that Trump, together with Netanyahu, were chosen for a particular task for a particular time, and the results are in, beautifully.

"Then why so gloomy? Read your own books."

I was having a bad day. The wrong man got elected… by hook and by crook.

"Do you really believe that with Biden as president, it's really the end of the world?"

Not immediately. Give him time.

"Are you aware that his grandkids are Jewish?"

Yes, but not really. And they don't sit in his Cabinet. John Kerry does.

"We've had worse, and survived. Remember Obama?"

"Who can forget. But they keep coming back."

"Faith, man! In your own *Indecent Proposal*, you have this marvelous section where Joshua Kane summons King David to ask him why he is being punished. David explains that Joshua has it all wrong. Joshua's flaw… the punishment, if you will… is that he lacks faith, and faith is a two-way street. You wrote this."

I was having a good day.

"You've had many as a writer. Your readers depend on your best days, and they bless your successes."

If only the world stood still. All of us who write commentary too often take our cue from the latest headline, which almost always portends doom. We ride it when we forget that everything has its time; re Koheles. The good and the bad take turns. On Sunday Trump won't sign the Relief Bill and America is ruined; Monday he signs it and America is saved. We are guilty… myself included… of forgetting that tomorrow is another day.

"Good line."

It's from Margaret Mitchell, *Gone with the Wind.*

"So there is hope. Even when all seems lost. You say so yourself. In your own books. So you are an optimist."

Today, maybe. Tomorrow… who knows?

Let's Hope the *NY Post* is Right and I'm Wrong

***Dec. 17, 2020 – Remember Fukuyama writing that this is "the end of history," that the world has come to its senses?. So the *NY Post* says BDS is dead.**

Just when I started to despair, about everything, along comes the *New York Post*'s Op-ed editor, Sohab Ahmari, to say, so far as Israel, everything's going to be just fine.

His column of the other day, runs with this headline – "Trump's peace deals mean the anti-Israel boycott movement [BDS} is dead."

So says an optimist. If only it were so, says me, a pessimist, and I hate to bring this up, but pessimists get it right about 80 percent of the time.

We get no kick saying, "I told you so."

But Francis Fukuyama was wrong. He wrote that we've approached "the end of history" because post-Cold War, the world has come to its senses.

No more battles to be fought because "tolerant democracies" are sprouting up all over, and if I'm off target with his message, so is he. He has since retreated from so sunny a point of view.

I hope the *Post*'s Ahmari never has to second guess himself upon his own upside view regarding the end of BDS. He is right to cheer an Age of Aquarius ("a coming together on our planet") at this time of normalization and tranquility between Israel and the UAE, Bahrain, Sudan, Morocco, and more to come.

Yes, thanks to Trump, and another big hand for teammate Prime Minister Benjamin Netanyahu.

If only the planet would quit spinning… backwards.

A pessimist will tell you that, alas, Trump is out, and Biden is in, and so all bets are off the table. John Kerry, Susan Rice, and that whole gang are back, and getting ready to pounce.

---

* Originally published in *Arutz Sheva* English site (israelnationalnews.com).

John Brennan and James Comey are licking their chops.

My next column ought to be – "Waiting for Godot and the Durham Report" for the low-down on the swamp that never arrives.

They are not finished with America, nor with Israel.

Who told you so? I told you so. In the weeks leading up to the election, I kept telling good friend and top author Linda Shelnutt that Trump's campaign is failing.

The Democrats are up to something.

Linda kept saying not to worry. Trump's got everything in hand. Yes, he knows crookedness is afoot, and he's on top of that, too. Trump is a shoo-in.

There you go… and among pessimists there is the standard belief that everything that can go wrong, will go wrong, and so it does, and so it did.

Here is what we do not believe, that in the end, talent and goodness will prevail. Pessimists laugh when they hear this. Very funny.

Millions of talented people are never heard from, and the same number of good people never get a chance, but rather get trashed, scorned, and spurned.

I say this after reading Barbara Amiel's *Friends and Enemies*, a bravely written cautionary tale about what happened to her and husband Conrad Black. (Lovers of Israel, both.)

Think the Book of Job.

What happened to them can happen to anyone once the Establishment (aka the swamp) for no good reason, decides to dump on you with a ton of bricks.

So something else we don't trust… people in authority, people in charge, people with titles and degrees who know nothing, or know but don't care, or care only to do harm.

Does it sometimes feel that the cheats are everywhere and in control of everything? It's in all the channels and in all the papers.

That attitude may be so for being a Child of the 1960s. But being an adult of 2020… the world of Pelosi, Hunter, Joe, Swalwell… inspires no confidence that anything has changed.

Nor does a rigged election where no judge comes to the rescue, offer much hope that change is over the horizon.

I'll take Martin Amis' word that to be a true pessimist, it helps to be Jewish, and so I remember growing up in Montreal and coming home with a black eye every day.

That was courtesy of the French gangs who waited for the Jewish kids before and after school.

Did that stop the harassment? For a time, yes. But it was never really safe, and it never really is safe, and it never really ends. They only regroup.

So bless Sohab Ahmari for his optimism. But fate has other plans and I know other things.

Hunter, Pelosi, Swalwell, Omar – Pick A Scandal

***Dec. 11, 2020 – The crime of the century began in US newsrooms. The media are the villains, guilty of fixing an election as never before in US history.**

Let's pretend you're the editor of a major American newspaper and one day find yourself swamped with four stories, each worthy of a stop-the-presses headline.

Can't run them all… not all at once. You'll need your nose-for-news to feature which scandal tops them all as being most despicable.

Let's pretend further that you are an honest and fearless journalist, which mathematically puts you in the one percent category. Pretty near one-of-a-kind.

But as we said… fearless… and here she comes again, Ilhan Omar (D-MN), always with a story… a who's who between husband and brother… and this time a real whopper.

Then of course those insinuations of hers that Jews are money-hungry when, of all people, we read that when it comes to money, no one scoops it off the table as smoothly as she does.

She can smell a "Benjamin" a mile away.

I am not good with math, nor with money, so I rely on the *New York Post* to explain how it works with her, this money-grubbing cookie from Somalia who learned awfully fast how to game the American Enterprise system… and how to spread even stimulus money, intended for needy Americans… among family.

That would definitely be my top story. How about this for a headline? – "From dirt poor, to filthy rich."

However, within hours, along comes the story that tells how Hunter Biden, son of Joe, is under federal investigation for tax fraud related to his "overseas business."

What business? Don't ask. The media certainly didn't. Word of the shenanigans could have spoiled it for Joe and kept Trump in the White

* Originally published in *Arutz Sheva* English site (israelnationalnews.com).

House another four years.

There is also a grand jury looking into Hunter's "business"... specifically as tied to China... and, just a guess, as tied to Joe, Hunter's dear old dad.

But now Hunter's follies are trickling out and what looks bad for Hunter could look worse for Joe, the man who would be president... but already under a cloud.

If you ask me, that is the topper.

But wait. Does the name Eric Swalwell ring a ball... the same bell that tolls for Adam Schiff? Not yet for Schiff, but Karma has found Swalwell.

Swalwell (D-CA) was the congressman who, high on smugness, never missed a chance to accuse President Trump of being a spy for Russia.

He was dead wrong on Trump, of course, but when it comes to spies, Swalwell should know. He's been caught dallying with an alleged Chinese spy.

We don't know what sweet nothings were whispered and exchanged, but for sure he is a compromised member of the House, and of the House Intelligence Committee.

Not Foreign Relations?

Anyway, that... Swalwell... should surely be the boldfaced banner.

However, Nancy Pelosi pretty much said, "Let them eat cake," when she admitted that she sat on a stimulus package intended for starving Americans... because it might help Donald Trump.

That is as low as it gets... except...

As we suggested in this column, a day too early, the entire election could have gone the other way if voters had been told about any of these wrongdoings... mainly the Biden scandal.

But the media suppressed the story. The media are the villains over and above all the rest... guilty of colluding and fixing an election as never before in American history.

In a perfect world, every single editor and reporter who had a hand in this would stand trial and punishment for the crime of duping the American people.

The crime of the century began in this nation's newsrooms... with no end in sight.

Dancing in the Dark... Thanks to Big Media

***Dec. 8, 2020 – How Big Media's Iron Curtain feeds us spoonfuls of one-sided information to keep us knowin' nothin'.**

Turns out my neighbor up the road never heard about the Hunter/Joe Biden scandal that weeks ago was all the rage on the *New York Post*, and later *Fox News*.

That's the one where Hunter allegedly served as bagman for himself and his dad off money scooped up from China, Ukraine and Russia.

"How come you didn't know?" I asked this neighbor.

"Never heard of it," he said proudly. "I don't read the *Post*. I only read the *Times*, and I never watch *Fox News*."

If he knew the story, would he still have voted for Biden?

"It would have been something to consider."

Yes, it would… and I read somewhere that more than 60 percent who voted never heard of it, either.

Nor were they aware of the anti-Israel characters Biden is filling his cabinet… from a pool of Democrats now famous for their tolerance of anti-Semites.

Israel is properly bracing for a Biden administration as if a tsunami is looming.

Nor were voters hip to the fact that it was Nancy Pelosi who refused to sign on for a stimulus bill for millions of impoverished Americans… because it might help Donald Trump.

Makes you wonder what else they don't know when all they read is *The New York Times*, all they watch is *CNN*, and all they believe is Big Media…*CBS, NBC, ABC, PBS, NPR.*

Together those broadsheet and broadcast titans are determined to keep most of America dancing in the dark. This is after Big Media descends its Iron Curtain.

---

* Originally published in *Arutz Sheva* English site (israelnationalnews.com).

At what point do people get corrupted? I ask as someone who used to be proud of his role in journalism. I know the business… and can't remember it ever being this shoddy.

Suppressing the news… burying the story… welcome to the New Journalism… as we see *CNN* chief Jeff Zucker instruct his staff to ignore the Hunter/Joe scandal… nor to "humanize" Trump.

Same goes at *The New York Times* under Dean Baquet. Same all over.

They do it with no regret, no shame. The news is theirs to fiddle. The bosses? They actually tell their staffers to deceive and to lie. The staffers? They are just "following orders" – and where have we heard that before?

The trick is to dish Americans with spoonfuls of one-sided information, in order to keep us illiterate, or barefoot and pregnant, as they would say in the hills of Kentucky. Then, speaking of the Bible Belt, there must be some broken-hearted reporters remorseful enough to fess up for the sins of dirty reportage.

In their hearts they know they are wrong.

I've written a hundred columns on this, on media mendacity, mainly on media bias against Israel, but election finagling is yet another plunge.

The other day, I made the mistake of tuning into *ABC-TV*. The reporter said, "President Trump continues his made-up stories about election fraud."

Reporters now have license to interpret straight news… while disputing everything the President says.

Fact-checking was never done on the spot. Only after all the facts were in.

So next question… does anybody know that for the first time in ages it is relatively calm in the Middle East as to Israel and its neighbors, and that domestically, we are energy independent?

Trouble is, those were largely Trump (and Netanyahu) successes and therefore made no sound. The media would rather cover-up than cover a rightful story.

So no wonder nobody knows nothin'.

How do they sleep at night, these people who hide the news, or give the news so crooked aforethought? Do they go home at night and say to themselves, "Job well done?"

Or do they have a conscience that awakens them at night with nightmares over "What have I done? What am I doing?"

Besides Bari Weiss, who left the *NY Times* in disgust, and a few others, who else comes to decry the cynical rot decaying today's newsrooms?

Check out Sodom to find out what happens when even 10 righteous persons can't be found.

Political Sanity... Anyone, Anywhere?

***Dec. 3, 2020 – Dear Israel – you do not have to do everything we do. We are flattered, but this is not the best time to play follow the leader.**

So it's back to that – Prime Minister Benjamin Netanyahu must go.

How many times are they going to keep trying? Well, this would be the fourth, in under two years.

Israel, at the moment, is doing okay so far as peace and security, thanks to some wonderful teamwork between President Trump and Netanyahu in terms of rapprochement between Israel and her neighbors, the UAE and others, but the politicians won't leave well enough alone. No, there must be chaos. There must be upheaval. There must be reckoning.

Led, it appears, by Benny Gantz and friends, there's a serious move afoot to dissolve the Knesset in order to dissolve Netanyahu, and hence possibly another round of elections.

You've heard this before? Don't blame me… and yes, together, we are all hearing it again… again, and again, and again.

Gantz, by the way, already serves as defense minister, and as alternate prime minister, eventually to get the seat, but not soon enough, apparently.

So it's back to Netanyahu's "corruption" and "indictment" for cigars, and his desire for more leniency from the clamorous Hebrew press, and whatever else they can cook up.

For all that heckling, might as well be Trump we are talking about… as someone who gets nothing but incoming day after day. Still.

They're even angling to put Trump on trial AFTER he leaves office for the crime of being Donald Trump, and same goes, we hear, for Netanyahu.

Dear Israel – you do not have to do everything we do. We are flattered, but this is not the best time to play follow the leader.

---

* Originally published in *Arutz Sheva* English site (israelnationalnews.com).

Right now, politically, we are so dysfunctional that we have no right to teach anybody about anything.

Now it is Georgia on our minds.

Soon, Jan. 5, voters in Georgia will decide who will run the Senate, which means partly the Congress, which means the Republicans, and if it falls to the Democrats, we all fall down.

It means that Biden will have a free hand to do anything he wants, and with John Kerry back in the picture, nobody is safe. Nobody in America. Nobody in Israel. Nobody in the world.

He's to be in Biden's cabinet as the expert on climate and on everything that walks, crawls and flies.

Kerry… the "architect" of Obama's Iran Deal, which forked over billions for the mullahs to enrich their uranium, their pockets, their Hezbollah, their global terrorism… Kerry is by far the stupidest or most sinister US politician, ever. The prospect of having him back in action, is terrifying… as we see already through Biden's readiness to get back to the old Iran Deal as manufactured by Kerry. Disaster.

"Bad for America, bad for Israel, bad for the world," Netanyahu warned the US Congress back on March 2015 – but perfectly all right for Biden 2020 and beyond.

Voter fraud did this? Oh, surely.

The same scoundrels who gave Trump no rest all these years… you expected them to keep hands off an election… THE election?

Rather, this is what they'd been plotting in the back rooms since, and even before, Trump got sworn in.

I say "back rooms" but the fix was in right out in the open… starting with the free-for-all "mail in ballots" racket. So that everybody can vote, by hook or by crook.

All that, while the whole world has been watching… watching the superpower of freedom decompose into third world harlotry.

Biden's other cabinet picks are beginning to scare people, and, probably too late, people are starting to miss the good old days under Trump.

Yes, Megyn Kelly, who won't speak to me ever since I wrote that quick novel *News Anchor Sweetheart* imagining what it must be like being married to her, now speaks up for Trump.

For some time, she was his number one media nemesis. She has come around.

We seem to agree that as Trump won the people, he was never a fit for the Establishment.

Trump, even as president, and for all his successes, was always the outsider, and apparently, through no fault of his own, it will cost him.

To lose Netanyahu under the same circumstances would be a double kick to the head.

Barack Obama's 760-Page Love Story

***Nov. 29, 2020 – The book is a perfect gift to Americans who believe that America was never special or great. Only the writer himself, Obama, is great.**

You would think that after two books about himself, Barack Obama would be finished with his story, but no, there was more, 760 pages about himself in *A Promised Land.*

A title like that you'd expect from Theodor Herzl, since that term… promised land… has always meant a particular place, specifically Israel, and Obama will never be mistaken for a Zionist.

For that it's back to Herzl, who announced his vision and advocacy through the book, *The Jewish State*.

It was originally a pamphlet, and runs 96 pages. That was all Herzl needed to kick off a campaign, a summons to Go Forth, that led to the creation of Israel, and it succeeded because it was a story about a people, rather than a self-serving autobiography about a singular man… in which his writing on Israel, by the way, Obama gets nearly everything maliciously wrong.

The book is a perfect gift to Americans who believe that America was never good, exceptional, or great. Only the writer himself, Obama, is great.

What you get in Obama's latest door-stopper is a love story. Obama loves Obama. He will tell you about it in print, or through audio, I am told, that runs 28 hours.

That's like watching a man comb his hair for 28 hours. If music comes with the oratory, perhaps Carly Simon's *You're So Vain.*

Pity the editor who was in no position to tell a former president, and a man still so full of himself, "But, sir, is there anywhere we can cut?"

"Your job."

So no cuts, apparently. So maybe it's in there who he really is. We still don't know.

---

* Originally published in *Arutz Sheva* English site (israelnationalnews.com).

Not sure how he appeared out of nowhere except for a talent to ingratiate himself from one step up the ladder to another. He knew how to work people. He knew how to hobnob the swells. He knew how to make up stories for the lack of substance or pedigree. He'd be their diversity gem for cocktail hour.

Columbia U can't or won't produce any of his grades or papers. The media never asked, never bothered, never cared. They had their man. O come let us adore him.

(Of Michelle Obama's illiterate university papers, someone quipped, "We don't know what language this is.")

When Muhammed Ali proclaimed, "I am the greatest," he said it with a wink and a smile. Obama isn't joking.

You can be sure that the boys and girls in the media lap up every word of Obama's opus. Their reviews are already in and the frenzy of adjectives keeps piling up. Naturally, for them, and him, the Nobel Prize for Literature is next, and as deserving as the Nobel he got for Peace, all for showing up with nothing to show.

For eight years they deified him, and the worship starts all over again now that he is back with a bang. His book is number one. So, in terms of the Swamp, he is number one.

Obama… his narcissism now so blatant… never liked being upstaged, even by Biden, and so now we understand, more fully, why he resented and detested Donald Trump so terribly much.

Trump removed him from the spotlight, a development utterly intolerable for a man who feeds off adulation… and dines off the applause from a Jimmy Kimmel Late Night audience. There he cracked that the Navy Seals may have to be called into action to remove President Trump from the White House. The big-eyed grin when he said that masked a mile of catty bitterness.

So much for a "gracious" transfer of power… and behold how he glorifies himself now that he's making the rounds for his book and back in the saddle, politically.

Would it, then, come as a surprise to find that all along it was Obama who was behind all the Dirty Tricks against Trump? Not Strzok. Not Schiff. Not Comey.

Obama gave the order.

Obama refused to step aside, and thanks to Michael Goodwin, we learn that Obama and his wife have signed up with *Netflix* for Specials intended to further slam President Trump.

The man knows how to keep a grudge.

On his last hours in office he socked it to Prime Minister Netanyahu when he, Obama, refused to block UN Resolution 2334, which, on December 2016, named Israeli "settlements," even East Jerusalem, illegal. A US to Israel stab in the back no one saw coming, even from an administration seldom on the best of terms with the Jewish State.

Months earlier, March 2015, Netanyahu had addressed the US Congress and there spelled out his dismay at the Obama Administration's (misbegotten) Iran Deal, which he labelled bad for America, bad for Israel, bad for the world… even worse for Obama, apparently, who took it as a personal jab, for which he'd one day get even, and did, at UN Res. 2334.

The security of our two nations be damned, so long as Obama got his comeuppance. That's one for the books, though likely not his book.

As for me, I'm picking up a copy, of Herzl's *The Jewish State*. Thanks for calling it to my attention, Mr. Obama.

Amanpour's Blood Libel of the Month

***Nov. 17, 2020 – For years, *CNN* was PLO headquarters, and Hanan Ashrawi was a dial away from Ramallah to blood libel Israel. Now they're in the building.**

That was quite a mouthful from *CNN*'s Christiane Amanpour, harnessing President Trump's first four years in the White House to the two days of Kristallnacht, Nov. 9-10, 1938.

Right here about Kristallnacht, because I don't feel like going into it all over again, coming as I do from a family that went through the whole thing – as if she'd give a damn.

Right here about what she said and Israel's reaction. She doesn't need me to popularize her odious rant.

People want her to apologize. Mort Klein at ZOA wants her fired. I'm with Mort, for all the good that will do, as after all, at *CNN* they're thinking what she's thinking. Certainly, about Trump. About the Holocaust, I don't know. *CNN* has plenty of Jews high and low, but they sold out years ago, and for a job of journalism that has no conscience.

Should she apologize? She did, but I don't care. We know what's in her heart, and that's enough, or too much, for me.

Anyway, you cannot come clean after airing thoughts like this. The stain will always be there, and it will always be part of her legacy. Her bed to sleep in.

What should offend me more, the Holocaust inference, or the Trump reference? I don't know. As a Jewish-American Trump supporter, I'll take a spoonful of each.

By way of saying that we do not watch *CNN* in our home. So we do not know what goes on in that universe, and when something like this gets out, we say, "consider the source."

For decades, *CNN* was PLO headquarters, where Hanan Ashrawi was only a dial away from Ramallah to blood libel Israel.

Now they are in the building. Well, they always were, but Amanpour's obscenity amounts to doubling down.

---

* Originally published in *Arutz Sheva* English site (israelnationalnews.com).

Oddly, by the way, she said what she said at about the time when Biden's Antifa and BLM goons were beating up MAGA men, women and children on the streets of DC.

Shades of the Reich's Brown Shirts, if you ask me… speaking of Kristallnacht.

But I do not think Amanpour is hip enough to get the timing, nor the connection.

I have read the articles where she is being implored to understand the pain she has caused by bringing up the Holocaust… all useless to closed minds and deaf ears.

You can lead a cow across all the wonders of the world, but when it comes back it is still a cow.

I offer up Roger Waters for Exhibit A when it comes to scoffers of the Jews, and Robert De Niro when it comes to perversion against Trump.

Nothing will change these people, which is why I don't even try. They will always be among us, and if it wasn't Amanpour, it would be someone else.

Seems to come up about once a month; someone uses the Holocaust as cash for a cheap trick.

Let them yap. We've been called names before. We've been called names throughout. I was called names growing up as a kid in Montreal.

There was a time when they had us on the run, and when their slanders scored direct hits.

But it doesn't count anymore, because we've got Israel, and they don't, and with Israel we've got the power…. no matter where we live… against their sticks and stones.

That's the entire story – Israel. With it, everything is different. Let them sneer. We're big. They're small. They exist only if we let them. They can't reach us. They can't touch us.

Israel – our shield and secret weapon against all slurs.

Am Yisrael Chai.

No Voter Fraud, Says *The NYT*

***Nov. 15, 2020 – How stupid are we supposed to be?**

We're supposed to believe the same crowd that gave us four years of false charges against President Trump has suddenly turned kosher.

Not just kosher, but super kosher… glatt kosher… of the kind blessed by *The New York Times* with the following seal of approval… "No Evidence of Voter Fraud in Any of the 50 States."

That, of course, is a bald-faced falsehood. Suspicious ballots… into the millions… are under review in all the contested states… PA, AZ, GA, NV, WI, MI.

Some 600,000 votes in Michigan that were marked for Trump ended up for Biden. Oh, machine malfunction. Aha. Funny how it never malfunctions in Trump's favor.

Plus, not a single state has yet certified the vote.

But typical of the *Times* to know best... a paper that does try to fool all the people all the time… and too often comes too close to succeeding.

Millions buy in, often not knowing what they're buying.

So if you voted for Biden, you may be a decent, loyal Democrat or… you may have been brainwashed. Newspapers, the *Times* in particular, can have that effect.

Probably your uncle, usually at Thanksgiving, won his arguments by forcefully insinuating – "It says so in the paper." And that was that.

Can the paper ever be wrong? If it's the *Times*, frequently.

The same paper saw no evidence of wrongdoing on the part of Hunter Biden, nor even Hillary Clinton and the 33,000 emails she unlawfully destroyed.

The same paper saw no evidence of mass starvation in Ukraine when millions died from famine under Stalin's Five-Year Plan.

Walter Duranty, the paper's Man in Moscow, used the power of the press to misinform and to deceive, but he was so good at it that he got

---

* Originally published in *Arutz Sheva* English site (israelnationalnews.com).

himself a Pulitzer. Then the truth came out, and the *Times* admitted that Duranty's reporting was disgraceful… but refuses, to this day, to revoke the Pulitzer. Lesson learned? Never.

The same paper, which could have alerted FDR and awakened the nation, instead mentioned the Holocaust while it was happening sparingly and reluctantly, which is more than journalistic malpractice, but a sin of Biblical proportions. Lives could have been saved. The rails to Auschwitz could have been bombed.

Yes, books have been written about the *Times*' infamy – but nothing sticks and nothing gets fixed.

People still believe what they read in the paper, if it's the *Times*. For the Networks, the *Times* is the received word.

Sunday's headline becomes Monday's talking points… and the official policy of the Democrat Party.

"There is no evidence of voter fraud" for instance continues to be the chant all across the channels.

It is all coordinated between the *Times*, the media, and the Party, and it is never happenstance, not while Dean Baquet is in charge.

Outside of the president, Dean Baquet may be the most powerful man in America.

He is the most powerful Democrat in America. Runs most of it behind the scene, like a ventriloquist, as executive editor at *The New York Times*.

Nobody in the Party makes a move before consulting Dean Baquet. He sets the table.

Upon Trump's ascent four years ago, Dean Baquet gathered his staff… almost all of them fanatically Liberal… and instructed them to forget Old School Journalism.

Instead, they were to focus on their "feelings." Which is the most flagrant departure from the norms of American Journalism since Benjamin Franklin… or even Adolph Ochs.

Objectivity can be such a drag.

So it was like recess, now that they could go wild and OPINE even on the Front Pages and let it rip, how they felt about Trump and all Republican/Conservatives. Never anything good.

These days they feel that “there is no evidence of voter fraud” and so, case closed, we are to accept Joe Biden as our president, no further word needed, because?

Because it says so in the paper.

Israel is Heading into A Perfect Storm

***Nov. 10, 2020 – After Trump, who watches Israel's back? Hearing Biden's crew, I am already nostalgic for Trump.**

For all these four years there was a sense of warmth and comfort knowing that Israel was going to be all right so long as Trump was in office.

Israel… certainly America… would be tucked in safely so long as Trump was boss. No more sleepless nights with John Kerry and the entire Obama gang on the prowl.

That nightmare was over. So we thought. So I thought, and I guess I should speak for myself since mine are entirely private views.

So that's how it was during the dark days when nearly every Democrat was Israel's judge and executioner… and no need to mention Omar and the Squad.

That was to be done. Finished. Old Business. Never to come around again. It did not occur to me… it dared not occur to me… that here we go again.

If indeed Biden wins, the same people are BACK… and coming with a vengeance. They will be coming with scores to settle.

They won't be happy until all debts are paid.

A perfect storm is coming.

Say it ain't so? But it is.

I am already nostalgic. Like Young Love that only happens once, I miss those four golden years when between Trump and Israel it was nearly all honeymoon. I thought it would go on forever, forgetting that presidents and administrations come and go. But not this one, I believed. This one would stay. At least four more years. How silly of me, I know.

But that's how comfortable I felt knowing Trump was in office and all is right with the world. Before that, everything was so wrong.

We had been through eight years of curses. How about an equally long run of blessings?

---

* Originally published in *Arutz Sheva* English site (israelnationalnews.com).

Along came Trump. Thank G-d. Thank G-d. Thank G-d.

No harm could come to the Jewish State so long as Trump was its Night Watchman. Over and over again he proved himself more than a friend, but as Israel's brother.

It's the kind of older brother who puts his arm around you, and says, "Don't worry, kid, I'm always at your side."

Yes, he was… and speaking of Trump in the past tense is verily heartbreaking.

By only a few thousand (suspicious) votes, the world is turned upside-down. Though the media would rather you ignore the recounts that could change everything back again, and set the world straight again.

Like Gary Cooper in *High Noon*, Trump was that lonesome figure who acted heroically for Israel while the rest of the town cravenly fell away, one by one, and deserted him.

He would be Israel's cowboy… traditionally the mythic he-man who in one person reflects the ideal American.

A reader writes: "I always thought I was stronger than I feel now, but the thought of Biden, Harris, the Clintons and Obamas, the Schiffs and Schumers all partying with the Ayatollas and Abbas.... the licking of chops by all those who literally own Biden and Harris.... it's tough to stomach."

Do you understand what he means? Of course you do. So do I, particularly the thought on strength, and how at this terrible moment strength has been taken from us.

Taken from me, for sure.

Trump at my side, I felt free to take on all of Israel's enemies, and I felt safe to express my love for Israel cheerfully, full-throated and unconditionally.

I knew the informers were watching. But they did not have the power. Trump had the power. So I had the power. So we all had the power who bled and rejoiced for Israel.

We celebrated Israel without fear of being placed on an enemies' list – which is being developed by AOC and her crew, even as we speak.

This will take some getting used to… a world without Trump, nor pity.

Bonus Engelhard Classics

Engelhard's Guide to Writing
(for a world gone berserk)

"Everyone is a genius at something.
The trick is to find out what it is."

[*]**NEW YORK**, September 18, 2013 – Tips on writing, from any writer, should be ignored. But here we go anyway because the world needs you.

1. Keep it simple.

2. Write for yourself. If you do not trust yourself, write for your best friend.

3. Do not write for the public. There is no such thing anyway.

4. Never worry about bad reviews or spiteful comments. Recognize that there are quite a number of stupid people out there who think they should be heard.

5. Every book – even a novel – is really a long newspaper article. That is where the word novel comes from – news. So the first task is to come up with a lede. Yes lede, for lead. Never mind why we put it like this. But once you have the opening thought, the rest follows. Moreover, every type of writing begins and ends with journalism – fact upon fact.

6. Drop the embellishments. Write the way you speak.

7. Do you like sex? If you are British or Jewish obviously you do not indulge. Otherwise, fear not, but write it as if you invented it.

8. Write your heart out. After that, cut it by half. You will be amazed to find that by subtracting you are adding.

9. Free yourself from worrying how your book will end. A book is smart. It knows when it is done.

---

[*] Originally published in the Communities section of *The Washington Times*.

10. Never approach your typing unwashed. Remember, writing is prayer; writing is holiness.

11. Consider yourself special, but also typical. Whatever hurts you, hurts the entire world. You embody the universe. Your job is to light up the place.

12. Yes, the world is tumbling all around us. Nothing makes sense. Remember, a simple candle brightens a darkened room. Be humble, but remember that in a world gone berserk, we need you. But never mind the answers. The questions you ask are more important.

13. Surprise yourself from one page to the next. If you can't surprise yourself, no way you can astonish your reader.

14. Write the outline to make your editor happy. Then discard.

15. Begin by approaching the mainstream (NY) publishers. After they have thanked you and rejected you, get it done by small press and/or digitally.

16. Read the classics. Then read the pulps. Read everything. Keep writing. Eventually you will find your own voice.

17. Study the movies. Screenplays show you how to condense.

18. Find the type of writing that suits you best. You are good at describing? Describe. You are good at dialogue? Do that.

19. Are you sure you want to write a novel? If nothing but dialogue keeps happening, maybe you wrote a screenplay.

20. Do not be a perfectionist. Perfection never comes. So why wait? The Liberty Bell is most famous for its crack.

21. Be kind to yourself as you write. Imagine your mother peering over your shoulder as you type – not your mother-in-law.

22. Grammar is important, but people forgot to tell William Faulkner and James Joyce about this and they did okay.

23. You will find that virtually every paragraph that runs five sentences or more can and should be cut to two.

24. If you write a sentence and must think it over more than three times, it is sending you a signal that it does not work. So give it a fresh start.

25. Actors should never be caught acting. Same goes for writers. Never get caught *writing*.

But the first rule to remember is that you stand on the shoulders of literary giants who came before you, but still, you are on your own.

Now shut up and write.

Salinger is Back and PBS Has Got Him

***NEW YORK**, August 27, 2013 – The theme of despair runs throughout literary and even biblical history. So J.D. Salinger, who excelled in writing about the melancholy of human existence, mainly so in *The Catcher in the Rye*, was not the first to approach the topic of futility.

Raised as a rich kid in Manhattan, something changed when he returned from serving heroically in World War II. Was it all of it or was it mostly *Dachau*? We can argue that after that singular experience *he came back a Holocaust survivor*, and as such we will never know what he knew and we will never know what he saw – except what he told his daughter, that the smell of burnt flesh never leaves your nostrils.

Salinger left us in self-imposed silence some three years ago at age 91, but he still manages to make headlines. A new Weinstein Company production of Salinger will be distributed to 200 theaters Sept 6 in advance of a PBS documentary set for January. The accompanying biography, written by dubious experts David Shields and Shane Salerno ("slapdash," according to *The New York Times*) is to emerge in print September 3.

The buzz has it that Salinger wasn't done. More Salinger books are coming one of these days, but never too soon for Salinger buffs. Apparently, if the reports are accurate, Holden Caulfield and members of the Glass family will be with us again, updated and refreshed. If the reports are inaccurate, this won't be the first time high hopes were dashed.

As for this Salinger devotee, no biography on Salinger says it better than Kenneth Slawenski, who, it appears, holds to the opinion "not so fast" about a Salinger Second Coming. Slawenski's biography is still the authoritative word on Salinger and his chapters on Salinger's wartime exploits can perhaps be duplicated, never surpassed.

But what is it about Salinger that so fascinates us? We never stopped bothering him when he was alive and when dead we will not let him rest in peace.

---

* Originally published in the Communities section of *The Washington Times*.

He wrote those novellas and those short stories – all of it first-rate American literature – and then only one full-length novel, *The Catcher in the Rye*.

Repeatedly we are told that *Catcher* is about "adolescent angst." Really? Is that why, published in 1951, the book still sells around a million copies a year?

There must be something else, something deeper that keeps us coming back and wanting more. I suggest that Salinger hit on the very thing that we would rather not touch by that touches us all – despair. Remember, happiness is only a pursuit. Despair comes without an invitation and we all know the feeling. This is the truth Salinger had the guts to reveal. He may have couched it in teenage lingo, but *The Catcher in the Rye* can be read and appreciated at any age.

Stylistically, Salinger was mostly on his own, but owes much gratitude to Mark Twain and Walt Whitman and others who articulated American vernacular.

Onto the depth of despair, here Salinger had tradition on which to rely.

In *Ecclesiastes*, King Solomon was the first to awaken us to human frailty and futility. What profit is there in all this toil when we all come to the same end? Rich or poor, the same end awaits us all, and from wisdom to foolishness, it is all the same at the time of reckoning.

Centuries later Erasmus picked up the theme of futility, arguing in praise of folly, and in favor of foolishness above wisdom. It is the fool that gets it right.

Tolstoy admired the "holy fool."

Later on we come to F. Scott Fitzgerald, mostly in *The Crack-Up* and Samuel Beckett, mostly in *Waiting for Godot*, who extend the thought that everything is useless.

"I can't go on. I'll go on," from Beckett's *Unnamable.*

No wonder Salinger turned to Eastern Religion to find some purpose, namely the Vedantic branch of Hinduism.

Did he not know that Judaism is the original Eastern Religion?

Maybe he found the purpose, after all, and that is what is hidden in that great big box that we all want opened. Did he find the secret?

Hemingway never found the secret and by his own hand refused to go beyond 61 years.

In his last years, Salinger's search was a search for God, or simply godliness, a life of constant prayer. Did he not know that in Psalms King David is the father of prayer?

The sages who codified the 24 Books of Hebrew Scriptures tried to suppress King Solomon's *Ecclesiastes*, on the obvious notion that it was too pessimistic. They changed their minds and even declared that it was among the holiest books of all, because, despite harsh truth, it ends on a foundation of faith.

In his quest, did Salinger find that moment of divine clarity? Is this our pursuit and what keeps us waiting and wanting more?

In Praise of Jeff Bezos

*NEW YORK**, August 9, 2013 – By now most people know that Jeff Bezos took a giant step into the world of journalism by purchasing the *Washington Post*, and nobody covers all the ramifications of such a bold move better than my colleague Rick Townley here. Townley offers an overview and an appraisal that, in my view, is right on.

As a writer who was there nearly at the start, I may have something to add, and it is all good, good for Bezos, good for readers and very good for writers. That part, the part about writers, is seldom mentioned when talk gets around to Amazon, the online company that Bezos started back in 1995. A personal observation may be worthwhile, and it amounts to this:

Jeff Bezos saved books as much as Johannes Gutenberg saved printing.

Through Amazon, Bezos started off by selling just that, books. Today he sells everything under the sun, and nobody does it bigger or better.

But on publishing and bookselling, there has been talk that Amazon trampled the competition. That is nonsense. Publishers began losing traction back in the 1980s through faults all their own when the big fish began swallowing the small fish. Today, on Publishers Row in Manhattan, where once there were thousands of different and varied imprints – today there are five.

There are rumors that soon the Big Five will be whittled down further, to the Big Four. If you are a writer, good luck.

As for bookstores, same thing. The shops-on-the-corner began disappearing before Amazon came along, all through mergers, acquisitions and consolidations.

Amazon came in just in time. Millions of books that were destined to die, got sold. Thousands of writers out in the cold, got published.

I got the call (actually an email) around 1996/97 asking if I would mind having my books (starting with *Indecent Proposal*) listed and for sale on Amazon. Are you kidding? Of course! But there was nothing

---

* Originally published in the Communities section of *The Washington Times*.

so special about me. By the multitudes, writers from all over were invited to participate; their books listed and for sale.

Where has this been all our lives?

In those early years, Amazon introduced its Amazon Shorts program, where writers were urged to submit their short stories. In other words, if you wrote well enough, you were getting published – and what a new world was this for writers who had been teased and trifled by the big-time houses, and whose works were doomed from start to finish.

Now writers had a home. This is a big thing! Writing is tough enough. Getting published can be brutal in a world so uncaring. Hundreds, soon to be thousands, participated. Digitally, this is where I met some first-rate writers, John W. Cassell and Linda Shelnutt to name just two. We exchanged our stories, shared opinions, and a big bad world got friendlier.

A new universe of literature had opened up, and soon readers, actual readers, began buying our short stories and our books, digitally and in print.

All that was unthinkable until Amazon came on the scene.

Following the Shorts program, another new beginning – the Kindle. We know that readers love it, but writers love it even more, for Kindle offers another means to get published. No longer are writers at the mercy of the Big Five, whose doors always seem shut. Now writers can bypass the snobs and go directly to Kindle.

Even big name writers, fed up with the slow and grinding process of mainstream publishing, have turned to Kindle. This includes Pulitzer Prize winning author David Mamet. He went straight to Kindle with his latest, as have many others. This is, after all, the digital age.

Theologian Abraham Heschel provides a near perfect definition of a prophet. A prophet is a person "who knows what time it is."

Jeff Bezos is no prophet, okay. So what is his secret? He knew what time it was. The 21st Century.

Hemingway and A Lost Generation

*NEW YORK, July 2, 2013 – In the end, the will to die was stronger than the will to live. On the morning of July 2, 1961, Ernest Hemingway aimed a double-barreled, 12-guage shotgun at his head, pulled the trigger and thus ended the short happy life of America's most famous writer. He was 61 and we do not know what would-be books he took to his grave.

Fittingly, he often spoke of the power of silence, or as biographer Kenneth Slawenski reminds us about J.D. Salinger, the secret to great writing resides in the "fire between the words." On the temptation to write long, Hemingway remarked that there are times to resist and to "say no to a typewriter."

Was Hemingway a great writer? The greatest? That is an argument, so let us leave it at that, but without a doubt he was a prose stylist par excellence, even though his most beloved work, *The Old Man and the Sea,* was more poetry than prose, and it earned him the 1954 Nobel Prize.

He was the Babe Ruth of American literature. Often enough he did swat it out of the park. He was a boozer and a brawler but turned devotional when he sat down – or stood up – to write. Famed for that granite-like style, he claimed to have no style, only the blood, sweat and perseverance to cobble together the cleanest sentence possible. In virtually all his paragraphs there is a sense of urgency. This is also how he lived.

Writers who came along during his heyday and those that followed owe him a debt. Only with trembling fingers did we dare type even page one in the shadow of Henry James and Herman Melville. Hemingway taught us to be unafraid. By example, he proved that saying it simple, straight and true is far more authoritative than razzle-dazzle.

Thanks to his matter-of-fact articulation, we stopped being intimidated by the flowery prose of the past. If he could say it so plainly, so could we.

---

* Originally published in the Communities section of *The Washington Times*.

Depart from embellishments, was his message, just tell it *as it is* – and this was the lesson he learned early on from the *Kansas City Star*. Later, he complained that journalism "blunts the instrument" for fiction, and yet all his novels and short stories show the hand of newspaper reporting, like this, from the opening of *The Short Happy Life of Francis Macomber:*

"It was now lunch time and they were all sitting under the double green fly of the dining tent *pretending that nothing had happened.*" (Italics added by author)

Something did happen. So now we are drawn in, and in journalism that is a lede, or lead.

On war, Hemingway's novels do not match up against Tolstoy or James Jones. Sentence-by-sentence, however, Hemingway pioneered a unique American voice.

Hemingway illustrated that simplicity, directness and repetitiveness, if done wisely and properly, can be powerful literary tools. Surely he learned some of that from Gertrude Stein, "rose is a rose is a rose," but much of his rhythmic prose was biblically inspired, like this from King Solomon's *Ecclesiastes*:

"All is futility and vanity… A generation goes and a generation comes, but the earth endures forever."

One paradox follows another in the life of Ernest Hemingway. He is still America's most famous writer and yet, most of his years were spent overseas.

He was at war against nearly all his contemporaries, but gave time and even money to literary fledglings.

He was synonymous with virility but in his first novel, *The Sun Also Rises*, hero Jake Barnes cannot satisfy Lady Brett Ashley. Moreover, in real life Hemingway was stricken by bouts of impotence. A visit to a Catholic church cured him and he remained a somewhat devout Catholic until the end.

How did it all fall apart? He became depressed and paranoid. At the peak of his fame, wealth and glory, why the onset of despair? He must have known this from the wisdom of the Hebraic *Midrash*: "Man has no profit for all his toil under the sun, for life and fortune on this earth are transitory."

He complained that the FBI was tailing him. People said he was wrong. Turned out he was right. Depression and physical ailments made him increasingly incoherent and enfeebled. His doctors tried everything, including electroconvulsive therapy. Even at his worst, he was able to persuade them that he was well enough to go home, back to Ketchum, Idaho. A few days later he shot himself.

In accepting his Nobel Prize, by letter, he wrote: "Writing, at its best, is a lonely life."

Ernest Hemingway was not afraid of writing. He was only afraid of living.

Casino "Eye in the Sky" Knew You Before NSA

*WASHINGTON, DC, June 12, 2013 – If you get that creepy feeling that you are being watched, bet on it; you are.

The Shadow Knows. Nationwide, casinos have known you like a brother, or Big Brother, even before the FBI or the NSA or the DOJ or the IRS snuggled up to you without even a kiss. If they did not do it earlier, casinos certainly did it better in what is chillingly known by dealers and gamblers as "The Eye in the Sky."

Banks of surveillance monitors are up there atop every casino in the United States watching every move you make.

They will catch you misbehaving. They surely will catch you cheating and they won't call you Shirley. They will pick you out of a crowd and make you cry uncle. Gambling has always been a metaphor for life – sometimes you win, mostly you lose – and casinos have always served as a microcosm for life in the real world.

Apparently, we, that is, gamblers and non-gamblers alike, cannot be trusted to behave properly unless we are being shadowed. Acts of lawlessness are rare in the casino, any casino. People know. So they are careful. Does this argue in favor for the massive snooping going on in America today?

Heck no. Some privacy, please. We did not bargain for Sweet Land of Tyranny.

But already we are being far more cautious in the messages we send by text, email, and by telephone. That is good and that is bad. Bad because this is America and we ought to be able to say whatever we want. We should not be like so many other countries where people have to whisper.

We should not have language police.

So what's the good? Maybe it is time to bring it down a notch, all that unfiltered garbage talk that floats throughout the Internet, and maybe every idiot that has a grudge to announce against his neighbor

---

* Originally published in the Communities section of *The Washington Times*.

ought to think twice, and maybe every imbecile who has nothing to say but says it anyway ought to just shut up.

Has there ever been so much road rage in America, on and off the road? Has there ever been so much stupidity in 140 characters or less?

Consider it a gain if the "eye in the sky" stops the next fool from seeking his or her 15 Minutes of Infamy.

Headlines come and headlines go, but there is still nothing new under the sun. We have it from Eugene Ionesco and H. G. Wells and George Orwell and Arthur Conan Doyle who, through their fiction, saw what was coming – arbitrary and unrestrained use of power, as happened before and will happen again. Is this where we are headed?

Franz Kafka gave us a world where first we prosecute and then hear testimony. Are we there yet?

France's Robespierre was sure that everybody was *guilty* of *something* (and he had a point there) hence, White Terror, in which everybody spies on somebody else. We get an especially chilling quote from him, which goes something like this, "Show me 20 words written by any man and I will find reason to hang him."

That is something to think about if we allow our government to get out of hand – and also, this, from Hebrew Scriptures (Mishna):

"Know what is above you…an eye sees, an ear hears, and everything is recorded in a Book."

Scary.

Me and Esther Williams

[*]**WASHINGTON, DC**, June 7, 2013 – Right now she is probably teaching the angels how to swim. Esther Williams is dead. She left us last Thursday at the great age of 91.

I met her many years ago and am still star struck. Bill Holland, my editor at the *Burlington County Times* (NJ), scanned the newsroom and found no one else around. I was the new kid. "You'll do," he said even before handing me the assignment. A star had come to our neighborhood to promote her swimming pool business.

"How would you like to interview Esther Williams?" Bill asked.

Could this be a joke?

"There is no such person," I protested instinctively. "She is a movie star."

Where I came from, movie stars were not people. They were gods. Gods cannot be approached, and some of them were so magnified that their names alone signified a mystique that was strictly and awesomely American… names like Clark Gable, Gregory Peck, John Wayne, Elizabeth Taylor, and right there with them was Esther Williams!

Esther Williams – goddess of the waters!

Such divinities truly walked among us?

"Yes, there is such a person," said Bill, laughing, and off I went to the interview, dizzy with anticipation.

Apparently, then, celestial beings did come down once in a while to visit the world of mortals.

But I still thought it had to be a joke. Me? Esther Williams?

But there she was. No longer was she the young darling that swam in all those MGM extravaganzas. But she still radiated.

Oh brother did she radiate!

But I still had a job to do. I was here as a reporter, for gosh sakes.

I had a list of questions, but forget them all. My mind was zapped. I just stared at her.

The manager of the swimming pool operation, a terribly annoying man, hovered over me, afraid of what? Was he worried that I would

---

[*] Originally published in the Communities section of *The Washington Times*.

make a play for her? That would be logical. Was there a chance our eyes would meet, *me and Esther Williams*, and that the attraction would be so irresistible that, despite everything, we would link up and run off together?

That may have entered my mind, yes. Fernando Lamas – big deal! When you are 21 you want to have every woman.

But there would be no future for *me and Esther Williams.* I can't swim.

Finally, I came around and asked some questions – but only pertaining to the swimming pool business. Those had been my orders anyway, plus this tip-off: she was wearing a business suit. No bathing suit. Driving over, I had thought, catching Esther Williams – *Esther Williams*! – in a bathing suit would be as close as I'd ever get (at that time) to the entertainment divinity that is Hollywood.

There was so much I wanted to know. But I was an absolute tenderfoot. If I asked the wrong question, might she storm off?

Might word get back to Bill Holland, to have him say, "How dare you talk this way to a movie star?"

Anyway, that creepy manager kept breathing down my neck. I did ask her if she was planning to do any more movies. The guy tried to intercept. "I can answer for myself, thank you," she told him to brush him off. Offering a generous smile, she replied that yes, there will be other movies, and that I would be the first to know.

I have been waiting.

So now she is in heaven. But wasn't she there all along?

On Writing A Novel in Six Weeks

***NEW YORK**, March 28, 2013 – Jack Kerouac told people that he wrote *On the Road* in three weeks. Never mind Truman Capote's dig: "That's not writing; it's typing."

Is it possible to write a truly good or great novel in that period of time, in one non-stop flourish of heat and inspiration?

There is a catch to Kerouac's claim: He spent *seven years* on the road before he wrote *On the Road*, so all the material he included in the book was already distilled and waiting to pop.

I could argue both sides. On the one hand, a novel needs to be revised and polished a thousand times before it can be declared done. The other argument is that the first bloom, the first rush of excitement, tells the real story. Writing a novel is like being in love. Enjoy the romance and don't ask too many questions.

Love happens and novels happen by the same inexplicable combustion.

As a horseplayer will tell you, your first choice, follow your first instinct (there is no *second* instinct) is the most reliable, and when you start second-guessing yourself, you ruin the honest moment that came in a flash, a moment that will never come round again.

Kerouac chose his speedwriting method to attain spontaneous prose. He wanted to match the improvisational rhythm of jazz and bebop.

Conventional critics dismissed Kerouac and his fellow Beats, but today *On the Road* is deemed a classic.

Back in the mid-1800s in Russia, Fyodor Dostoyevsky had no choice but to write fast. Broke and desperate, he had 26 days to produce a completed novel. If he failed, the earnings from all his works over the next decade would revert to an exploitative publisher, Stellovsky, who insisted that the work be done by November 1, 1866, and not a moment past midnight.

Dostoyevsky met the deadline by dictating his prose to a stenographer, whom he later married, but when he presented the work at the

---

* Originally published in the Communities section of *The Washington Times*.

publisher's office, the publisher was conveniently not in. Dostoyevsky then rushed to a police station to have his manuscript certified in the nick of time. He called it Roulettenburg. We know it today as *The Gambler.*

This is now a minor classic. This writer, Dostoyevsky, had no qualms about degrading himself, and when he wrote about the harrowing days and nights at the roulette wheel in the flesh pots of Europe, he knew what he was talking about. This greatest of Russian writers, along with Tolstoy, was a gambling addict, prone to bad luck. That is partly why he'd been in debt in the first place.

The novel is largely autobiographical. Dostoyevsky had this novel in mind years before he found himself in desperate straits. Though the writing, the sprouting, took three weeks, there were years of seeding and planting. So we cannot say the writing was fast, only the typing.

The Gambler illustrates that really great novels proceed liberated and unafraid. They tell it uninhibited, blemished, warts and all. Even the hero can be as flawed as any villain. There are sections in the book that make the reader cringe, both for the blunt honesty of the hero and for the choppy, uneven prose. We can tell that it was rushed. But we are hooked *because* it is so honest and unvarnished.

Or as Hemingway said of Dostoyevsky in general, "How can a man write so poorly and still make you feel so deeply?"

Readers who follow these pages will recall that I confessed to having ditched a novel that wasn't working. But what I didn't say, for fear of the kibosh, was that the very next day I picked myself up and started all over again. I started a new novel. I finished it in six weeks. I sent it off to the publisher (typos and all) before I could change my mind.

I knew that if I let it sit I would re-work it to *perfection.* No, I would rather it be imperfect – imperfect but true.

But did I really write it in six weeks? Let's say I *typed* it in six weeks and started on it at the moment of a relentless brainstorm. But to get there, it took years of gathering material, consciously and subconsciously – material that was already percolating and seething in my mind for years, even decades. Then the right moment came for it to explode onto the page. I will only say it too is about a hero obsessed by an addiction.

On average I spend two years on a novel. *Indecent Proposal* took three years. By far my shortest work, the memoir *Escape from Mount Moriah*, took 20 years.

This new one just burst. Is it good, bad, great? Usually it takes generations to find out.

My enemies will surely be waiting for the result. But we also have friends.

Don Imus to Frank Rich: Regrets for Butchering Broadway?

*__NEW YORK__, March 6, 2013 – Still after all these years my early mornings begin with coffee and Don Imus on Radio or TV. He's still tops, especially in getting his guests to open up as if there's no microphone picking up deep dark secrets – as he did again this morning with Frank Rich, who used to be known as the Butcher of Broadway, and for good reason.

Rich so affably offered his confessions and condolences a second time, and that made it no tidier or prettier than the first time. Rich now sings a different Broadway melody as a writer for *New York Magazine*, but back then, between 1980 and 1993, he served as senior drama critic for *The New York Times*, and here the word "critic" is not used in vain.

For more than a decade Broadway shuddered at what that man Rich might say next.

A play that opened on Friday could be shut down on Saturday after Frank Rich had his final say, and in those days *The New York Times* was most firmly the final say. Not so anymore, as *New York Post* theater reviewer Michael Riedel told Imus just the other day, noting that *The New York Times* does not enjoy the same singular power anymore, at least on drama.

Riedel, who has a knack for telling it good, straight and honest for the *Post,* is no fan of Frank Rich. He still thinks the man was too brutal.

Here's the kicker: Frank Rich thinks so himself.

This morning he told Imus and that on second thought, all those plays he savaged – well, maybe they weren't all that bad, after all.

Now we hear this? A bit late, no?

Actually we heard this before, and it's still not funny, even though Rich laughs when he says something like, "Yes, I could have been wrong."

---

* Originally published in the Communities section of *The Washington Times*.

That is not an exact quote, but it is the gist.

Years ago I heard Frank Rich make the same confession, accompanied by giggles and laughter. As a member of the fraternity of writers who knows how ruinous a bad review can be, I was not amused by the carefree and whimsical condolences Rich offered to the many Broadway artists who'd been destroyed by the might of his heartless pen.

The topic came up again this morning, on Imus, because Rich has written a book, and in it, apparently, he discusses his "second thoughts."

Yes, on second thought, maybe those plays did not deserve to be killed, along with the people whose years of artistic work were cursed into the netherworld.

I covered that in a book I wrote in 2007, where editor in chief Jay Garfield confronts his drama critic for getting to be too much like Frank Rich. I never thought those words would come back to life, or maybe I did for life has a habit of repeating itself for the good, the bad, and the vicious, like this, from page 211:

"Yes, Frank Rich. This man had been the theater critic for *The New York Times* but was better known as The Butcher of Broadway. In his day he had scorched nearly every play under his withering eyes, sending thousands of writers, actors, directors, producers, stagehands and angels into the pit of eternal damnation. Most were never heard from again, so all-powerful was this executioner for *The New York Times.*

"Finally (and for whatever reason) he got switched to another beat and now he could speak his mind, and so on a morning radio show – Imus, I believe it was – relaxed and entirely happy with himself, he confessed that most of these plays, on second thought, weren't all that bad. Some were even good and maybe excellent. But he destroyed them and why? Well, because he felt like it and because he could.

"Then, after saying all that, he laughed, never mind all the people he had ruined, and all the dreams he had dashed."

So once again Frank Rich gives his regards to Broadway – and still not funny.

Dear Writers: Suppose Your Novel Sucks?

***NEW YORK**, February 26, 2013 – All things considered, it could have been much worse. Some writers put 10 years into a book, and only after giving it all that blood, discover that it was all in vain. I only put in a month of sweat, or thereabouts, and woke up one morning with something of an epiphany, like this: hey, this novel sucks!

This would have been my 11th published book and my ninth novel and I had it figured from beginning to end, which is mistake number one. If you've got it all figured out so perfectly then surely you can never surprise yourself, and if you can't surprise yourself, how can you expect to amaze the reader?

A novel has to breathe and if you've got every scene charted out, you're suffocating the baby.

Besides, a novel should never be perfect. It is usually the imperfect ones that are the great ones, like James Jones' *From Here to Eternity*, which is full of bad writing, but incredibly alive. Like Hemingway said of Dostoyevsky, "How can someone write so poorly and make you feel so deeply?"

Beethoven's Ninth Symphony was full of mistakes, he thought so himself, and yet it turned out to be his preeminent triumph.

Hemingway thought his *Across the River and into the Trees* would be his finest work. He was thrilled about the progress he was making. He kept reminding A.E. Hotchner that passage for passage, chapter for chapter, he had never written so well — and what happened? The book turned out to be about some grumpy old colonel, which nobody liked. (Well, some did and some do.)

I stopped the bleeding before it was too late. Each morning when I'd start back to work on it, I found that no matter how many pages I'd written the day before, I was still on page 66. This was inexplicable and entirely weird. How can I still be on page 66 after hours of writing?

---

* Originally published in the Communities section of *The Washington Times*.

But it proved that I wasn't skipping along as I usually do for the works that succeed, and I have had successes and failures, and haven't we all?

I even went back to those novels of mine that did succeed (I number them at nine) and in them tried to figure out what worked before against what wasn't working out now. In all my novels from before, something got turned on, something clicked. The secret was simple (especially for *Indecent Proposal*): in one place my heart was in it, I was aflame, full of passion, and in this place, this new place, I was simply writing to conform to plot.

The characters never talked back to me, never argued with me, never stood up for themselves, and when none of that happens, you're writing cardboard.

I found this attempt at a new novel to be drudgery, and no matter how many times I told myself to keep going, that I will find the people, I will find the passion, I will find the excitement, I will find the voice, the novel refused to give itself up and refused to move. Still page 66. Nothing was *happening.*

(By the way, the working title for the novel that will never happen was "Welcome to Sogora." If you ever see a novel by that name, it wasn't mine, or my fault.)

Lesson number two on writing: If you can change the names of your characters midway, you've got nothing going. You are inventing, not creating. You are faking it, and with this discovery I went to bed that night. In the morning I glanced over a few pages and declared them to be officially dreck. I announced myself done with this project. I actually felt good.

I actually felt creative for making such a decision. Yes, knowing when a thing isn't working, and being done with it, that too is part of the creative process.

I talked to the primo novelist John W. Cassell about this.

"Didn't we agree?" he said, "that it's on page one hundred that we can tell if a novel is working or not?"

Eureka! That's how it was when Joan insisted, against my wishes, that she was going to take up the sultan on his million dollar offer, even as I kept saying no, and she kept saying yes. She kept saying yes and I could not stop her. She won, as did the novel. All that happened on page 100, when I stopped typing and began channeling, or rather when I gave in, stopped being in control and judgmental, and instead, let people behave as people behave.

Inspiration can't be the moment of clarity that happens only at the start. Inspiration, if it's real, has to keep moving you page to page.

I've already got a new novel started. I will let you know when I get past page 66.

JFK, Marilyn, Elvis: Trashing the Dead With Books

***NEW YORK**, February 20, 2013 – I slept with Marilyn Monroe.

Can you prove otherwise? That's right. You can't, and that's my point.

Or, as they'd say around my home, "Too much information, Dad."

I say the same about books that keep coming out about dead celebrities, told by people who were intimate with them, or so they say.

I do not need all that information.

Let me depart from books for a second to talk about a film that was made for HBO about Hemingway and Gellhorn, starring Clive Owen and Nicole Kidman. This was okay as these specials go, but I did not need those sex scenes, and I turned my head when I knew what was coming, a momentary glimpse of Owen's back end, meant to convey Hemingway in heat, in addition to his posterior.

Thank you, but I don't need that about an American legend. Nor do I need all those tell-alls that defame the reputations of people we revere and idolize.

Is this an American thing, this need to destroy our heroes? I call it Sleaze Lit.

Again on HBO, here we have Alfred Hitchcock as "mad about that Girl" – and nothing else. He comes off hateful and humorless and now dead, of course.

In other words, we get one side about people no longer among the quick.

Out comes a book by Rita Moreno (one of my favorites) and today I learn that Brando was a sex machine and that Elvis was a dud.

I may never visualize Brando the same way again, and certainly not Elvis who, over the years, I've come to appreciate.

There is a good and legit bio of Elvis by Peter Guralnick, but that is literally a different story. In fact, real biographies by real biographers belong in a different category than gossip mongers, and frank-

---

* Originally published in the Communities section of *The Washington Times*.

ly, I don't know what to make of Kitty Kelley and Andrew Morton. I will more or less trust that the research was done.

Norman Mailer did his book on Marilyn (guessing all the way), and Peter Manso did his book on Mailer, but these are biographers who make no other claim.

We're talking about those authors who claim to have shared their lives, and bedrooms, with our gods. Can we believe what they say?

Remember, they can say whatever they want....anything about anybody...as long as that person is gone.

The actor Frank Langella wrote a book in which he makes mincedmeat out of nearly everybody, particularly those who are no longer around to defend themselves, like a particular sweetheart of mine and of the silver screen, Anne Bancroft. Do we really need to know that she was so vain that only the mirror was her friend?

More important, is this really true?

Or is this just one man's opinion? Or is it one man getting even?

Mel Brooks can't be happy and I'm not happy, for this is not biography and it is not memoir, it is bitchery.

Yes, I know, that's what sells. I also know that when a prospective peeping tom approaches a publisher the question goes like this:

"Can you spill the beans? Can you dish the dirt?"

Langella also scandalizes John F. Kennedy, and who hasn't? Seems to me that nearly anyone who was in or around the 1960s has since "revealed the truth" about our handsome 35th president. For a time I believed all those stories about his supposed lechery. But as these books and movies started piling up and piling on, I began to wonder.

If true, when did Kennedy have time to inaugurate the Peace Corps and get us to the moon?

I am starting to think that Kennedy was absolutely loyal to Jackie, like a monk, and that he planted the gossip himself to distract us from knowing that he was in constant pain. Either way, some respect maybe for a president who was assassinated?

Not quite. A lady named Mimi Alford caused the latest stir. She wrote a book (who hasn't?) and appeared with Meredith Viera on TV to talk about her steamy affair with Kennedy, some of which got into perversion. As we get it, she started off as an intern, then named Mimi

Beardsley, and next thing you know she was canoodling with the president in bed and in swimming pools. (Oh those interns!)

That happened in 1962. She broke the news 2012.

Is all that true? Maybe it doesn't matter as long as we enjoy watching the dead squirm. How reliable are memoirs anyway?

Now it's back to my book, "How I Scored with Ava Gardner."

Adultery, Anyone?

***WASHINGTON, DC**, February 8, 2013 – In a book just published, and getting deservedly good reviews, *I do and I don't: A History of Marriage in the Movies*, author Jeanine Basinger asserts that we can't seem to get it right at home or at the movies. Infidelity lurks from bedroom to silver screen, and, as I define it, the love of sex and money is the root of all great fiction.

In real life, surveys mislead as to who is misbehaving, but online there are hundreds of website choices for "hooking up," single or married. On surveys and statistics we only know what people are saying, not what people are thinking, especially when it comes to sex.

Writers of fiction do it best, and on this topic I do have a say. I've been told that I started a new baby boom from what gets started on page 228 of *Indecent Proposal*. Too often I've been asked to define the novel and my standard response is that if I could define it in a single paragraph I would have written the paragraph instead of the book.

However, *temptation* comes close to the mark, and as I've already written, sex is nothing. Temptation is everything…and anyway, sex is not for girls.

I'm okay with Basinger naming David Lean's *Brief Encounter* as perhaps the best take on infidelity at the movies, even as the film was minus any scenes of lovemaking, drawing chuckles from reviewers in France who found it so "very British" for a film to feature sex but without the sex.

Ditto for *Madame Bovary* and *Anna Karenina* as contenders. There, too, most of it was flirtation and temptation.

Likewise, in books or in film, presenting married couples in the act of sex, does nothing. Who cares? That's what people are supposed to do, to be fruitful and multiply. *When it gets illicit*, that's when the fun and the drama begin. "All happy families are alike" – Tolstoy's opening line for *Anna Karenina.*

So thrilled as I was to be mentioned in the same pages as Leo Tolstoy, and Gustav Flaubert, and astonished that she missed James M.

---

* Originally published in the Communities section of *The Washington Times*.

Cain's *The Postman Always Rings Twice*, Basinger was mistaken to surmise, on page 142, that *Indecent Proposal* (the movie) "floats on an unlikely story."

Not quite. After my novel came out, followed by the Paramount movie, I counted a hundred letters spilling the beans on oil rich sheiks who offered a million dollars (more or less) for a night of love — and the many Hollywood actresses willingly sharing their bedroom charms for the cash.

I had no idea that this was going on (and still going on) when I wrote the book. We may think we are creating when in fact we are merely taking down dictation.

All that got me to wondering where we are, ethically, in this Real Housewives/Page Six world where nearly everything goes. Is there anything left that's taboo? The movie *Indecent Proposal* premiered April 7, 1993, so we're approaching a 25th anniversary. The novel was published four years earlier. In each instance, there was shock.

Someone out there said it better than I could.

Writing for *NPR* (National Public Radio), Jimi Izrael ranked *Indecent Proposal* number one on a list of "Five Great Films about the Perils of Infidelity." Izrael complained (as did I) about Amy Holden Jones' "jerky script" but cited the novel as "a gut-wrenching study on love, money, and trust that sparked dinner party conversations for years afterward here."

Back then, women's groups blasted me for sexism, even when they'd only seen the movie and not read the book. To my defense comes a recent Amazon UK review from Thomas Hardy for the Kindle edition of the novel: "Indecent Proposal is probably the ideal example of why a screenwriter should never be allowed near a great writer's work." (His words, not mine.)

Still, back then, even as the novel kept selling and getting fine book reviews, and even as the movie broke box office records, I took it on the chin from movie reviewers coast to coast. *The New York Times* and Roger Ebert were overly generous about the movie, but the rest of them were overly hysterical.

My guess was that people simply did not want to be challenged like this – like what would you do if you were impoverished and were offered a million dollars to perform a sinful act that could change your entire life? Movie reviewers expected a popcorn outing and were vexed and offended when asked to go back home to *think* and face up to a too-near-to-home moral dilemma.

Robert Redford, though I had nothing like him in mind, rather an oil rich sultan, even liked the script and especially the novel despite or maybe because of its "hard-edged writing" and "flagrantly sexual theme." He said, "Yeah. It will work." Sure did. The movie took in $260 million at the box office worldwide and made everybody rich in Hollywood, and sales of my book zoomed here and around the globe.

So nobody got hurt except for the critics.

The novel, and even the movie, got personal, and touched America deep into its Puritanical soul. On live TV, Matt Lauer chuckled and asked me if my novel was based on personal experience… hell no!… and on live radio, Larry King asked, "Why only a million dollars?" True, I had not thought of inflation.

I also did not think that we'd turn as blasé as the Europeans, who take sex casually and often.

When I asked columnist Liz Smith to please get women's lib off my back, she wrote, "What are you complaining about? Your book is a runaway bestseller."

Nowadays every sitcom comes with overt sexual titters and nearly every movie opens with two or more people in bed and nudity is ho-hum.

I refuse to rate my book or my movie on the scale of infidelity and I refuse to judge the behavior of my characters.

Sex is about love and nothing else and let someone else, not me, be the judge.

I write and I publish because there may be one person out there with whom I've made contact in a world so brutal and lonely.

Salinger, Roth, Hemingway and the Wilderness of Writing

***WASHINGTON, DC**, January 16, 2013 – Philip Roth has quit writing and nobody knows exactly why though I can guess. Salinger wrote only for himself, for his own pleasure, and considered getting published a nuisance, a bother and an intrusion. F. Scott Fitzgerald's last royalty check amounted to something like six dollars and change. He said, "Why am I doing all this writing. No one's reading me."

Hemingway was so unimpressed with his Pulitzer, his Nobel, his wine, his women, his fame, his books waiting to get written, that he committed suicide.

John Kennedy Toole ("A Confederacy of Dunces") won his Pulitzer too late. He kept getting rejected and answered right back with his own suicide.

Dear world…How's that for rejection!

Both a doctor and an auto mechanic (people I admire) marveled at the fact that some of us can turn emotions into prose.

I explained that we are all geniuses at something. The trick is to find out what it is.

Writing novels, as I do, is fun, and more than that, once the inspiration kicks in there is nothing compared to the exhilaration when the words begin to flow, and there is no stopping us once we get started. There is no choice but to write and as I have said plenty of times, you don't choose writing, writing chooses you.

But that's the writing itself that I'm talking about, and in that period when the going is good and the words (from above?) keep coming so fast that even the keyboard can't keep up – in that period we are charmed and blessed. At these moments, as we write and lose track of time, we create a universe and discover continents. We become gods and kings.

In the publishing we turn ourselves over to our readers and trust that we will get a fair hearing. We don't ask our readers to love us, on-

---

* Originally published in the Communities section of *The Washington Times*.

ly to understand that a novel is tender and precious and easily broken when trashed. We worked long and hard to get it done and deserve leniency for the effort alone – and for having the guts to stick our necks out where there may be multitudes waiting to do us harm.

This is an especially tricky time for writers. We find ourselves squarely into the teeth of a technology that permits anyone to comment on our work without telling us who they are, so that by remaining anonymous they enjoy a tyranny. Bygone writers faced their accusers.

All around I have been lucky with reviews though we don't know what a new day will bring, but on getting published it has been a drag from day one, and yet there have been some astonishing successes, which only recently I have come to appreciate. I keep saying that every work of art is a failure because we never get it exactly right, but even so, sometimes we click and our books get praised, become best-sellers and get made into movies…and for that much I can vouch.

But generally all true writers – all true artists – are failures. We are dependent on the mercy of strangers.

I even wrote a novel about a novelist, his triumphs yes, but oh brother the rejections, the hardships, the bills. I knew what I was talking about.

I am reading the biography of David Lean the great director of "Lawrence of Arabia" and am astonished at his feelings of inadequacy even after scoring success after success. Even at the height of his fame Hemingway had trouble getting a press pass to cover World War II. Even after *The Catcher in the Rye* Salinger had to keep proving himself at *The New Yorker*. (Read Kenneth Slawenski's fabulous bio on this.)

Today I have begun writing a new novel and I wonder if it's worth the trouble. I keep hesitating as I consider my predecessors and about their weariness and despair and the uselessness of it all. Fitzgerald in *The Crack-Up* extended King Solomon's despair in Ecclesiastes. All is futile and futility.

Readers will misunderstand, as is to be expected, but some will misunderstand the work purposely and viciously.

Once the work has been done and is out of your hands you have no say. Onward your readers become gods and kings. They, not you, interpret your work, and this is their duty in this, the final act of intimacy, more intimate than sex, this give-and-take between writer and reader.

But who will be around to read this book of mine? Will we all be tweeting by the time it's done – tweeting instead of reading, and tweeting instead of writing? Already the language has changed and already we have a generation trained and conditioned to express themselves in 140 characters or less.

I notice this even at the movies where a typical scene in today's films runs no more than about 10 seconds. Our attention spans are devoted to the next commercial.

I also notice that the finest writing these days comes not from our novelists but from our screenwriters. (Is this why Roth quit?) True that so many films are junk but also true that good films keep getting done, and the writing is good and sometimes very good. I cannot write a screenplay because to me words are notes, sentences are music, and I need rhythm to keep moving from paragraph to paragraph.

Rhythm is something you have or you don't. Read the first paragraph of Hemingway's *A Farewell to Arms*.

Read the opening lines to James M. Cain's *The Postman Always Rings Twice*.

Read Kafka to find that a writer does not and should not care if his works get read. Kafka died before seeing his novels in print.

The work – it's only the work that counts. Forget the rest.

Tips for Becoming A Better Writer from A Writer

***NEW YORK,** November 6, 2012 – Writers and editors periodically ask me if I have any advice about writing and I usually, actually always, say hell no. Writers, speaking mostly of fiction writers, don't like to be told.

We don't like rules and we don't like tips. We are all different and respect must be paid for the uniqueness in all of us.

That said, as a public service and free of charge, here are some tips and rules gathered from my years in the trade.

Jack Engelhard's Tips and Rules to Become A Published Writer

GET TO THE POINT: Get that hook going right at the top. This is how it works in journalism. We want to grab the reader's attention immediately if not sooner.

TAKE YOUR TIME: When writing a work of fiction (or fact) remember, you've got all the time in the world to win the reader's attention. There is no need to get it all said right at the start. You've got plenty of pages to go. Don't get fooled by people who tell you that the hook is how it works in journalism. You are writing a book.

WRITE SHORT: Short, tough sentences always succeed. Think Bukowsky, Fante, James M. Cain, but most of all, Hemingway. He learned how to condense from Scriptures and from Gertrude Stein. Fitzgerald's dreamy type of writing is old hat and it is Hemingway who is now regarded as our greatest writer.

WRITE LONG: Every writer has his or her particular style, so it makes no sense to heed advice from anyone who tells you that writing short, clipped sentences is the way to go. Ridiculous. Today, it's Fitzgerald who is regarded as our greatest writer. Hemingway is old hat.

---

* Originally published in the Communities section of *The Washington Times*.

KEEP YOUR READERS IN MIND: You want to reach a wide public. People are waiting for your first or next book. So unless you are writing a diary or a laundry list, you want your work out there, to be appreciated by all. You want to cover all the bases so that you can please as many people as possible.

WRITE FOR YOURSELF ONLY: If you write with your readers in mind you are cheating both yourself and the reader. You will never make everyone happy, and you shouldn't even try. Remember, people are not waiting for your first or next book. Nobody cares. It's a jungle out there, believe me.

GO TO SCHOOL: Learn from the experts, first high school, then college. Let the professors tell you how it's done.

FORGET SCHOOL: Professors will scuttle every original thought that runs from your mind to the page. They are killers. It's all about grammar and punctuation with those people. Our best writers never went beyond high school and this includes Hemingway, Faulkner and Salinger. Fitzgerald stayed at Princeton for maybe a cup of coffee. If they had gone to college you never would have heard from them again.

DO NOT WORRY ABOUT POLITICAL CORRECTNESS: Say it all. Don't be afraid!

BE AFRAID: Editors will accept only so much boldness and controversy. If you really write what you think you have no shot. If it's politics, think Mahmoud Ahmadinejad as your editor. (Say it all anyway. This is still America…until the United Nations lords it over your Internet.)

GET AN AGENT: Traditional publishers will accept your work only if it is submitted to them through an agent. Agents are easy to find online.

NEVER MIND AN AGENT: Literary agents are impossible. They cannot be found and when they are found, they never respond. If they do respond they do so after you have aged by some three to four months. After this, they will tell you that your work is quite wonderful – but not quite right for them. Then they will wish you "good luck" but they don't really mean it.

GO DIRECTLY TO A MAINSTREAM PUBLISHER: Fat chance. There are only seven publishers left in the United States of America and each time I check the list, I find that the number has been reduced – so that by the time you read this there may be only three or two left, or maybe one. Meanwhile, there are a thousand opportunities by going Independent – and this, small press and e-book publishing, like Kindle, this is the future. Truly great writers like Mark Twain and Walt Whitman self-published.

SO FORGET MAINSTREAM PUBLISHERS: Period.

GO MARKETING: If you get published, you are sure to land on TV and get big sales.

FORGET MARKETING: Sure you ought to try. But chances are you won't get on TV unless you are a TV personality and have your own show.

LET YOUR SPOUSE OR MOTHER REVIEW YOUR BOOK: Good idea.

LET YOUR EX-SPOUSE OR MOTHER-IN-LAW REVIEW YOUR BOOK: Not a good idea.

TAKE ALL THE ADVICE YOU CAN GET: Learn from other writers, especially those who have succeeded.

NONSENSE: Go it alone…and besides, all writers have mostly failed…but never give up!

The Obit Uris Never Got

NEW JERSEY, July 1, 2003 – Leon Uris deserved better. The obits were a disgrace. They read more like a spiteful book review, rather than an appreciation for the man who gave us the romance of Israel. But let's not be fooled -- for these obits were an attack upon the Jewish State, not Uris, who merely served as a prop, a decoy.

The cheap shots came from intellectual stormtroopers who decide for us what is good, what is bad, what is high-minded, what is low brow... Like this, which appeared all over the news media: "Uris is not well regarded by critics, many of whom consider his writing crude and simple. People who think Saul Bellow, Bernard Malamud and Cynthia Ozick are major Jewish writers would say he's just a popular writer... He tells a good story, but he's not of lasting literary value."

Huh? This belongs in an obituary?

For my money, Uris towers over Bellow and others on the strength of Exodus alone. And if Exodus is not of lasting literary value, I don't know what is.

Oh, I know what they're talking about. He was no stylist. First of all, there is no such thing as style. Of course there is, but that's for us, the readers, to decide. There is no Supreme Court to rule on style, and anyway, style is no factor in deciding a book's greatness. Dickens (in my view) was a terrible stylist, as was Dostoevsky, and James Jones was a terrible writer, but a great novelist by weight of *From Here to Eternity*. These were all great novelists.

No, the snotty obits were reprisals upon Israel, and had nothing to do with literature and everything to do with politics.

How many writers "created" a nation within the pages of a book? Non-Jews by the millions (never mind Jews) know and love Israel only through Exodus.

Uris died at the wrong time; anti-Semitism is up, Israel is down. Today it is not proper to glorify Israel, as Uris did. Today it is proper, it is fashionable, to slap Israel around.

Here's a secret: Newsrooms carry obits well in advance for people of achievement. As I write this, there's news that Katharine Hepburn just died, but you can be sure that the obits for her were written years ago. Back a generation, someone was in such a hurry to present his beautifully-written obit on Hemingway that he got it published all over the wires while Hemingway was merely recovering from a plane crash.

Hemingway, very much alive, said he loved what was said about him. Uris would not be so pleased.

Surely, over the years Uris' obit kept being rewritten in reflection of how the world viewed Israel and the Jewish people at the moment. Back then, a guilt-ridden world embraced the romance of the Jewish people returning to the land of their Fathers and Mothers. The mood has changed. The mood is ugly and the obits on Uris symbolize that change and that ugliness. Our tenured intellectual elite (think Oxford, Columbia, the BBC, NPR....) have fallen in love with homicide, terrorism, anti-Semitism.

Uris showed us David winning against Goliath, but this world covets Goliath... Hence the scorn upon the man who wrote Exodus.

In a class that I visited as a lecturer, a student mocked Proverbs. "Anyone can do that," he said. "Go ahead," I said, "write one." Of course, he was stumped.

I say the same to Uris' scholarly critics. "Go ahead, write me an Exodus."

We have lost a great man, a great writer, and he deserves to be hailed.

www.ingramcontent.com/pod-product-compliance
Lightning Source LLC
Chambersburg PA
CBHW031238090426
42742CB00007B/244
* 9 7 8 1 7 7 1 4 3 5 5 3 6 *